UNDOCUMENTED

A DOMINICAN BOY'S ODYSSEY

—————————— *from a* ——————————

HOMELESS SHELTER TO THE IVY LEAGUE

UNDOCUMENTED

DAN-EL PADILLA PERALTA

PENGUIN PRESS

New York

2015

PENGUIN PRESS
An imprint of Penguin Random House LLC
375 Hudson Street
New York, New York 10014
penguin.com

Photographs courtesy of the author

ISBN 978-1-59420-652-8

Printed in the United States of America
1   3   5   7   9   10   8   6   4   2

Designed by Marysarah Quinn

---

*Penguin is committed to publishing works of quality and integrity.
In that spirit, we are proud to offer this book to our readers;
however, the story, the experiences, and the words
are the author's alone.*

4324816

Tyndarus: *Sed tu dic oro: pater meu' tune es?*
Hegio: *Ego sum, gnate mi.*

Tyndarus: But you, tell me, please: are you my father?
Hegio: I am, my child.

—PLAUTUS, *The Captives*

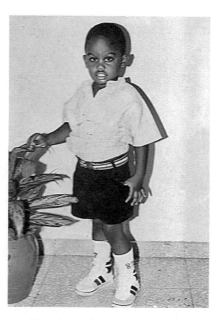

Dan-el, age three, Santo Domingo

Fundamentally, almost no one coming from the
Dominican Republic to the United States is coming
because they have a skill that would benefit us and that
would indicate their likely success in our society.

> —SENATOR JEFF SESSIONS (R–Ala.), remarks on the
> U.S. Senate floor, May 22, 2006 (*Congressional
> Record–Senate,* Vol. 152, pt. 7, p. 8955)

PROLOGUE

EVERY WEEKDAY MORNING of my high school years, I left my apartment building in Spanish Harlem and took the subway or bus to Manhattan's Upper West Side, where I attended private school.

Whenever I wasn't navigating the streets on autopilot, I'd be confronted by the differences between HarlemWorld and the Upper West, no matter how hard I tried to shut them out. The streets around my Upper West Side private school were mostly clean; the streets in my hood were littered with trash. Broadway had ritzy shops and clean storefronts; 116th Street had 99-cent shops, dusty and crusty storefronts. The Upper West had white kids loitering around Zabar's; my block had black and Latino hoodrats loitering outside apartment buildings. And the police! I'd see one or two or (on a truly exceptional day) three on Broadway—usually hitting up the bagel spot between 79th and 80th—but the baton-wielding Blue rolled deep where I lived.

During the school day, my private school made it easy to forget about these differences. Science classrooms decked out with the newest technology, an Upper School student center trashed in a way I was beginning to recognize as the mark of entitled brattiness, the guitar- and bed-equipped office of my high school adviser—I inhabited daytime spaces that bore not a single trace of that other life I lived on weeknights and weekends. Sometimes, though, *that other life* intruded into the realm of my immersion in white-boy privilege. The hood would come knocking—or just smash through the door.

"Dan-el, the police just searched our apartment for drugs!"

I took Mom's call outside my school's computer room, where I'd been proofreading the school newspaper. I'd ignored the first ring of my cell phone, thinking Mom was just calling to ask when I'd be home for dinner. But when she rang a second time, I'd grown worried and picked up.

"What? What happened? Why did they think we had drugs? Did they say?"

"*Mi'jo*, it's going to be okay now. They made a big mistake. They had one cop who speaks a little Spanish explain to me what went wrong. They'd received a call from someone who told them dealers were stashing drugs in an apartment in our building. The cops thought the informant said 'Apartment 2B,' so they came to our apartment—"

"So they were there when you got home from church?"

"They'd knocked down the door. They were searching everything. They searched my bedroom, the table where I have the candles for the *santos,* the living room, the kitchen, the bedrooms. I'm just so happy that your little brother was at chorus rehearsal and not at home, thank God."

"Do they still think we're involved with drug dealers?"

"*Ay no, mi'jo.* So they're searching everywhere and I'm telling them over and over again that they're wrong, that we're a family of God and I'm just a single mother raising two children. I showed them all your books, I told them you go to a famous private school on full scholarship. But they wouldn't believe anything I told them. They just kept asking where the drugs were. But finally, finally—thank you, Virgin Mary—one of the police officers took out his radio and spoke with the police officers standing outside our building. That's when another cop came up to me and said they were extremely sorry. That it had all been a mistake, that they were supposed to be investigating another apartment instead. And you should have seen them, Dan-el, how nice they were when they realized their mistake. They're even going to pay to have our door fixed."

"Those *sinvergüenza* cops!"

"Dan-el! They were doing their job, my son. It's over now."

"Did they ask about our immigration status?"

"Thank God, no, my son. They didn't ask me for *papeles* or anything like that."

I let out a small sigh of relief. Mom continued:

"But I must have interrupted you, my son—you're still at school working on the newspaper, right? Everything's okay, I just wanted you to know what had happened. Get back to what you were doing and I'll see you at home for dinner. *Dios te bendiga.*"

I returned to the computer room. All eyes were turned to Britney Spears, who was shaking and dancing on one of the computer screens. One of my friends asked me if anything was wrong.

"Me?" I replied. "Nah, kid, I'm good. Britney can hit-me-baby all she wants."

He laughed. I took my seat a few computers away from the Britney show and admired her moves. By the time the gyrations came to an end, my newspaper buddies and I were hard at work. When we were done editing an hour later, I packed up, told my editors-in-arms that I'd see them the next day in class, and peaced for the afternoon.

At no point then or after did I seriously consider telling any of them—or any of my other classmates—what had just taken place back home.

I was seventeen. In my teenage negotiation of the divide between hood life and school life, I was carefully managing which aspects of myself I'd present to the people around me. In conversations and interactions with family members, mentors, friends, I tried to be a normal, slightly immature kid with a healthy interest in pop culture and a passionate love of reading. To them all, I simply wanted to be a slang-dropping, rap- and pop-versifying, slightly nerdy, Britney-loving teenager. And this front would stay firmly in place for years.

Then and later, I didn't want to go to the trouble of explaining to people the lives I was living: skeptic son of a pious mother; undocumented immigrant; Dominican in Harlem; food stamp recipient at a New York City private school; Ivy Leaguer; Dominican expat without papers. A part of me worried that those closest to me wouldn't fully understand; another part, that they wouldn't care. And a third part was busy cultivating some ironic distance from it all. Why did I even have to sweat myself and my situation? Was I even that special? It was so played out, this whole hood-boy-in-richy-rich-school saga; my story was just a variation on a familiar theme.

This book is about how I came to embrace and celebrate the variety and contradictions that make up my life. If the essential arc is of an undocumented Dominican immigrant who became captivated by the study of the Greek and Latin classics, the parallel narrative is of how a boy so fearful for so long of sharing the real story of himself with others decided to let it all hang. Complexity is daunting, and, to paraphrase T. S. Eliot's Prufrock, it can be impossible to say just what you mean. But I would rather run after the impossible than live as a string of labels: undocumented, hoodrat, Dominican, classicist. I am all of those things; no one or two of them define me.

PART I

CHILDHOOD

Dan-el, age three, pre-K graduation,
Santo Domingo

—— CHAPTER 1 ——

*Dan-el and his mom celebrating his fourth
birthday, Santo Domingo*

WHEN MY PARENTS first traveled to the United States, I was four.
They left me behind in our blue house in Santo Domingo with two
babysitters to keep me company. Every night, Mom called to check
in. I would ask her, "Are you coming back tomorrow?" and press the
phone to my ear as hard as I could to catch her faraway voice.

"No, *mi amor*," she'd reply gently, "but you'll see me soon."

I'd cry into the phone.

"Just a few more days, *mi'jo,* and we'll be back. I promise."

On the day Mom and Dad were set to return, I stood on the couch next to the window and refused to budge until I caught a glimpse of them coming down the block, dragging their suitcases. At that moment I ran out of the living room, through the front door, and into Mom's arms. She swept me up, kissed me, and told me how much she'd missed me.

On my parents' second trip to New York, I came along. I didn't know why we were making the trip. Mom's belly was enormous. I'd heard her and Dad talk about doctors. They told me we wouldn't stay in New York for long—just long enough for me to get to know Tía Altagracia and Tía Mercedes.

"Do you want a baby brother or a baby sister?" Mom would ask.

"Sister."

During the flight, I listened to the people speaking English in front of us and across the aisle. I wanted to talk to them, but I didn't know English, so I imitated the sounds coming out of their mouths.

"Shhhh, Dan-el!"

My parents didn't approve. But I wouldn't stop. I tried repeating every English word I heard. For the brief stopover in Puerto Rico, where we took on more passengers, and then for the remaining three hours in the air, I was an English-garbling machine. Mom and Dad were ashamed and surprised: I was usually so well behaved. But first one compliment from a stranger, then another, and soon my parents began to soften up.

"*¡Ese niño va ser un genio!*"

Egged on by their compliments, I kept at it. Mom and Dad relaxed into helpless embarrassment. Four-year-old me, twenty-nine-year-old Mom (swelling with child), and fifty-one-year-old Dad landed at John F. Kennedy Airport on June 15, 1989.

Family portrait: Mom, Dan-el, age four, and Dad, Santo Domingo

EVERYTHING ABOUT NEW YORK seemed so complicated: the street names, the neighborhood names, the distances you had to travel to get anywhere. My parents patiently explained to me that Tía Altagracia and her husband, Jesuito, lived in *El Bron,* and that *El Bron* was different from where Tía Mercedes and Tío José lived, in *Queen,* where we stayed for a short while before moving to *Ma'hattan* for the rest of Mom's pregnancy.

For our trips to the Bronx, we took the D train, got off at 167th Street and Grand Concourse, and walked to Altagracia and Jesuito's apartment on 165th and Grant. But my favorite was the trip to Queens: whenever we took the N train, my parents would let me stick my face to the window and stare at the streets and cars and people flying beneath us as the train shot out from under the East River.

Every time we went to see my aunts, the adults had the same conversation.

"My sugar is really high," my mother would tell her sisters.

They'd nod somberly.

One late-fall morning, I woke up to Mom's moans. Out of a closet, Dad swiftly pulled out a wheelchair. He bundled Mom up, helped her into the wheelchair, and bundled me up. With one hand he held me; with the other he wheeled Mom into an elevator, through the lobby of our apartment building, and down Audubon Avenue and Broadway until we reached Columbia-Presbyterian Medical Center, on 167th Street.

Mom had one last question for me before the doctors took her. "Do you want a baby brother or a baby sister?"

"Sister."

"But you'll love a brother, too?" She smiled, her face wan.

"Yes, Mamá."

Dad took me to a room, where we waited. Every few minutes he got up and paced. I fell asleep.

Finally, we were called in to see Mom. She lay in her hospital bed, looking very tired but smiling faintly, holding the newest member of our family. His name was Yando, and he was very light-skinned, unlike me, with large curls of hair on his head, also unlike me. He was beautiful. I kissed him on the forehead. He smelled funny.

A FEW DAYS AFTER Mom's release from the hospital, we took a cab to Tía Altagracia's apartment. Dad held and propped up Mom most of the way there. She was hot to the touch. When we arrived, Mom pulled up her blouse to show her sister the healing wound from her C-section. It was bloody.

"We have to call an ambulance!" my aunt yelled. "It's infected!"

An ambulance came and took Mom away. Dad told Tía Altagracia to take care of Yando and me and left with the ambulance. I cried.

Dad came back a few hours later and told us that Mom was being kept at the hospital for the night. When she came back to us the next day, she seemed a little better. We returned to *Ma'hattan*. For the next few weeks, Dad did all the household chores every day while Mom slept.

About a month later, Dad packed our suitcases, loaded us into a car he'd rented, and drove us to a new apartment in the Bronx, five minutes away from Tía Altagracia. He then enrolled me at the local public school. I was placed into the Spanish-language kindergarten classroom.

I didn't like it that much at first. At my pre-K in Santo Domingo, they'd let me read on my own. Now I had to do activities with other kids, and that wasn't as much fun. But when we began to practice saying letters out loud, my teacher was impressed that I already knew how to read. In my report card she wrote that I was an expressive reader. Mom and Dad read her comments and told me they were proud of me.

MY FIRST WINTER in the States, I was fascinated by ketchup. I loved it so much that I wanted to pour it all over everything I ate. Mom wouldn't let me: I was restricted to a *chin-chin* with every meal, and if I so much as tried to sneak in a little more, the ketchup bottle would immediately be snatched from my hand and returned to the fridge.

One night, while Dad was out, Mom put on her clothes to pick up a few things at the corner bodega. She called me to the kitchen, gave me my dinner, and told me to keep an eye on Yando, who was asleep in his crib. The moment she stepped out, I hurried to the fridge, grabbed the ketchup bottle, unscrewed the cap, and emptied it all out on my rice and beans. Finally I could live my dream.

I had one spoonful, then a second. All that ketchup didn't taste as good as I thought it would. I drank some water to make the funny aftertaste go away. I kept eating, but soon I began to feel woozy, and within minutes my stomach began to hurt. When I couldn't make myself eat any more, I took my plate to the garbage bin in the kitchen, cleared it off, and shoved the food to the very bottom. Then I placed my plate in the kitchen sink and washed it just enough to remove traces of the ketchup.

When Mom returned, she saw the empty ketchup bottle and searched the garbage. I was summoned into the kitchen.

"¡Qué desperdicio!" she yelled. "You didn't eat your food! Who told you to put so much ketchup on it?"

I felt too ashamed to say anything. She continued talking, more to herself than to me: "We're poor, we don't have much money, and here he is wasting food. I leave him alone for a few minutes and this is what he does."

Mom at her office at the pension fund, Santo Domingo, 1989

I hadn't known we were poor. Mom and Dad had had office jobs in Santo Domingo. I remembered Mom's work colleagues pinching my cheeks. What had happened?

BY THE SPRING, Mom and Dad were arguing almost every day. In the mornings I would hear them through the closed doors of their bedroom. The topic was always the same: *We don't have any money; we need to return to Santo Domingo.*

I listened closely, even to what I didn't understand. Their bosses in Santo Domingo had offered to hold their jobs for a few months while Mom received treatment for her pregnancy in New York; but she'd needed more treatment than she expected, and then she'd come down with that infection after giving birth to my brother. We'd been in New York for nine months; their bosses couldn't hold their jobs any longer. But Mom wasn't all that anxious to head back. She kept saying that she'd made powerful enemies.

"You know those union leaders never liked me," she'd remind Dad. "People were saying something would happen to me if I kept doing what I was doing. I was trying to be an honest pension director, and all I got were threats."

She was worried about her health, and about life in Santo Domingo.

"How would you feel if I got sick again in Santo Domingo? You know that if we hadn't come up here, I would have had to abort Yando. You know how terrible the doctors are down there! And what about the crime? Do you even remember that time we were asleep at home and thieves tried to break in? We had to reinforce every single window with steel bars! What kind of life is that? How could we live with ourselves if something ever happened to our children?"

Dad's voice sounded much like it did when he scolded me for

being messy or not eating all of my dinner: deep, patient, ever so slightly irritated.

"I'm *licenciado,* I taught accounting, I had accomplishments to my name—and now I'm driving a taxi and selling fruit to make some money. And you: director of the Pension Fund for Port Workers, your whole career ahead of you. Now you write little pieces for a local newspaper. We don't have enough money. We have to head back. We don't have a future here. We don't have *papeles.*"

I had no idea what *papeles* were, but I knew Dad had been trying to get them. He'd been gone for most of one Friday and Saturday on a trip to meet with a man who'd told him he could fix our *papeles.*

"I paid the man," he kept saying, "but we still haven't heard back from immigration."

Mom brought me up.

"Dan-el likes going to school here. He's learning English! Don't you see what his teachers write about him? You know what an education in Santo Domingo is like."

"Muchacha," Dad said, his voice rising, "but we don't have *papeles!"*

And so they went at each other until they saw the feet through the gap under their bedroom door and guessed that I was listening. Then Dad would say, "Come in, *triunfador."* We'd snuggle together for a few minutes before one of them got up to make breakfast.

AROUND 7:00 A.M. EVERY WEEKDAY, Dad would sit at our kitchen table—legs crossed, trousers on, and shirt half-buttoned—and sip from a cup of coffee while he read *El Diario* or any other Spanish-language newspaper he could get his hands on. When Mom told me to get ready for school, he'd rise from his chair, put on a coat or a blazer, and head off to drive cabs.

Usually, he'd be home by the time school let out. In the evenings, he'd watch baseball if a game happened to be on—Yankees, Mets, Dodgers; it didn't matter. He'd invite me to sit next to him on the couch and watch the games. He was passionate but restrained, never giving way to any extreme of emotion, even when he questioned a particular pitch or complained about a player's performance. And I thought it was so cool that he knew so much: whenever I pointed at a batter or pitcher and asked his name, he'd immediately give me a profile, tell me where the player was from and what position he played. And if I happened to ask about a Dominican player, he'd tell me about the player's city of origin, his accomplishments to date, whether he had any siblings or relatives in the majors or minors.

Every day I came home from school in the spring or summer, there was baseball to watch, and that made me happy.

We watched baseball wherever we happened to be living at the time. Dad kept driving cabs at night and working a fruit stand during the summer to make more money, but we always seemed to be short when it came time to pay the rent. Every time we fell behind, we had to move. From Tía Mercedes's place in Queens, we'd moved to our first New York City apartment in Washington Heights; after Yando was born and Mom had fully recovered from her hospital stay, we moved to Sedgwick Avenue in the Bronx; then to Corona, Queens; then to Jackson Heights; then to another place in Jackson Heights. And every time we moved, I changed schools: kindergarten at PS 226X, first grade at PS 143Q, second and third grades at PS 148Q. Any friends I made, I left behind.

On the weekends, while Dad worked and Mom ran errands, I spent a lot of time by myself or playing with Yando. From time to time, Dad brought me a book to read. Otherwise I conjured up imaginary friends, studied the roses growing in front of our apartment building in Queens, circled our block on the bike Dad taught me to ride. And every school night, I did all of my schoolwork as neatly and correctly as possible. Mom and Dad took turns supervising me.

OUR FIRST THREE YEARS in America flew by. Around the time of my seventh birthday, Dad took a part-time factory job. A few months later, he was injured when a heavy piece of machinery came loose and fell on his foot. He came home hobbled and took to bed. Mom wrapped his foot in gauze.

"*Basta,*" he told Mom. "*Muchacha,* I can't keep going like this."

I noticed for the first time, as Mom nursed Dad back to health, that he was aging. He moved and spoke so slowly compared with Mom, who always had enough energy to take Yando and me on walks to the park. Dad had white hair, seemed tired all the time, and talked only about heading back to the Dominican Republic.

"We have to go back to Santo Domingo," he'd tell Mom.

"Let's keep trying, please," Mom would reply. "Dan-el's doing so well in school! Yando will go to school here and do just as well. I'm staying right here with them. For them and their future. You can go if you want."

Dad bought a plane ticket back to Santo Domingo and began packing his clothes. One night he pulled me aside and spoke to me with a very serious look on his face.

"You have to take care of your mom and little brother. You're going to be the *hombre* of the family now. You promise you'll behave and do all of your homework?"

"Yes, Dad," I assured him.

Was he just making a short trip to Santo Domingo? Was Mom joking when she said that he could go down there and stay but that she would remain in New York with us? When would we see him again? My mind was swirling with questions. But I couldn't bring myself to ask any of them. I was too scared.

"Your mother and I believe in you," he said, kissing me on the forehead.

A few mornings later, a cab was waiting for him outside our apartment building. He brought two large suitcases out of the bedroom and carried them downstairs. Coming back up, he hugged me, picked up Yando and kissed him, and hugged Mom.

"If you change your mind—" he began to say, but Mom cut him off. "May God protect you."

From my bedroom window, I watched as the cab drove off.

It was January 31, 1993. Mom sat down on the living room sofa and cried for a few minutes. Then she got up and made us lunch.

ON WEEKENDS, Mom, Yando, and I would usually head to the Associated Supermarket in our neighborhood to buy groceries. Yando had become a hit with the supermarket staff, because he danced up and down the grocery aisles whenever they played bachata and merengue over the PA.

He was also the only reason we could shop. Back when Dad was still around, Mom had made a few trips to the local welfare office and signed Yando up for the Special Supplemental Nutrition Program for Women, Infants, and Children (WIC). I didn't really understand how the program worked; I just knew that we got help from the government. Once a month, we'd get a check in the mail and use it to buy food. There were things we could and couldn't buy with it. Milk, cheese, bread: yes (but only certain kinds). Candy, quarter waters: no. We also couldn't use the check everywhere, only at places that had a WE ACCEPT WIC sign in the front. But the biggest problem was that the amount on the check was barely enough for Yando's food. He was getting WIC because he was under the age of five. Mom and I weren't eligible: Mom wasn't breastfeeding anymore, and I was eight.

The WIC helped, but once Dad left, we didn't have much money for food shopping. One day that winter, Mom had brought me along to a meeting with a Spanish-speaking caseworker to explain our situation. We had no money. Mom couldn't find a job because she had to take care of us. We were hungry.

The caseworker asked a few questions.

"Are you *ciudadanos*? Do you have a green card?"

Mom replied, "My son Yando is a citizen. My son Dan-el and I are not."

The caseworker looked up from her desk. "Green card?"

"No."

"Hmmm."

For a moment the caseworker was silent. I wondered if she was going to ask more about our *papeles,* but instead she simply said, "Only your son Yando will be eligible for public assistance."

Then she had Mom fill out paperwork for the Aid to Families with Dependent Children (AFDC) program. I saw the full name on one of the forms, but no one called it that—not the caseworker, not Mom, not her sisters when she talked to them about it later that day. It was just "*welfer.*"

When Mom finished signing the forms, the caseworker announced, "You will receive a fixed amount in food stamps and in cash twice a month: sixty dollars in food stamps, forty-two fifty in cash."

Mom's face turned bright red. "Is that all my son Yando is eligible for? That's not enough to feed a family!"

The caseworker shrugged. "That's all."

So, between WIC and *welfer,* we ate because of Yando.

Our route to the supermarket was always the same. We'd pass the same flea market and church, the same bar, the same brick houses and carefully tended gardens of crisp yellow sunflowers and thorn-studded roses.

One Saturday, we were just past the bar's entrance when I heard running feet behind us. A skinny young man slipped between Mom and me, yanked off her purse, and flew down the street. As he turned left at the end of the block, I took off after him. I had no idea what I would do if I caught him, but I chased after him anyway. I ran as hard as I could.

Even though I narrowed the gap between us with my initial burst, he began to pull away. My feet flew over the pavement. I'd never moved that fast in my life. But it wasn't fast enough; the gap grew larger. Two blocks up, I saw him jumping into a car and driving off. I stopped. My lungs were on fire. I turned around and saw Mom and Yando hurrying to catch up. In a minute or so, she was standing at my side.

"Mom, I couldn't catch him," I panted. "I'm sorry."

Yando on the playground slides,
Jackson Heights, Queens, spring 1993

The purse contained our *welfer* benefits card. Without it, we couldn't shop. At our local bodega, Mom bought some food on credit until a new card came in the mail.

WHEN I WASN'T IN SCHOOL, Mom, Yando, and I would go on trips to the American Museum of Natural History, in Manhattan, and the Aquarium at Coney Island. I had no idea where the money for the trips came from, but they were so much fun. The greatest thrill came on the early June day that we went to Coney Island, spread out our towels on the beach, and took dips in the water.

"*Cuidado*," Mom cautioned me. "You don't know how to swim."

Staying close to her, I kicked up the cold ocean water with my feet. A small crab pinched my foot. I shrugged it off and laughed.

We'd also make trips to see our family scattered across the boroughs. Mom's great-uncle and his wife, recently arrived in the States, lived in Bay Ridge and cooked the best *moro* I'd ever tasted. Tía Mercedes and Tío José still lived in Astoria, and we went to see them often. But Tía Altagracia's apartment in the Bronx was where it went down almost every single weekend. Mom and her sisters would cook *arroz, pernil,* and *bacalao* in the kitchen while Tío Jesuito's sound system blasted bachata and merengue.

Whenever the music began to hurt my ears, I'd retreat to my cousins' bedroom to watch Jean-Claude Van Damme movies. *Bloodsport* helped me work on my English. I enjoyed and repeated to myself the insults characters tossed at one another: "scumbag," "dickface," "asshole," "shithead." I puzzled over the phrase "Put up your dukes."

During one of our visits, I was watching a Van Damme movie when the conversation among the adults suddenly became very animated. Through the doors of the bedroom, I couldn't make out what they were arguing about at first. Then the bachata was lowered. I heard shouting.

"You are *not* raising those children right, Yani! They need a man in their lives!"

I stepped out to see what was going on. Mom was glaring at one of my uncles.

"I'm raising them by myself, with God's help, and I don't need your or any man's help."

Mom dragged Yando and me out of the apartment. At the corner of 168th and Grant Avenue, she hailed a cab back to Queens and haggled with the driver until he was willing to take us for the twenty bucks she had in her purse. The entire ride home, she muttered angrily under her breath.

I THOUGHT WE would never be going back to Altagracia's, but a few phone calls and apologies later, we were back at her apartment eating *moro* and *pernil*.

On one of our first trips back, Altagracia and Jesuito introduced Mom to Carlos. He was an auto mechanic who owned a shop just around the corner from their apartment. He wasn't super-dark-skinned like Dad or me, but he was plenty *moreno*. He also had bulging biceps, sported a goatee and a Wesley Snipes–style flattop haircut, and wore long gold and silver chains.

Mom and Carlos began to talk. I tried to listen in on their conversation while pretending to play dominoes with my uncles. He'd grown up in a small *campo* in DR, near Santiago. He started working on cars as a teenager to support his family. In the eighties he moved to New York; after several years, he'd saved enough to open up his own *taller*. He still had a few businesses in Santo Domingo.

Dan-el, age eight, to the right of center,
PS 148Q Arts Day, spring 1993

As we got ready to leave at the end of the night, Altagracia endorsed him:

"Hombre de trabajo," she whispered to Mom as I stood nearby.

We started seeing more of Carlos. He'd come to Queens, take us around on drives in his Chevrolet Corvette, and buy Yando and me all the junk food we wanted: Sour Powers, plantain chips, quarter waters. Sometimes he even held Mom's hand while we were hanging out. She'd beam at him. And whenever he called our apartment, she'd be all smiles on the phone.

SHE DIDN'T HAVE that same look on her face when Dad called.

"We're not coming back!" I heard her saying into the phone one day. "Dan-el is doing well in school! Ask him about his project." She passed the receiver to me. I had news.

"Dad, they're printing an assignment of mine in the school newspaper!"

"Very well done, *triunfador!* Tell me about it."

I told him about my school's newspaper, *The East Elmhurst Echo*. I'd wanted the paper to publish a booklet on snakes that I'd put together for my third-grade class project. Under my very own colored drawings of every major species of snake, I'd written a short paragraph on how to identify them and how they behaved: color pattern, poisonous or nonpoisonous, preferred places of habitation.

"What I wrote," I told Dad, "it's like what you read in the encyclopedia."

My teacher said the newspaper couldn't take the snake book, because they wouldn't be able to print the drawings. But the paper was more than happy to print an assignment I'd completed on rain forests. "When I finally got my copy of the newspaper," I announced to Dad, "I found my essay on the sixth page!" I began reading it out to him. Somewhere in the back of my mind, I knew that Dad's English wasn't that good, but I read on anyway.

"Muchacho," he said when I was done, "you are a *triunfador!"*

I handed the phone back to Mom. She went into the bedroom and closed the door. I drew close to the door and caught snippets of her whispering.

"Are you going to send your children some money?"

A pause.

"Fine. I'll pick it up at Western Union."

She'd pick it up and come back home, sometimes muttering to herself. On the good days, I wouldn't hear much of the muttering— she'd stop within a minute or two of getting home. On the bad days, the muttering wouldn't stop.

"Mojiganga. Saying he can't send a lot because he has his relatives to take care of. His sons are here!"

The phone calls became less frequent.

Mom made fewer and fewer trips to Western Union.

———

WIC AND *WELFER* weren't enough, plus Mom wasn't having any luck finding a regular job beyond the babysitting she was doing for a family in our neighborhood.

For a while, the owner of the local bodega let her run up a tab. Whenever we were low on food, Mom wrote out a list of items on a piece of paper and sent me down the block. Once or twice a week, I'd walk over, pick out what we needed from the store aisles, and bring it to the counter. The owner would take out his pad, write down the prices of the items on a page with Mom's name on it, and help me bag the food.

By summertime, though, Mom still hadn't found a job and was still buying on credit, and soon the tab was too long for even our indulgent bodega friend. One day, he had a message for Mom when I came to the counter:

"Until your mother pays some of what she owes me, *no más.*"

I walked back home and told Mom that the owner hadn't allowed me to take any food on credit. We went back to the bodega together. She pleaded with the owner.

"Seven hundred dollars is too much," he said.

"Would you like to take our TV and VCR as payment, please?" Mom asked. "They work fine."

"No."

Mom and I walked away empty-handed.

On our walk home, I felt so embarrassed to have seen her beg. I began to worry that we wouldn't have any food to eat once the little we had in the refrigerator ran out. That night and for the next few nights, until it was time to pick up Yando's WIC and food stamps, we had rice and small pieces of chicken for dinner. On one of those nights, I noticed that Mom wasn't eating. I didn't want to ask her why.

JULY ARRIVED, and Mom couldn't make rent. Our landlord posted an eviction notice on our door. One afternoon, when we came back from a daylong trip to the park with Mom, our furniture was sitting on the street. Mom salvaged our papers and photos and pleaded with the men throwing out our belongings to spare her a few boxes. Yando and I sat together on the curb while Mom packed and tried to figure out what to do. Finally she walked to a nearby pay phone and called a Puerto Rican landlord she'd met earlier that spring. He offered to put us up in his building's basement until we landed on our feet.

Our stay in the basement lasted about three weeks. One August night, the water and sewage pipes on the ceiling of the basement burst while we were sleeping. Mom woke up just as the water level began to rise. She roused Yando and me from the cot that we were sharing and moved us onto a table. In the rising water I saw my book of snake drawings crumbling into pieces, the ink bleeding every-where. Wading through the water, Mom rescued our belongings and crammed them into a suitcase.

We went to the nearest police station. With me as her translator, Mom asked the police for directions to the nearest shelter. We were pointed to the Emergency Relocation Center for homeless families in the South Bronx.

— CHAPTER 2 —

WE RODE THE SUBWAY to 149th Street and Grand Concourse, then walked three blocks to 151st and Walton Avenue. On our walk from the subway, I realized that we weren't far from Tía Altagracia's apartment. I wanted to ask Mom why we weren't just going over to her place until we could find a new apartment, but I couldn't bring myself to.

The Emergency Relocation Center, a two-story structure of dusty brick and mortar, took up the entire block. Across from it was a bodega, surrounded by apartment buildings and the occasional two-story row house. At the building entrance, we were waved through a metal detector and directed to sit in a waiting room until it was our turn to be processed. The room, roughly the size of my public school cafeteria, was poorly lit and very stuffy. Two whirring fans provided some relief. Kids were running around everywhere, bawling until they were nursed to sleep or demanding food and candy. Every chair and corner was taken up by a family. Some had pieces of luggage; others had packed their belongings into large backpacks or black garbage bags.

When we entered, we couldn't find any spare seats, but after a little searching we rounded up two folding metal chairs. I sat on one; Mom sat on the other, with Yando on her lap, our bags of clothing at her feet. After about an hour we were called to one of the small windows at the front of the room. Mom asked me to translate for her.

"We are homeless. We were evicted from our apartment."

"No, I do not work."

"Their father is not with us; he returned to the Dominican Republic in January."

"I am thirty-three years old. My younger son is three, turning four in November. My eldest son, Dan-el, is eight, turning nine in September."

No questions about our *papeles*. Our interrogator complimented me:

"Your English is very good, young man."

"Thank you," I mumbled.

We retreated to our chairs until the next round of questioning. We were lucky to have seats—with not enough chairs to go around, the newcomers being admitted had to sit on their luggage or on the floor—but the seats were no protection against the buzzing flies tormenting everyone.

Day dragged on into evening. Called back to another window, we were told that it would take two to three days before they could assign us to a shelter. Until our assignment, we'd be allowed to sleep at the relocation center. No beds were available, but there'd be food.

At dinnertime, we sampled the milk and Wonder Bread slices in the center's small cafeteria. The main meal was a mostly inedible beef stew. The few families who had a little money to spare headed outdoors and returned thirty minutes later with McDonald's. I envied them.

To relieve the boredom, I took Yando on short walks around the waiting area. *"Pórtense bien,"* Mom would say to me before letting us go, in such an exhausted voice that I didn't dare think about misbehaving.

AFTER THREE DAYS of sleeping in chairs, with Mom standing guard over us, we were called to one of the windows and told to get ready: we'd been assigned to a shelter in downtown Manhattan. Outside the center's entrance, a van was waiting for us. We boarded with four other families, and the van took off. After a few minutes we crossed a bridge into Manhattan and then joined the traffic streaming down the FDR. The van exited the highway in the 130s, dropped one family off, exited again in the 60s to drop another family off, then rumbled to its final destination. Pressing my face to the van's window, I gazed in the direction of the setting sun, its rays playing with the glass and concrete of the Manhattan skyline.

Soon the bridges and streets of Chinatown came into view. Finally we pulled up to a large gray building at 78 Catherine Street. An employee of the center stepped down from the van and accompanied us to the front door. We were waved through a few metal detectors before being allowed inside and registered as residents. We weren't asked about our immigrant status; all we were asked for was our names, ages, and dates of birth.

Our first stop after that was the shelter's clinic, where Mom was asked for our immunization records.

"Aquí están," she said, signaling for me to take them out of the small plastic bag in which we carried them along with my report cards and a few family photos. I handed them to the nurse on duty, who reviewed them and told us that Yando and I needed a few more shots. I took mine in silence. A Spanish-speaking member of the shelter's staff then came by to bring us upstairs. As we walked through

hallways and up staircases buzzing with the chatter and arguments of the shelter residents, our guide gave Mom an overview of the shelter's rules: hours, curfew, and mandatory drug testing for parents—the news of which made Mom wince.

"I've never used drugs in my life!"

He shrugged and continued talking.

"These," he said, pointing to his left as we came out of the staircase onto the third floor, "are the bathrooms and showers on your floor. This"—he pointed to a door at the end of the third-floor hallway—"will be your room."

We walked into our new home. The furniture consisted of a table, two steel closets, and two beds. Our guide left us to ourselves. Mom helped Yando take off his sneakers; I kicked mine off. After about a minute, Mom picked my sneakers up from the floor and tossed them into one of the closets.

"*Mi'jo,*" she said, smiling, "your sneakers smell so bad! They can have a closet to themselves."

I knew why my sneakers were smelly: I hadn't showered in weeks. But Mom's words didn't make me feel self-conscious. Instead they brought a smile to my face. I was proud of my smelly feet. Together we laughed.

Within minutes, I fell asleep.

A FEW DAYS after we'd arrived, Mom enrolled me in the fourth grade at nearby PS 2 and Yando in a pre-K program. To get ready for school, we'd wake up at 6:30 every morning. Yando would be first out of bed; I'd follow. Mom would fold our towels and underwear, place the shower soap and toothbrushes in my hands, and walk us to the communal men's bathroom, where she'd wait by the door.

Mom had fought to be allowed inside the men's bathroom with

us whenever we went to shower. But shelter staff insisted that it was safe for us to shower and refused to grant her permission to step into the bathroom with us. So she'd ordered me to scream as loudly as I could if anyone came near Yando or me—she'd heard that really bad things happened in the bathrooms, especially to children left unprotected. Also on her orders, Yando and I would keep our sneakers on while we showered and brushed our teeth, to keep our feet from touching the pools of urine and the streaks of shit on the bathroom floor.

After showering, we'd return to our room and get dressed. Mom had somehow hustled an iron to press my public school uniform: white shirt, blue slacks. Then the breakfast bell would ring, and the hallway would crowd with families on their way to the cafeteria. The selection always consisted of Wonder Bread, small cereal boxes, and little cartons of milk. From time to time, fruit appeared: apples, bananas, oranges. You could also serve yourself some mashed potatoes or some sloppy joes, alone or on a bun.

At the long dining tables, the residents would clump together by ethnicity and complain. "Staff sure loves the white families." "These black druggies can't get their shit together." "*Blanquitos* get all the good stuff." "We're all being treated like shit, so who fucking cares?" Sometimes fights broke out.

I didn't eat much. Under Mom's gaze, I willed myself—I didn't want to disappoint her—but on some days it was simply too hard: the food tasted nasty, and the milk was expired. Mom wouldn't reproach me the way she used to when we lived in Jackson Heights and I happened to leave *unos granitos de arroz* on the plate after dinner. But Yando wouldn't eat anything. At best he would peck, and no amount of pleading could induce him into eating more.

Our first month at Catherine Street, Mom repeatedly took us to the staff office in the mornings and aired her frustrations to the Spanish-speaking employees. "If only," she'd tell them, "I could cook, my children would eat. Don't you see"—and here she would hold my or Yando's arm—"how thin they're getting?!" Mom kept making herself a nuisance until she'd wrung a pot and a hot plate out of them. And so Yando and I woke one morning to a delicious smell and Mom's joyous exclamation: "I boiled some *platanos* and *huevos* for you!" Plantains and eggs bought with the food stamps she received for Yando. We smiled at her and licked our plates clean. But we couldn't afford to eat plantains and eggs every morning, and we still had to report to breakfast in the cafeteria.

After breakfast, we'd put our coats on and head out to school. Mom would drop me off first. PS 2 stood on the corner of Henry and Pike Streets, in the shadow of the Manhattan Bridge. Every day on the walk, we'd pass a comic book store. I'd always slow down a little to take a closer look at the Batman comics in the window display.

"*¿Eso te interesa?*" Mom had asked me once.

I'd shaken my head. I knew we didn't have money—how could I ask Mom to buy me a comic?

One morning I'd noticed a new comics cover on one of the shelves. Batman was bent over a hulking beast's knee, on the verge of being snapped like a toothpick. His eyes were closed, and his face was bloodied. I couldn't stand to look at it. I hurried away and tried to avoid looking at the comics every day after that. How could Batman lose? How could someone crush him like that? I didn't understand.

We'd arrive at the PS 2 schoolyard: time to ask for Mom's blessing.

"*Bendición,* Mamá."

"*Que Dios te bendiga, mi'jo,*" she'd reply, kissing me on the forehead.

I'd line up with my fourth-grade classmates. Mom would go to drop off Yando at pre-K before reporting to the mandatory employment orientation sessions held at the shelter.

EVERY FEW WEEKS, Mom would call Tía Altagracia and Tía Mercedes from a pay phone in the shelter. But before we'd placed our first call to them, Mom had pulled me aside.

"Remember, no one needs to know our business. You don't talk to anyone about where we are or what we're doing here unless I tell you to, okay? We don't need their help. And I don't want their pity. When everything is back in order, we'll see them and spend time with them, but for now they don't need to see us. They don't need to know what we're going through. They'll ask too many questions."

On the phone with them, Mom didn't say much. Yes, we were all fine. Yes, they could come visit us one day, but not soon. No, unfortunately, we wouldn't be making it for the holidays. We had other plans, and life was just a bit crazy at the moment, but come the new year, we'd see them again. Yando? Great—he's very healthy. And Dan-el? Perfect report card.

Then Mom would pass the phone to me. I'd say "*Bendición, Tía*" to each of them and answer their questions about school. They would compliment me and tell me I was becoming quite the *hombrecito*.

The rules in force for the calls to my aunts also applied to conversations with Dad, whom we called from time to time with phone cards purchased from a Chinatown bodega. Everything was fine, school was great, I was reading many wonderful books—that was it. It felt strange not to tell the full truth, to talk about everything except the new experience that dominated every aspect of our lives. But how weird would it be to explain to my aunts or to Dad where we were living?

———————

I WAS TOO EMBARRASSED to tell my fourth-grade classmates that I lived in a shelter. I imagined they all had nice apartments like our old one in Jackson Heights. If they asked where I lived, I said I lived just off Catherine Street and left it at that. If they asked any more questions, I told them that my family used to live in Queens. Then I made a point of telling them that I was Dominican. I thought I'd seem cooler if they knew I was from Santo Domingo.

"Oh, so you speak Spanish?" they'd ask.

"Pero claro que sí," I'd reply, in my most *tíguere* Dominican accent.

My few memories of Santo Domingo—the faces of my cousins and old neighbors, the sounds and smells of my old neighborhood—were fading with each passing day, but I took pride in being able to speak Spanish. And I really tried to show off my Spanish-speaking skills to the two cute girls in my grade; one was Puerto Rican, the other Venezuelan.

I enjoyed school most during reading time, when I could go to the tables in the back of my classroom and pick out any book I wanted. I loved reading Roald Dahl, and every so often I'd daydream of being James in a giant peach, or Charlie in a great glass elevator. I enjoyed recess, too: the boys in my grade would always get together and play football. I could run fast, but I wasn't great at making catches, and sometimes the football would hit me right in the face and I'd have to go to the nurse.

I was saddest when Mom came to pick me up at the end of the day. No one asked me to hang out with them after school. But I didn't ask anyone to hang out with me, either, because Catherine Street had a rule forbidding visitors from entering the shelter. And even if the shelter hadn't had that rule, it would have been so strange for them to come over: I didn't have anything to show them. No toys, no Nintendo, no comics, nothing.

EVENINGS AND WEEKENDS I spent reading and talking to Mom. Through regular, bilingual pleading with the shelter staff, Mom had managed to score a very small TV, which was perpetually set to Univision. But she set rules: we could watch the *noticiero* and from time to time *Primer Impacto,* but *telenovelas* were off-limits. And I had to read.

The shelter had a library on the top floor whose books residents were allowed to borrow on their honor. Most weekday nights, I'd prowl through the stacks in search of something interesting. I looked for what I thought were real books: grown-up, fact-filled books, not the bunny-rabbit children's softcovers that crowded the shelves. One of the first books I checked out was a children's book on Spain. From this book I learned not only that Spain had the highest average elevation of any country in Europe (Switzerland included) but also that weekdays in Spain were organized around the siesta. Everyone took naps right after lunch! So cool.

"Mom," I asked one night in our bedroom, "do people in our country take siestas, too?"

"*Claro,*" she replied. She described our siesta time in Santo Domingo: how she'd leave work and head back home to find the babysitter minding me while I napped, naked, on the floor of the blue house. The days were very hot, and the living room tiles were very cool. The babysitter had tried to get me to move to my bed, but Mom and she had finally talked it over and decided that, yes, I could sleep on the floor.

Mom explained to me that in many other respects, Spain and the Dominican Republic were very different. We spoke Spanish, but our Spanish was different—it was *no tan refina'o,* because we peppered our sentences with *"dique"* and dropped every *s* we could. Plus our *patria* wasn't all that far from the United States, but Spain was an ocean away, in Europe. And Europe was funny, because over there people spoke so many languages! Not just Spanish and English, but French and Italian and Greek and Russian and Polish.

The next book I borrowed from the library was a textbook called *Exploring World History.* After I finished reading it, I came back to Mom with more questions. It was strange to me that *Exploring World History*—and every history textbook I came across in the shelter library—had so little to say about the Dominican Republic. I knew the name of our current president, Joaquín Balaguer, but who was president before him?

"Antes de Balaguer," she began, "there was Salvador Jorge Blanco, but he was corrupt. Francisco Caamaño, Antonio Imbert—Balaguer outlived them and replaced them. Before that, there was Juan Bosch, but the Americans wouldn't let him be our president. Balaguer was there, he'd worked under Trujillo, and so they picked him over Bosch."

Rafael Trujillo was evil. One night, Mom told me the story of why her dad, Abuelo Memo, hadn't been around when she was born. Trujillo's men had beaten him and left him for dead in a ditch, all because—*dique*—Abuelo had been overheard complaining about Trujillo. Memo had come to his senses, fled the country in a *yola,* and spent a few years in Cuba. But what happened to him, Mom said, had also happened to a lot of men and women back then. Abuelo was lucky: he'd lived.

"But before Trujillo," Mom was now telling me, "we were a Spanish colony. Columbus came to our island. The first university in the Americas opened up in Santo Domingo—that's the same university I went to. We were a colony until 1821, when we won our independence. But then the Haitians conquered us, and we had to fight them to regain our independence in 1844. Juan Pablo Duarte and his companions set Quisqueya free."

Mom knew so much history. I was in awe.

ONE EVENING, I came across a book in the shelter library titled *How People Lived in Ancient Greece and Rome*. I took it down from its shelf and brought it back to our room to read. Most of the front cover and the first few pages were covered in doodles and scrawls, but the opening, doodle-free paragraphs of the text were set against illustrations of a man in a toga reading a scroll; a young man strumming a lyre, with another laurel-crowned youth looking on attentively; a black vase, decorated with a band of warriors; an open scroll; a spear- and shield-wielding warrior; an aqueduct; fortifications; and a temple. The first few sentences grabbed my attention:

> Western civilization was formed from the union of early Greek wisdom and the highly organized legal minds of early Rome. The Greek belief in a person's ability to use his powers of reason, coupled with Roman faith in military strength, produced a result that has come to us as a *legacy,* or gift from the past. This legacy has grown and blossomed into a smooth, colorful way of life—covering equally the arts and the sciences, the one and the many.

My eyes were glued to the page. I hadn't had quite that same experience of intense focus when learning about the people and customs of Spain or about the Dominican Republic's presidents. It had been fun to learn those things; it was even more fun to know that I knew them. But this book talked about a *legacy* and a *way of life.* Those words made Greece and Rome seem much more important than anything I'd read about before.

The book began with a chapter on sites in early Greece and Rome. There were maps of the Mediterranean in the time of the Roman Republic and Empire, regions shaded in blue and purple and orange that were dotted with cities whose names were familiar—Rome, because that's where the pope lived, Mom told me; Athens, because Dad had once said to me that the most famous Greek philosophers were Athenians—and others that were unfamiliar: Corinth, Mycenae, Thebes. There were descriptions of the climate, followed closely by an end-of-chapter question for further thought: "Do you think the locations in which these cultures developed had anything to do with the advanced nature of their civilizations? Why?"

I paused for a moment, stumped. I was encouraged when I saw that one of the book's previous owners had traced a box around the "Why?" I kept on reading, about the invasions of the Persians and the domination of Athens, the Peloponnesian Wars that pitted Athens against Sparta, Alexander the Great and his conquest of the entire known world. With the help of drawings and maps, I imagined what it would have been like to fight in Darius's army, to drink wine at a symposium while poetry was recited, to talk with philosophers. But then a recap question on page 41 left me searching for answers that I couldn't seem to find in the book itself: "In a civilization such as early Greece, where man was so highly respected, why were some people made slaves and treated cruelly? Is it possible for people to act in the same way today?"

I'd read about slaves in library textbooks on American history. I'd come across the word *discrimination* and learned about its roots in slavery. Talking to Mom, I'd learned that in Santo Domingo there had been slaves, too: *negros* from Africa, *indios* from the island. The white slave owners had had children with them—black and white slave children, *moreno* and *trigueño* slave children—and that's why Dominicans now were so many different skin colors. Now I was learning that the Greeks had slaves, too. All the good things that they had done to create modern civilization—and they'd had slaves.

Next in my new book came the Romans. They'd conquered the Greeks. They'd conquered everyone else in the Mediterranean. I learned that kings had ruled them first and that, after the kings were kicked out, Rome had become an *oligarchic republic,* usually headed by consuls but also, in emergencies, by a dictator. The Roman dictator wasn't like a modern one; not even Julius Caesar was like Trujillo. In my mind I heard Mom's favorite joke:

"Desde que Brutus mató a César, ¡los brutos viven sin cesar!"

When Mom first told the joke, I laughed because I felt it was the grown-up thing to do. I didn't really get what was so funny about it. Now I got it. I read and reread the book and never returned it to the library.

DURING THE HOLIDAYS, Mom volunteered at the shelter's main office and helped staff pack and wrap the little packets that each family received as a gift from the shelter. The packets were going to be handed out at the Holiday Dinner, to the delight of parents and children alike. Right after the dinner, the curfew rule would be waived, and families would be allowed to spend a few days with relatives and friends in the outer boroughs or suburbs.

One of the shelter staff, a slender Puerto Rican woman with graying hair, was curious to know where we were going for Christmas.

"Do you have any family you and the kids can stay with, Maria Elena?"

"No," Mom said, while I stood next to her. "We'll be staying here."

I couldn't believe we were going to remain in that miserable building with awful food for the entire holiday season! But I knew better than to complain. That was a fast track to the *pela*. Besides, Mom had promised Yando and me a surprise. It was revealed on Christmas Day: she'd saved enough from the $42.50 bimonthly welfare cash payments to take us on multiple trips to McDonald's. Christmas morning: the first trip. New Year's: a second trip. The day of the Tres Reyes Magos: a third trip. My meal of choice was the Big Mac with fries and a large soda; Yando's, the Happy Meal with a toy.

But our main holiday diversion was walking. Rain, snow, or shine, we strolled all over downtown Manhattan, from the base of the Manhattan Bridge to Canal Street, up into Little Italy via Mott and Mulberry, past the restaurants and trinket shops. From Madison Street to St. James Place and Pearl Street, then up the stairs to the massive headquarters of the New York City Police Department; next, down the Avenue of the Finest, staying parallel to the Brooklyn Bridge rampart, until we hit City Hall Park. Across Chambers Street to the West Side, crossing the West Side Highway; Nelson A. Rockefeller Park, the Esplanade, the Twin Towers, Rector Street, Wall Street, Battery Park, South Ferry, Water Street, Fulton Street, South Street Seaport.

Mom loved the sight of the rivers most, I think, and Yando loved any park with slides; but I loved the adventure of the walk itself, the ever-present possibility that I might come across a new street or park whose name I could recite and commit to memory. So I'd plead with Mom to keep walking, even when our feet started to hurt.

THERE WAS SOMETHING very weird about my brother: he didn't really talk. It wasn't like he was *sordomudo*: if you talked to him, he'd say a few words in response; sometimes he'd even put a full sentence or two together. Most of the time, though, he didn't say anything. If he wanted to tell you that he didn't like his food or that he didn't want to keep walking or that he wanted to sleep, he'd pout or cry. He was *caprichoso* like that; everything had to be his way. His crying was soft and low—silent tears—because Mom kept telling us over and over again that we couldn't be like all the other shelter children, *dando carpeta* and being so dramatic.

The pickiness Mom could deal with, but the not talking bothered her. She didn't show any concern while the three of us were together, but on the way to pick him up from pre-K in the afternoons, or late at night when he was asleep, she'd worry aloud:

"*Dios mío,* please, I hope the medicines I took when I was pregnant didn't hurt him. Those doctors said those medicines might have some side effects. *Ay, Dios mío,* what did I do?"

I didn't quite understand why she was saying that. If she looked my way, I'd usually nod and try to look serious.

On one of the days I had off from school, Mom brought me with Yando to his pre-K. She was taking him to see a speech therapist there that day and wanted me around in case she needed a translator. While we waited in one of the classrooms, my brother went off with the therapist. Thirty minutes later, Yando came out and went straight to his pre-K playmates. The therapist came up to Mom and said:

"Your son is okay. He doesn't have a developmental problem. He just doesn't *like* to talk. He'll be fine."

Mom wasn't so sure.

"He *doesn't* have a problem? He's going to be okay? He'll talk more?"

"Yes, Mrs. Peralta: he doesn't have a problem. Some kids just don't talk as much. But I can assure you that he doesn't have any developmental problem."

On our way home that afternoon, Yando said barely a word. That night at the shelter, barely a word. But little by little over the next few months, he began to talk more. At shelter dinner, he'd turn to Mom, point to his plate, and say, "I don't want to eat that."

In our room, he'd turn to me and say, "Will you play with me?"

IN FEBRUARY, Mom came down with a cough.

"It's just a cold," she'd say whenever I turned around in my bed at the sound of her coughing. "It's going away. Don't worry."

But it didn't go away, and within a few weeks I was waking up to the sight of her hunched over and coughing in a corner of the room. Eventually she dragged herself to the shelter clinic for a checkup. When she mentioned that she was having blood coming up with her phlegm, we all had to be tested for tuberculosis. Her tests came back positive. She was immediately placed on a course of antibiotics and ordered to rest as much as possible.

Our trips and walks came to an end. She'd take me to school, drop Yando off at pre-K, and return to the shelter to sleep. Her recovery was slow. She didn't have much of an appetite and began to lose weight. I didn't know how antibiotics worked and began to worry that she wasn't recovering fast enough. That maybe she wouldn't recover. That she would die and Yando and I would be left all alone to fend for ourselves.

One night, Mom put Yando to sleep early and called me over to her bed.

"Dan-el." She looked me in the eye. "You have to be prepared if something happens to me. I want you to pay attention to me. This is serious. I could die."

"No, Mom, you're not going to die. *No.*"

The tears began to stream down my face.

"Listen to me: no crying. Be a man. You have to be strong. If I die, you have to take care of Yando. You have to be a father to him. Remember that. Promise me that you're going to do well in school? And that you'll always behave well?"

"Yes, Mom," I said through my tears.

"Now go get ready for bed. Don't forget to pray."

I prayed my hardest, angriest Angel de Mi Guarda that night. I couldn't understand why God and Saint Michael would want to take my mom away from me.

THE ANTIBIOTICS ran their course, and Mom slowly returned to health.

In the spring, we began to meet regularly with caseworkers at the public assistance and housing department offices. When I didn't have to go to school, I accompanied Mom to translate.

"We need to get out of the shelter," Mom had me say. "It is not good for our health. I am only now recovering from tuberculosis. My younger son has asthma attacks. We have to be transferred out of Catherine Street before one of us gets sick again."

We'd been put on a waiting list for low-income apartments, but Mom wanted to make it clear to the caseworkers that we simply couldn't wait any longer. The shelter air had triggered Yando's asthma. And the crowded living spaces, the filthy bathrooms, the congested cafeteria all helped to spread disease. She reminded them that she hadn't been alone in coming down with TB: it had flashed through the shelter during the winter, sending several adult residents to the hospital.

"We are doing the best we can" was the usual reply. "Once we find you an apartment, or if a place opens up in another shelter, we will contact you."

Other times, we were simply met with stares and the shuffling of paper.

In early May, eight months into our shelter stay, an outbreak of chicken pox swept through 78 Catherine Street. Yando and Mom had relatively mild cases and recovered quickly. But I woke up one morning to pain radiating from sores on the ceiling of my mouth and the insides of my cheeks. A few mornings later, as I got ready to shower in the men's room, I stared for a moment at my chest in the mirror over the sink.

To my initial horror, I was completely covered in sores.

After thinking about it for a little, though, I was happy again. I knew getting the chicken pox meant I wouldn't have to go to school. We were doing these math units in class, and I hated them—it was just worksheet after worksheet after worksheet of fractions and long division. Because of the chicken pox, I'd now have days of freedom during which I could simply read to my heart's content in the shelter library.

But as I became sicker, reading stopped being fun. In a few days, my skin felt like it was burning, and I couldn't fall asleep. If I tried sleeping on my back, the sores on my back hurt; if I tried to sleep on my side or chest, those sores itched and chafed. I'd scratch until Mom slapped my hand, scratch even after she had rubbed down the sores with VapoRub, scratch when she wasn't looking or had fallen asleep. Then my throat became sore and my tonsils swollen; strep throat was also making the shelter rounds. Soon I couldn't swallow solid food, and I struggled to drink the liquids Mom brought me. Nausea set in. I started vomiting.

The sequence of hours and days grows blurry: I remember Mom crying and holding me to her chest, shelter staff coming into our room, Mom yelling at them that her son was sick and that it was their fault, shelter staff helping me into an ambulance, a trip to Gouverneur Hospital. I remember an attending nurse saying, "Now, stay very still," and I remember being frightened out of my delirium by the large needle that I could see moving toward me. It hurt, but I didn't cry—not until after, when a wave of pain spread through my abdomen and I held my stomach tightly and tried to squeeze the pain out. I fell asleep.

I woke up back in the shelter, Mom talking to me and petting my head.

The sore throat went away. Soon I could eat normal food again. And one morning I woke up and discovered that the sores inside my mouth were gone. I touched my sides and chest: the sores had shrunk to scabs that I picked until they oozed pus. It was almost time to return to school. I'd missed two weeks.

IN LATE MAY, we were called to a meeting with our caseworker and notified that we were being reassigned to the Bushwick Family Shelter, in Brooklyn. When Mom complained about my commute back into Manhattan for the final weeks of fourth grade, the caseworker assured her that I could easily obtain a student subway pass, and that the trip would take only about twenty minutes each way.

Once I was well enough to travel, we were moved into our new home in Bushwick: a large first-floor room with windows that looked out onto the shelter's garden. The shelter was much cleaner than Catherine Street, the families friendlier, the cafeteria quieter. But, most important, we had a kitchen.

"I can cook again!" Mom announced, beaming, on the day we moved in.

For the remainder of the school year, Mom took me to school on the J/Z line, from Bushwick to Chinatown and back again. I'd beg her to let us ride in the first train car: I wanted to peer out of the front window and see the tracks flying under us, the steel snapping and locking into place whenever the train switched from one track to another. Usually, Mom would laugh and humor me.

On our rides, I'd stare hard at the names of the stations speeding by: Chauncey, where we boarded; Halsey, Gates, Kosciuszko. I'd wonder why the stations had those names. But before long I'd usually return to reading my school history textbook, or one of the books I'd smuggled out of the Catherine Street library. My second or third time through the chapters on early American history in my textbook, though, the meaning of the train station names suddenly became clear to me: each station was named after a general who fought in the Revolutionary War! I couldn't conceal my pleasure at having cracked the riddle.

I shared my new insight with Mom, who smiled and said: "*¿Oh, sí?*"

I wondered if any of the other kids in Bushwick had noticed the names. I wanted to share my discovery with other people.

THE SCHOOL YEAR at PS 2 wound down. On one of the last days of class, my fourth-grade teacher held an awards ceremony for her students. The two students with the highest scores on the citywide reading and math exams would each receive a twenty-five-dollar check. First came the prize for the math exam. When Mrs. McGill called out, "Alena Chen!" I wasn't surprised. Everyone knew she was the best math student. But my stomach suddenly knotted up. I was jealous of Alena for winning the math prize. I began to pray that I wouldn't miss out on the reading prize, too.

"Dan-el Padilla!"

I walked up to the front of the classroom and took my check from

Mrs. McGill. The final few minutes of class that day lasted an eternity. I couldn't wait to see the expression on Mom's face when she saw the check. Twenty-five dollars! When she picked me up at school that afternoon, the first thing I did was pull the check out of my backpack and show it to her. I told her I'd won it for earning the highest score on the fourth-grade reading exam. She smiled and kissed me on the forehead.

"Look at my smart son! You're amazing! This is wonderful!"

We went to Canal Street in search of a check casher. We were turned down at the first few places we went because I didn't have any identification, but finally one place cashed it for a five-dollar fee. We headed straight to McDonald's. Yando ate his Happy Meal, I ate my Big Mac and french fries, and Mom asked me to tell her the story of the check and the awards ceremony. I couldn't wait to win another reading prize.

——— CHAPTER 3 ———

ONCE THE SCHOOL YEAR ENDED, Mom signed me up for the Bushwick shelter's arts program, which was held in a first-floor recreation room not far from the building entrance. While there, I'd follow Mom's orders and keep to myself unless I was talked to. The other kids would yell at the top of their lungs or talk nonstop about sneakers or basketball or new toys or Nintendo or their friends who didn't live in Bushwick.

One afternoon, the other kids and I had finished our art projects for the day and had a bit of free time before the program let out. I retreated to a corner of the room to read a biography of Napoleon I'd borrowed from the local public library. I was deep into the book when our art teacher came up to me. I hadn't paid him much attention before. He was a tall white man with wavy light brown hair who'd asked us to call him Jeff. I'd seen how some of the other kids in my class tried to rile him up by being disrespectful, shouting and hollering whenever he asked us to be quiet, running around whenever he needed us to stay in our seats. I felt bad for him. He was the only white person I knew in the shelter.

Dan-el, age nine, Bushwick Family Shelter,
Brooklyn, spring 1994

"What is your name, young man?"

I rose from my seat. Mom and Dad had taught me that it was polite to stand when greeting someone.

"My name is Dan-el Padilla."

It was strange to me that the teacher suddenly wanted to talk to me and me alone, but I didn't want to be rude. Maybe, I thought, he'd like to hear about the things I like. Maybe we could talk about books.

"Where are you from, Dan-el?"

"I'm from the Dominican Republic. Do you know the size of the population?"

"No."

Quisqueya pequeña en tamaño pero grande en corazón: The Dominican Republic is small in size but big in heart. I'd heard that line in a Univision commercial. I wanted to share my pride in being Dominican with Jeff.

"The population is 7,400,000. Do you know the country's size in square miles?"

"No."

"The Dominican Republic measures 18,705 square miles."

"Wow! Where did you learn that?"

Jeff's blue eyes were fully focused on me even as the other kids kept running in circles and throwing crayons.

"I read it."

"That's very interesting. I'm impressed."

I didn't see what was so impressive. I learned everything from books.

"And what's this right here?"

He gestured toward the book I held in my hand.

"It's a book about Napoleon," I replied. "He was a famous French leader and a military genius."

He kept asking questions. I kept answering them. I began to think that maybe I had a new friend. There was something about him that convinced me he was actually interested in what I was saying. He seemed different from the shelter staff Mom and I normally interacted with.

Most afternoons, Mom would be waiting for me, Yando at her side, at the door to the rec room when the art program let out for the afternoon. Not long after our first conversation, Jeff came with me to the door to introduce himself to Mom.

"Does she speak English?" he asked me.

"No, but I can translate."

"Mrs. Peralta? I'm so happy to meet you. You have a very smart son."

"Thank you," Mom replied.

"Your son is extraordinarily gifted," Jeff continued. "I would like to help him apply for a scholarship at a private school I attended, the Collegiate School."

I translated. Mom looked at me, then back at Jeff.

"Ask him," she finally told me, "what the Collegiate School is."

"The best all-boys school in the country," Jeff had me reply, "with many famous alums. John F. Kennedy Jr. is an alum."

"¿Oh, sí? ¿Y cómo se aplica? ¿Dan becas?"

"I'll help you through the application process," Jeff said after I translated Mom's questions. "And yes, they do give scholarships. Mrs. Peralta"—here Jeff paused, turned to me, and said, "Now make sure she understands what I'm going to say"—"your son must have the best education possible. I believe he will go on to do great things. I want to help you make that happen."

No one had ever said anything like that to me before.

Mom thanked Jeff, had me wish him a wonderful afternoon, and led Yando and me back to our shelter room. The moment the door closed, the questions came in a torrent:

"Who is he? Where is he from? Why is he interested in you?"

"He's nice, Mom. He asks me questions about the books I read."

"And what have you told him about our lives?"

"I told him that Dad left us last year and that we've been on our own."

"Dan-el . . ."

"Mom, I trust him."

AT THE END OF JUNE, we finally reached the top of the affordable-housing list. Shelter staff began taking Mom on apartment visits. I was happy at the thought that it would only be a little while longer until we moved out of the shelter and into a place of our own, but Mom was upset because the apartments she was being shown didn't meet her standards. Over dinner, she'd tell me about each visit and pepper me with questions. The first apartment she'd been taken to was in Canarsie. She didn't know where that was exactly, but when she mentioned that the shelter people were saying she'd have to take the L train all the way to the last stop to get there, I knew where it was. I'd memorized the subway map.

"*¿Queda muy lejos, no?*" she asked me.

"Yes, Mom," I replied. "It's far."

After each apartment trip, she told me she'd complained to staff: "No, *es* small. No like. *Es* no clean. *Es*"—and here she would point to her ears to indicate that the neighborhood or the building was too noisy. In meetings with shelter staff and caseworkers, she tried to make her expectations clear. I'd translate.

"We would like an apartment in Manhattan. Queens or Bronx are okay. No Brooklyn"—we hadn't spent much time there, and Mom didn't really know her way around. "The apartment can't be too far from the subway or bus. The building must be clean, safe, and quiet. We would like a three-bedroom."

Here the welfare and housing caseworkers asked me to explain to Mom that we weren't eligible for a three-bedroom apartment. Yando's public assistance benefits would pay our rent up to $215 a month for a two-bedroom. The cheapest three-bedroom apartments were considerably more expensive.

"If you had a son and a daughter," they added, "things would be different: we would pay for a three-bedroom. But since you have two boys, and two boys can share a bedroom, we will pay only for a two-bedroom."

They did start taking her to visit more apartments in Manhattan. They also told her that once she settled on a place, the paperwork would be ready for her to sign within a few weeks. All she had to do was choose. But Mom kept asking to see more apartments. Even if we didn't have many options, she wanted to evaluate every single one. She'd even ask me what I wanted in our new apartment.

I still wanted my own bedroom but didn't want to say so, not after Mom had tried to get Yando and me one each and failed.

"A desk?"

"I'll get you a desk, *mi'jo,* and a nice bookcase for your books."

IN EARLY AUGUST, Mom finally settled on an apartment and took me to see it. We rode the subway from Bushwick into Manhattan, switched to the red line at Fulton Street, and rode the 3 train to 148th Street in Harlem. The neighborhood was new to me; I'd never been to Harlem before.

At the corner of 149th and Eighth, as we waited for the light to change, I looked around and noticed an abandoned building on my right. Up and down Eighth, up and down 149th, I saw boarded-up apartment buildings. On Bradhurst Avenue, the next avenue over, there was a park—Jackie Robinson Park—that faced our new apartment building and ran from 145th to the Polo Grounds projects, a few blocks north. Our building itself was a run-down five-story tenement of brick, gray-washed with a layer of cement and bordered on the north side by a vacant lot covered with shards of glass. The fire escape snaking down the building's front facade hadn't been cleaned in years. On the landings, untended pots competed for space with rusting bicycles and bags of garbage.

Mom unlocked the outer door with her new key. We entered a dimly lit corridor and climbed a flight of narrow stairs. The corridor walls were painted one light shade of green, the stair rails another. On the second floor, we stopped at a sturdy metal door, also painted green, with 2B pasted over the peephole; she opened the door and I walked in behind her. We stood in the small front hallway, maybe three feet wide and seven feet high, and took in the apartment. Walls painted off-white, linoleum floors, a bedroom on our left.

"This will be mine," Mom said. "It's closest to the door."

Moving clockwise, we explored the larger room, with its windows facing out onto the fire escape and Bradhurst Avenue.

"*La sala,*" Mom continued. "We'll put a *mueble* along this wall, a table here. Your books in a bookshelf there, in that space between the windows."

Finally, the second bedroom.

"For you and Yando. We can put a desk right here, in front of the closet."

I was lost in excitement. We had rooms—several rooms—not just a basement or a single room with a kitchen! I'd have space to run around. I'd be able to read in the living room or the bedroom. We'd have our own bathroom.

"*Te digo a ti!*" she exclaimed in frustration. "They have to clean the bedrooms." She was standing over a streak of dirt on the floor of her bedroom. "And they said they would paint, but they still haven't done so. I hope they do that before we move . . ."

Suddenly she turned back to me:

"So, do you like it?"

She and I were almost at eye level now. The entire time we'd been in Catherine Street and Bushwick, I'd been growing, but I hadn't really noticed until that day that I was an inch or two away from shooting past Mom.

"Yes, Mom, I like it."

The move came and went in a blur. We didn't have all that much to pack at Bushwick: our clothes, my books, the small TV, kitchen utensils. But Mom had left behind a few of our old belongings with a friend in Queens, to be retrieved when the time was right. We made the trip to Queens and brought them to our new home. The beds came next, purchase and delivery paid for by the New York City Housing Authority. With a voucher, Mom then bought a hand-me-down couch, which she and I placed against one wall of our new living room. And somehow she also scored a white bookcase. Up on the shelves went my books—all from the Catherine Street shelter library or from shelter book giveaways—arranged in alphabetical order by title. We stood the case on top of a white cabinet with three rows of drawers and wedged our small TV into the bottom shelf.

This was home.

THREE WEEKS AFTER THE MOVE, Mom took us to PS 200 and enrolled me in the fifth grade, and Yando in kindergarten. He and I would be in the same school building for the very first time.

During the first week of classes, I discovered that kids at PS 200 spoke in a different language. I began hearing all these new words and phrases I'd never heard before, especially the N-word. If you weren't dropping it, you weren't cool.

"Ay yo, my nigga, you gonna kick game to shorty?" "My nigga, wassup." "You chillin', my nigga?" "I be good, my nigga." "We straight, nigga." "You ain't shit, nigga."

In the early going, my new classmate Victor was the only person willing to talk to me. At lunch and during recess, he gave me the scoop.

"See," he'd say, "but don't turn around so quick! That nigga right there, he got held back; he mad old and mad stupid."

Tracking my eyes as they followed a cute classmate, he'd interrupt my thoughts: "Yo, she got a real old man—don't mess with her."

Whenever my eyes followed a not-so-cute classmate: "She busted!"

He also told me many, many stories about people getting jumped. One dude he knew had gotten jumped by six cats. These cats, though, they didn't even beat the shit out of him. They just took his jeans and draws and made him walk back to the projects butt naked.

"The nigga walked back to the projects butt naked!"

Vic laughed. I laughed.

In the PS 200 schoolyard, cats were always trying to throw down. The few fights I'd seen before at PS 2 always ended when teachers separated the kids. But the fights that started at PS 200 continued after school, usually with an older brother or cousin bringing a little extra something to let you know who was the man. Beef started with a diss, and every diss was dissected at lunch in the cafeteria, along with the blow-by-blow of the actual fight:

"My nigga dissed this nigga, and that nigga came at him quick. You know what Tajuan said? 'Yo momma is so fat . . .'"

If the diss had been good enough, we would laugh and shout:

"Ay yo! Daaaaammmmmmmn."

Now, if someone dissed you in the schoolyard during recess or after school, you had to be ready with a quick response: "Yo momma is so broke . . ." Otherwise, you were a punk-ass bitch. People would think you were scared. You could even get snuffed in the face by another kid when a teacher wasn't looking. He might not even know you and still punch you in the face anyway. Because he'd heard you were a bitch. Because you hadn't stood up for yourself.

I wasn't creative with the *yo mommas,* but I learned when to drop the bomb on someone, the diss no one wanted to face: "Haitian booty scratcher." The baddest—the absolutely baddest—diss. Everyone acted like there was no recovering from that. But the most important lesson I learned was to keep a low profile and not say or do anything that would get me branded as a punk-ass bitch. I didn't want to get dissed, beat on, or jumped, so I wasn't about to start shit with anyone. And if people tried to start shit with me, I was gonna keep it real cool. I wasn't about to front like I was hard.

But the hard dudes were the ones who got the girls, who whispered into Rosemary's or Sugeily's ears during recess and got to see them after school. And the reports of what they had done with the girls made their way back to us, the kids who were too pussy to start real shit.

"Yo," one of my classmates would shout, "my man hit it!"

"Say word?"

"Yeah," he'd say, launching into his play-by-play. "My boy got all up in that at the park after school. She was like going *Uhhh* and everything, grabbing his shit."

I was jealous.

ONCE SCHOOL LET OUT for the day, I'd walk to the library to check out a book or two and then come home in time for dinner. After dinner, I'd go to a corner of the apartment—the tight little gap between my bed and the bedroom wall, or the edge of the living room couch closest to the window—and start reading. I wouldn't be far along before Yando came up to me. He'd have a toy in his hand—maybe one of the toy cars or Power Rangers Mom had gotten him for his birthday. He wanted to play. Usually, I didn't.

"No, no," I'd tell him, "leave me alone. I just want to read."

He'd stand there, looking at me as I turned away, and wait for a minute or two to see if I'd change my mind. Then he'd walk away. Sometimes, if I turned back around to see him leaving, I'd notice he was about to cry, and I'd feel bad. But I wanted to read. What was wrong with reading? Why couldn't he read, too?

One night, after we'd finished eating, Mom pulled me aside right as I was getting ready to head to one of my corners.

"*Mi'jo,* I understand reading is very important. But you have to play with your brother."

"Mom, I don't want to play with his toys! I want to read."

"He gets sad when you say no to him. You need to spend time with him. You only have each other."

"He should read."

"And he will, my son. But playing is important, too."

I started saying no less often. I mean, I still said no, because I didn't really want to play with Power Ranger figurines. If he wanted to play some baseball, though, I was cool with that. But we couldn't play in the park across the street after dinner. Not long after we'd moved in, we'd heard what sounded like gunshots one night; from that moment on, playing outside after sunset was not an option. And stickball with the hoodrats? Mom didn't want us even to *think* about hanging out with those *tígueres* whose parents let them roam the streets like a pack of *fieras*.

The solution? Stickball at home.

We didn't have a real bat, but we did have a miniature Mets bat, a gift from one of Mom's new parent friends at PS 200. We didn't have a ball, but we made one by crumpling up some paper and wrapping it in duct tape. In the demi-hallway that extended about six feet from the front door of the apartment to the front door of our bedroom, we took mighty swings. I threw the ball as hard as I could to strike Yando out. Most of the time, he did. Whenever he did make contact, I'd get mad and throw harder. And when it was my turn to bat, I swung lefty, holding the bat straight upright like my new hero Paul O'Neill and banging every pitch he threw right past him and into the bedroom door, until the ball began to fall apart and we had to tape it up again.

EVERY COUPLE OF WEEKS OR SO, the electricity in our building would go out in the evenings and I'd have to do my homework by candlelight. Or the tap would spew brown water, or the stove would refuse to turn on until the tenth try. But these problems didn't worry Mom nearly half as much as what she had me tell our new public assistance caseworker at our first monthly meeting.

"The drug addicts. Tell him how we're surrounded by them."

Walking into the building, we'd usually pass two of our neighbors on the stairs sharing a pipe. Sometimes the smell was pleasant, almost sweet; other times it was harsh, like burning rubber. I didn't know what lay behind the smells, but Mom pounced on me whenever she noticed me trying to sniff my way to answers.

"That stuff can kill you!" she'd admonish me on our way up the stairs.

I was curious, though: what was in that pipe, and what was in those little glass vials we crushed underneath our feet whenever we entered or left the building?

At the meetings with our caseworker, Mom was indignant.

"I'm a Christian, God-fearing woman," she had me say. "How can I raise my children in that environment?"

"That is horrible," the caseworker asked me to tell Mom. "Simply horrible."

But from the ensuing silence, I gathered there wasn't anything he could do.

I didn't mind the crackheads too much. They smiled their toothless grins at me whenever I came back from an errand to the bodega and were even polite enough to make way for me as I climbed up the stairs. While I normally tried not to engage them in conversation—I knew Mom would never let me out of the apartment again if she saw or overheard me talking to them—one afternoon a crackhead noticed the book about modern warfare that I was carrying under my arm as I returned from the local library. He read the title out loud, then said:

"You know, I fought in Vietnam."

This skeleton, I thought to myself—with his tufts of gray hair poking out of his wifebeater, arms covered in bruises, eyes protruding out of their sockets—*he'd* fought in Vietnam? I wanted to ask him questions, but then I heard rustling on the second-floor landing: Mom had opened the apartment door and was poking her head out. I nodded at him and hurried up the stairs.

I DIDN'T SEE OR HEAR Mom speak to my aunts on the phone for about two months after we moved to Bradhurst. She grumbled once or twice about her sisters not being as helpful as they should have been, but I didn't know why she was saying that. And Mom didn't explain her grumbles; she simply said she wouldn't call or visit her sisters until the time was right. I had no idea what that meant. It had been more than a year since we'd last seen my aunts.

One day, Mom finally picked up the phone and dialed. Standing nearby, I overheard Tía Mercedes reproaching Mom for not calling or visiting. When Mom finally passed the receiver to me, Mercedes told me that she'd brought her three children over from Puerto Plata. She and Tío José were living in a new apartment in Jackson Heights, not far from where we used to live. Mom had to bring Yando and me to visit.

The next call went to Tía Altagracia. On speakerphone—Mom was making dinner—Altagracia demanded that we come over immediately, the next weekend if possible. She and Tío Jesuito were still living in the same apartment. Her daughters were almost all grown up.

"And besides," Altagracia continued, "someone's been asking about you."

"Who?"

Mom turned off the speakerphone, put the receiver to her ear, and listened for a few seconds before finally saying "Okay" and telling Tía Altagracia they'd talk again soon. Later that night, our phone rang. Mom asked me to pick it up. When I said *"Buenas noches"* into the receiver, a man's voice greeted me.

It was Carlos.

About a week later, he pulled up to our building in a sports car, climbed the steps, and rang the buzzer. When Mom let him into the apartment, he greeted Yando and me with a hug, lifted us in the air, and let us swing from his tree-trunk arms. He smelled of auto grease, his hands were knotty from working under cars, and he was wearing his nicest gold chains.

Mom cooked dinner for him. They talked for hours about DR, Tía Altagracia, their families. He had two sons down there. He'd separated from his wife and had no intention of returning to be with her.

Soon he was staying over, first for a day or two at a time, then for a week or two. One Saturday, after he'd left to go to work at his shop, Mom pulled me aside.

"Do you like him?"

I didn't know what to say. He and I didn't talk much. He wasn't that interested in books, from what I could tell. But I didn't mind him, I saw that he made Mom happy, and he seemed to like me.

"Yes," I replied. Mom smiled.

At some point that year, I started asking for Carlos's blessing when I left for school in the mornings. I can't remember if Mom asked me to or if I began doing it on my own. Asking for the blessing, *besando la mano,* is how a well-behaved Dominican child shows respect and deference to the older members of his family.

"'Ción," I'd say.

"Bendición, mi'jo," he'd answer back, kindly.

———

OCCASIONALLY, my real dad would call from Santo Domingo. I was bound by a new set of instructions: I was not to bring up Carlos. Mom's instructions made sense to me. I figured it would only cause trouble if I did talk about him, and I didn't want Mom to have to worry any more than she already did.

On the phone, Dad and I talked about my latest report cards and about the books I was reading. He showered me with praise and called me his little *triunfador.* But I no longer looked forward to hearing his voice. A part of me still wanted Dad to be with us, but another part saw how happy Mom was with Carlos. And besides, Dad didn't say much about coming back. He did talk about his *compromisos* down there: he was consulting for a law firm part-time; he was doing some work in the port-administration-and-management sector; he had a very friendly secretary. But only occasionally would he say that he might be coming up to see us sometime soon. And then he never did.

The dad I told my teachers about at PS 200 began to feel truer than the phony dad who materialized on the phone every other week or so. In my stories he was the *licenciado,* alum of the oldest university in the Western Hemisphere; he'd gone back home to Santo Domingo, where he was a super-important person. But I didn't tell anyone that in my day-to-day life he was simply a voice. I didn't tell anyone how much I hated it that all I had of him, besides the few photos Mom had saved of us, were his words of encouragement on the phone.

By contrast, Carlos was *around:* to love Mom, to drive us around in his Chevrolet Corvette, to slip Yando and me the occasional twenty for junk food. I don't remember if Mom put me up to it or not, but a few months after his first visit to Bradhurst, I began to call Carlos "Dad."

———

OUR ONLY OTHER regular visitor at Bradhurst was Jeff, who came by every other weekend. Whenever he called ahead to ask if he could visit, Yando and I couldn't think of anything else. He always came ready with jokes and brainteasers, and he had so many interesting stories.

In his presence, Mom was guarded. Early on, she'd told me she was worried he might have a crush on her. But I knew that didn't make sense. It wasn't like he was trying to spend time with her. He just seemed to enjoy hanging out with Yando and me. And I knew I was right when, on his second or third visit, he asked me to translate something for Mom. He stood right by me as I translated.

"I would like to be their big brother. I know how difficult it must be for them not to have their father around."

"Thank you, thank you," she said to him. Then to me:

"Tell him I'm very grateful for the attention he shows you two."

After he left that day, Mom said to me over dinner, "He's a good man. God has sent him to us."

And she never questioned his motives again.

For my tenth birthday, Jeff bought me a book. It was a thick hard-cover: *The Complete Sherlock Holmes,* illustrated by Sidney Paget. I turned its yellowed pages, crowded with small print, and entered the world of Sherlock Holmes. I knew he wasn't real, but before long I began to hope he was. Every spare minute, I found myself reading about him, right until the Hound of the Baskervilles and the retired Indian Army colonel and the code of dancing men made appearances in my dreams. I began bringing my Sherlock Holmes everywhere, even to the dinner table.

"Dan-el, put the book down!" Mom would yell.

But I was persistent, and eventually she yielded: I was allowed to eat *arroz con habichuelas* while I read from cover to cover.

"How do you like Sherlock Holmes?" Jeff asked when he came over two weeks later.

"I finished it! I loved it!"

"You finished it already? Wow!"

Mom came to trust Jeff enough to let him take us on trips. On weekends, he sometimes brought along two sets of roller skates and took Yando and me skating in Central Park. The first time I strapped on skates, I couldn't stop falling over. Jeff was a patient teacher: "Do this"—and he would show me how to position my feet. "You brake like this"—he formed a T with his feet. It took me a while, but I got the hang of it. We'd roller-skate around the 72nd Street skating circle and then up and down hills, falling and laughing.

If Jeff didn't come around, Yando and I had to stay indoors. Late one evening we'd heard shouting across the street in Jackie Robinson Park, followed by a pop, another pop, a flurry of pops, and then silence. When we stepped out of our building the next morning, our whole neighborhood was a crime scene. Cops were all over our block. *"Gangas,"* the Hispanic women standing on Bradhurst whispered to one another. A teenager had been shot and killed. The body had been taken away, but there was blood on the pavement and more blood on one of the Jackie Robinson Park benches. Within a day or two, a makeshift memorial had been erected on the park bench: a framed photograph of the fifteen-year-old, surrounded by a few lit candles. Soon flowers began to appear. I never knew who kept bringing them.

No Jeff meant indoor stickball for us and more reading for me. I didn't mind—I didn't want to get shot. In a 1992 volume of *Reader's Digest* that I'd never returned to the Catherine Street library, I came across an abridged biography of Henry Kissinger and told myself as I read it that I'd be the next immigrant genius to make it big in government and politics. In another *Reader's Digest* volume, I read an abridged history of the Romanovs and imagined myself to be Rasputin, almost invincible in the face of poison and bullets. Then I checked out *The Count of Monte Cristo* from the local library and made Edmond Dantès my personal hero: like him, I was just counting down the days and hours until I could show everyone the kind of man I was.

—— CHAPTER 4 ——

I DON'T HAVE MANY MEMORIES of church our first few years in
New York. We'd tried going to Mass while we lived in the shelters,
but Mom couldn't figure out the Mass schedule for the Catholic
church closest to Catherine Street. After God gave us an apartment
on Bradhurst, though, Mom made a vow of thanksgiving: church
every Sunday. Initially, we took the subway to Our Lady of Fátima,
our old church in Jackson Heights—an hour-long ride each way. But
eventually Mom decided to look for a Catholic church closer to
home: commuting was expensive, and all that subway fare was money
we needed for food.

On a fall Sunday morning, we dressed up in the nicest clothes we
owned and took a walk around our neighborhood. In about ten minutes, we found Resurrection, two blocks from the main entrance to
PS 200. We started attending the 12:30 P.M. Spanish-language Mass,
and I was signed up for Sunday school to prepare for my sacraments.

The second Sunday of CCD, my new teacher, Ms. Cynthia,
opened class with a question: "What is the name of the pope?"

My hand went up.

"Karol Wojtyla," I answered. "But we call him Pope John Paul II."

"Yes, that's correct!"

When class ended, Ms. Cynthia came up to me and asked:

"How did you know the pope's full name?"

I was a little confused as to why she was asking. Was I not supposed to know?

"I read it in a book."

She took me down to the rectory to meet the pastor. I'd seen him before at Mass, but only from a distance. Standing in front of him, I was awed by how tall he was—basketball-player tall. And white. Jeff was tall, too. All white men had to be tall.

Ms. Cynthia interrupted my thoughts.

"Father Michael, ask him the name of the pope!"

He asked, and I answered. His eyebrows went up.

"What is your name, young man?"

"Dan-el Padilla."

"He's very smart," Ms. Cynthia said to him. "He loves to read."

I was both proud and confused. Yes, I'd read a name in a book and remembered it. What was so special about that?

"God bless you, Dan-el. When are you doing your Holy Communion?"

"Next year, Father."

"Keep reading. And behave yourself."

He smiled at me and headed off to celebrate Mass.

I couldn't wait to tell Mom that I'd met the pastor.

AT RESURRECTION, Mom made a new best friend, Carmen. They'd met before, in the PS 200 playground during kindergarten dismissal; Carmen's younger son, Peter, was Yando's classmate. But they didn't become really close until they started running into each other at Resurrection and learned that they'd both grown up in Puerto Plata, where my grandparents still lived. Carmen invited Mom over to her place on 147th and 7th. One day after school, Mom took Yando and me to visit. While we waited for her to buzz us in, I marveled at how much nicer Carmen's building was than ours: the front of the building was clean, the buzzer worked, and no one was loitering on the stairs. And Carmen's apartment blew me away: she had a large TV, a true living room with real, new furniture, and three bedrooms.

Carmen and Mom sat down at the kitchen table to trade gossip. Then I saw Carmen move her eyes from Mom's face to mine and back again.

"Maria Elena," she half-whispered, "is he your son?"

"Oh, Carmen, that's Dan-el!"

"He and Yando have the same father?"

"Claro que sí."

"Ahh. They look different, that's why I asked."

Mom seemed completely unfazed by the question. She and Carmen went on and on about the neighborhood and how unsafe it was, how the *tígueres* were everywhere with their pants falling to the ground, how you couldn't let the children hang out with the *negros* because before long your kids would start wearing their pants low and acting all disrespectful.

Meanwhile, I was steaming with anger. Who did Carmen think my mom was? One of those *cualquieras* who has kids with different men? Why didn't she think I was Mom's son? Didn't we look alike? Plus it wasn't as if she hadn't seen me before—I was usually with Mom when she picked up Yando at dismissal, and I was always standing nearby whenever they bumped into each other at church, so why was she so confused?

Only when we left Carmen's place to head back to Bradhurst did it finally hit me why Carmen was so confused. Carmen was light-skinned. Her children were light-skinned. Mom and Yando were light-skinned. I was black. And I didn't know many Dominicans who were as black as I was: Dad, maybe my Tío José.

I didn't want to be so dark. I wanted Yando's wavy hair and lighter skin.

Before long, Mom and Carmen were calling each other *comadre*. The word gave Mom the idea: Carmen should be our godmother when Yando and I were baptized in the spring. A little after New Year's, Mom asked her. Carmen eagerly said yes, and from that moment forward, Carmen was no longer "Señora" or "Doña," but "Madrina." But Yando and I still needed a godfather. Mom had one in mind:

"Would you like Jeff to be your *padrino*?"

I called Jeff to ask. He replied enthusiastically:

"Of course! I'd be honored!"

But when Mom introduced my prospective godparents to the pastor a few weeks before the baptism ceremony in April, Father Michael was a little surprised to learn that Jeff wasn't Catholic.

"He's not even Christian, Maria," he told Mom in the rectory as I translated. "He's Jewish. I don't know that it's a good idea to give your children a godfather who's not Catholic."

Mom was insistent.

"He's like a father to my sons, and I'm so thankful to God for that."

After mulling it over for a minute, Father Michael yielded:

"All right, but I'd like to have a talk with him first."

I never learned what was said in that conversation, but Father Michael signed off on Mom's choice of godparents.

For the ceremony, Yando wore a white suit and bow tie. I wore white slacks, a button-down shirt, and a bow tie, with a blazer to top it off. How Mom had saved up to buy our outfits and get us fresh haircuts, I have no clue.

Dan-el, age ten, and Yando, age five, with Jeff,
Resurrection Roman Catholic Church, spring 1995

At the Mass, I knew I looked good. But when it was time to stand up and walk to the baptismal font, I tucked in my stomach to make sure I looked as handsome as the other boys getting baptized. There were girls in the congregation.

"DAN-EL, do you have asthma?"

It was springtime. Jeff was taking us roller skating in Central Park. We had been going up one of the hills when I felt it: a tickle in my nostrils. I thought I was about to sneeze—but no sneeze came, my chest tightened, and I couldn't breathe. I braked and stepped off the roller-skating loop, gasping for air. Jeff helped me to a bench.

"No."

"Is this the first time you've felt like this?"

I nodded. Jeff pulled out a water bottle from his bag. I sipped. Slowly, my breathing returned to normal.

Sitting on the bench, I remembered what had happened at home a few weeks before. Mom, Yando, and I had just eaten dinner. I'd been doing homework in my bedroom and Yando had been watching TV in the living room. Then I'd heard a gasp. I'd rushed into the kitchen to find Mom turning blue and wheezing.

"Call 911!" Mom had gritted through her teeth.

I'd run to the phone, dialed, told the operator in an urgent voice that my mom was struggling to breathe, and given our address. I helped Mom to a chair and held her hand as she fought to control her

Yando celebrates his sixth birthday at Madrina's house while two of his first-grade friends look on, fall 1995

breathing. I'd tried to calm her as we waited for the paramedics to arrive. I'd told her that she was going to be okay, that they'd take her to a nice hospital. But the entire time, I'd been worried sick that Mom might die and I wouldn't be able to do anything to prevent it.

An ambulance had come, and paramedics had knocked at our door. One had fitted an oxygen mask onto Mom's face, another had checked Mom's vitals, and a third had asked if I had any family member who could come over and take care of Yando and me while Mom was taken to the hospital. Mom had whispered to me, in a barely audible voice, "Call your Tía Mercedes." I had called her while the paramedics brought Mom downstairs to the ambulance. Once I'd gotten off the phone, I told Yando that everything was going to be just fine and that we'd see Mom the very next day. He'd cried. Forty-five minutes later, Tía Mercedes, Tío José, and my cousin Sinelka had arrived from Queens.

I vaguely remembered the hospital trip to see Mom the first night after her asthma attack. At the entrance to her room, I caught my first glimpse of her: frail-looking in her hospital gown, pale, hair unkempt. My first impulse was to cry. But I didn't want her to see me sad. When she saw me approaching, she smiled, asked me to come closer to the bed, and kissed me on the cheek.

"Are you eating? Sini and your aunt have been cooking for you, right?"

I'd been eating, but I missed her food.

"I miss cooking. The hospital food is so bland, *no sabe a na'*."

"What did the doctors say?"

"It's those dirty staircases and hallways in our building."

A Spanish-speaking nurse had translated the diagnosis of the attending doctor. Mom's asthma attack had probably been triggered by dust mites. She was being kept for observation, because her lungs were still weak from the bout with tuberculosis a few years earlier. In the future, she would have to take precautions to ensure that she wasn't exposed to so much dust.

The next few days were foggy. Yando and I continued to go to school, but I couldn't pay any attention to my teachers. At the end of each school day, I picked him up after dismissal and we walked home together, where Mercedes or Sinelka would be waiting for us. They cooked us dinner, spent time with us, put Yando to bed. Finally, Mom was released, and within days we were joking about her hospital stay. But the jokes didn't last long.

One night not long after, Yando had problems breathing; Mom had called 911 and screamed into the phone; the ambulance had come and taken him to Harlem Hospital, on Lenox Avenue. There, the supervising doctor had informed us that Yando would have to carry an asthma pump—and that he, like Mom, would have to stay away from all triggers, especially dust and dust mites. Yando had been released two days later.

Within a week of Yando's release, Mom gathered up her own and Yando's medical reports and brought me along to a meeting with our caseworker, where she had me explain to him why we couldn't live on Bradhurst any longer. We had to be moved to a new building that wasn't falling apart, a building where the air quality would be better and the hallways and staircases better maintained.

"My youngest son and I have both been hospitalized with asthma! Living in that building is unhealthy for us!"

Our caseworker listened and nodded. After I'd finished translating, he said that as much as it pained him to hear what had happened, there was simply nothing he could do. We had to understand that we'd been lucky to land an apartment on Bradhurst. And besides, people came to him with far more serious medical conditions that actually justified an apartment relocation. He was sorry, but he just didn't see what he could do.

I'd felt so disrespected that day. There had been nothing more serious than seeing Mom, then Yando, struggle to breathe and worrying that they might die right in front of me. I couldn't imagine why this man refused to take us seriously—why he refused to heed the urgency in Mom's voice.

All those memories flashed through me as I sat on that Central Park bench. But I didn't tell Jeff that Mom and Yando had asthma. And I told myself that I definitely didn't have asthma. Being out of breath, wheezing—that was all just a one-time thing. I was healthy and strong.

"I'm ready. Let's go!"

And when Jeff brought us back home from roller skating that day, I didn't say a word to Mom about what had happened. She didn't need to worry about me.

OUR FORTNIGHTLY building blackouts reminded Mom of the *apagones* in Santo Domingo.

"When I was a little girl . . ." she'd begin, easing into story mode.

But I started to find it harder and harder to keep myself fully focused on her voice. A part of me wandered off into thoughts of the Air Jordans and Boss jeans that my PS 200 friends wore. I'd wonder how it could be that their parents always had money while Mom was forever broke. Even if they lived in the projects, they had nicer gear than I did. I'd been to the Polo Grounds projects with Mom to visit her new church friends: the elevators sometimes stank of urine and shit, a crackhead might be passed out in a staircase, but at least the apartments were big and clean.

I wanted to leave Bradhurst and live in a spacious, clean apartment, where the lights would never go out and the tap water would never turn brown and my closets would be stacked with fresh gear.

I'd have a study where I could read at my desk or on a comfortable sofa and admire bookshelves overflowing with books. Maybe I'd fall asleep reading on the sofa; Mom would wake me up and bring me a snack and a glass of lemonade, or I'd go over to our fridge and get them myself. The fridge would always be full—not just on the first of each month, after Mom bought groceries.

On his visits to our apartment, Jeff was constantly telling me that if I kept working hard at school and earning high grades, I'd make all of my dreams come true. I didn't tell him about my burning desire to escape Bradhurst, but when he said that he had a plan for my educational future, I listened very closely. He still wanted me to end up at Collegiate, the school he'd told us about at the shelter, but he warned Mom and me that admission wouldn't be easy.

"It's hard to get in. Not only would you be applying for a place, but you'd also be applying for a full scholarship to cover the tuition."

"How much is tuition?" Mom asked through me.

"Sixteen thousand dollars a year."

Dan-el, age ten, and Yando, age five, the Bradhurst
apartment, winter/spring 1995

I didn't even know families had that kind of money.

Jeff went on. "I think it might be a good idea to apply to another very good private school first. The Allen-Stevenson School is an all-boys school on the Upper East Side that goes up to the ninth grade. Would you like to check it out?"

"Yes."

A FEW WEEKS after our conversation, I received an invitation to come to Allen-Stevenson for a tour and a half-day of classes. On the appointed day, Mom dressed me in a blazer and tie. Jeff picked me up and took me in a cab to 78th and Lexington. The school entrance was just around the corner, on a street lined with trees and town houses. We were buzzed into the school lobby, where I saw boys in blazers and ties running around, bright fluorescent light reflecting from glossy, immaculate surfaces, and not a speck of dust marring the glass table in the reception area. Other than a fleeting glimpse of a black kid or two, it was all a sea of whiteness. I'd never seen that many white people in the same place in my life.

We waited in the lobby for about ten minutes, until a student my age and a woman from the admissions office came up to us. Jeff wished me luck and left me in their hands. The woman told me she was pleased to meet us and looked forward to chatting with me later. The student introduced himself as my guide for the day and took me to his classes. He talked incessantly as he led me around the hallways and into and out of classrooms. I tried to keep up with his questions about the books I was reading in school and my favorite and least favorite subjects, but I was too distracted to pay him much attention: everywhere we turned, I saw shelves lined with books, and desks with new computers.

This is it, I thought. This is where I want to be.

Soon it was time for lunch. I followed my guide to a table with eight other boys and a teacher. We stood up while grace was recited from the front of the cafeteria by a boy in a jacket and tie, then sat down to eat. From a basket at the middle of the table we drew and buttered slices of warm, fresh bread. At the salad bar, we loaded our plates with fresh vegetables and fruit. Back in our seats, we ate and talked about *The Count of Monte Cristo,* which the other boys were reading for their English class. I felt so in my element talking about Edmond Dantès that by the end of lunch I was absolutely confident I belonged at Allen-Stevenson.

But that cresting confidence crashed into a wall when I went to my afternoon interview with the school's headmaster, who stiffly welcomed me into his office and asked me to take a seat. From the bottom rung of one of the shelves in his office he pulled out a book and asked if I'd read it. I hadn't. He gave me a summary of its contents and then asked me what I thought. I couldn't put together a clear sentence. I grew frustrated with myself and stammered. It was only when

Dan-el attired in his finest while Jeff looks on,
the Bradhurst apartment, fall 1995

he asked me about the books I was currently reading that my confidence returned. I began telling him about my favorites and what I liked about each of them. He smiled faintly and took notes.

When Jeff met me in the lobby at the end of the school day, I was outwardly glowing with enthusiasm about the school, which I was sure would accept me. But on the inside I feared that I hadn't shown the headmaster I was smart enough to attend Allen-Stevenson.

A MONTH PASSED. On his next visit, Jeff came over to Bradhurst with news.

"Dan-el, they're interested in offering you a place, but they won't offer you a scholarship. It's a polite way of saying . . ."

I immediately felt stupid for thinking that I could ever get into a school as nice as Allen-Stevenson. I was never going to leave PS 200. I was never going to leave Bradhurst. My eyes began to fill with tears.

Jeff saw them and tried to cheer me up. "Forget about them! Everything is going to be fine."

But the tears started spilling. How could I believe everything was going to be fine when this wonderful school had just rejected me? I was doomed.

"Dan-el, they don't know how special you are! You're going to prove them wrong. They were a little worried about your math skills, so I'm going to work on finding you a math tutor. You'll take a few classes and everything will be fine. Don't be sad."

When PS 200 let out in June, Jeff came by again and took me to meet with a math coach at her brownstone offices on the Upper West Side. The coach introduced herself and opened with a question:

"What have you learned this year in math?"

I told her I couldn't recall having learned anything new in my fifth-grade class. At PS 200, we simply did multiplication and division sheets and worked on fraction problems. I was promptly informed that kids in private school were already starting on simple algebra. I had no idea what an algebra problem even looked like, but it sounded like grown-up math.

"You have some ground to make up," she said, "but we'll have you all caught up in no time."

She smiled. Her good humor was contagious: I smiled back.

Every two weeks, Jeff took me down to her offices for an hour of intensive drilling. The material was hard, and answers to the problems she set me didn't come easily—but I wanted to prove Allen-Stevenson wrong so badly that I didn't care how often I got stumped.

AFTER FOUR SESSIONS, Jeff came over to Bradhurst with an announcement:

"Ms. Cohen is very pleased with how quickly you've been learning the new material. Now you're going to start working with a tutor. He's a high school student at Collegiate. You'll meet with him on Wednesdays."

The beginning of sixth grade at PS 200 was a week away when Mom and I followed Jeff's directions to Collegiate for my first tutorial. We took the 3 to 96th Street, transferred to the 1, and got off at 79th and Broadway. The school was on 78th, past a Cuban-Chinese restaurant. As we approached the entrance, I took in the size of the main building: eleven stories!

After we signed in at the reception desk and stepped into the lobby, the first thing I noticed was the wooden tablets with the names of Head Boys affixed to the walls. Then I noticed the crush of teachers and students my age and older streaming into the lobby from several directions to board two elevators, little white kids running around everywhere in blazers and ties, and a mound of backpacks guarding the entrance to a courtyard. Through the reinforced glass separating the lobby from the courtyard I saw kids playing Butts Up—a game we played at PS 200—and a weirder game I'd never seen before that looked a little like soccer but with a tennis ball and didn't appear to have any rules.

Mom and I took a seat on a lobby bench and waited. A few minutes later, a lanky, stringy-haired teenager came up to us, shook Mom's hand, and turned to me.

"Are you Dan-el? I'm Louis. I'll be your math tutor."

Mom kissed me on the forehead and wished me well. Louis and I walked up the stairs in search of an open classroom.

Louis began asking me about my school and my math background. But I was distracted by the murals splayed across the walls of the staircase. Giants, monsters, students, faces, soccer balls: the images rose and fell as we passed the second floor, where students entered and exited in gym clothes; the third floor, where I heard the squeak of sneakers and the thud of basketballs; the fourth and fifth floors, where I saw classrooms messy with books.

Even more badly than I'd wanted to be at Allen-Stevenson, I wanted *this*.

Once a week for a month and a half, I went back to Collegiate for tutoring with Louis. I suspected that my meetings with Ms. Cohen and my tutorials with Louis weren't free, but I had no idea who was paying or how much was being paid. Jeff didn't dress like he was rich: he always wore jeans and a collared shirt, and he never talked about money. He'd told me a few times that he was a photographer, which didn't strike me as a job that paid a lot. So I was very curious to know where the money for the tutorials was coming from. Out of politeness, I didn't want to ask, but I sensed that Jeff was sacrificing his money and time to set everything up. That realization touched me and made me even more determined to prove Allen-Stevenson wrong.

AT PS 200, I was beginning to feel restless. When we weren't watching movies in class, we were doing reading and math worksheets that took five minutes to finish and didn't teach me anything new. My sixth-grade teacher, Ms. Terrence, saw the bored look on my face. One day she pulled me aside after class.

"You really need to be at a school that challenges you. Have you heard of a program called Prep for Prep? We can nominate you to take the test."

At the school guidance counselor's office, I'd read in a brochure that Prep for Prep was a fourteen-month-long academic boot camp—a summer session, Wednesday and Saturday classes during the school year, then a second summer session—with students just as smart as you. Plus Prep helped you earn admission to big-time private schools like Allen-Stevenson and Collegiate. At the end of your fourteen months of classes, you headed off to your new school. It sounded amazing. I told Ms. Terrence I'd be thrilled to do Prep.

It was early winter when Mom picked me up one day after school and took me to the Prep test—administered at Trinity, a private school less than a mile from Collegiate on the Upper West Side. Trinity seemed so similar to Collegiate: art and books everywhere, spotless surfaces, purposeful-looking students rushing to class. I felt that only in this kind of school would I ever have the opportunity to talk about books, to live a life of the mind. But I was jealous, too: why did the white kids get such nice schools?

I sat the test and waited for news.

THE NEXT TIME he came over, I told Jeff about how Prep would help me get into a great school with a full scholarship. But Jeff had news of his own for me:

"I think you're ready to apply straight to Collegiate. Louis tells me you've made tremendous progress in math. I'm confident you'll do great on the private school entrance exam. You'll be irresistible to Collegiate. Why don't we start working on your application?"

"Yes!"

I broke into a wide smile.

A few weeks passed. Jeff called to say that Collegiate had invited me to a day of classes and an interview with the admissions director, Ms. Heyman. Again I put on my blazer and tie. On the subway ride down, I was so excited that I could barely sit still. When Mom and I arrived at the Collegiate lobby, Ms. Heyman was waiting for us. Mom hugged me and whispered:

"May God and your patron saint Michael accompany you."

"*Bendición, Mamá,*" I whispered back.

I followed Ms. Heyman to the admissions wing, where several other applicants were waiting: four my age and another a few years older. To the assembled group, Ms. Heyman explained that we'd each have a student guide for the day. Soon enough, mine arrived: Zach, a skinny white kid who wore glasses and braces and had a slight lisp. Zach took me first to his science class, taught in a room unlike anything at PS 200: the lab desks were all a smoothly surfaced black, and test tubes and burners for experiments were stacked in the back.

The day's lesson was on the composition of the earth's crust and mantle. The teacher was young, pretty, and very energetic. With chalk in hand, she bounced around the front of the room, shooting questions. For one of the questions I raised my hand. She called on me. I answered the question correctly.

"Very well done, Dan-el," she said with a smile.

History was next. I'd read enough history books from the library to feel comfortable in Mr. Chambers's classroom, but I was amazed at the enthusiasm of the other students. Everyone seemed so engaged with the material. And the students who raised their hands to answer questions weren't teased by their classmates.

After history, I met with Ms. Heyman. Entering her office, I remembered my interview with the Allen-Stevenson headmaster and grew nervous. But Ms. Heyman welcomed me with a smile on her face and simply asked me questions about the books I was reading and the lessons I was drawing from them. I told her about the reading program I'd joined at my local library: "Solve Mysteries—Read." Each student in the program received a Reading Record sheet on which to jot down the title of each book he read. I had nineteen books on my record sheet. Most were biographies: Julius Caesar, Thomas Jefferson, James Madison, Abraham Lincoln, Teddy Roosevelt, Bill Clinton, and a book of capsule biographies of extraordinary Hispanic American men and women.

"I read them," I told Ms. Heyman, "because I aspire to be an important person who does good things in the world."

She smiled and scribbled away on her notepad.

On the walk back to the lobby, I couldn't wait to tell Mom about the science classroom and my interview with Ms. Heyman. And I was so smitten with Collegiate that I couldn't bear the thought of returning to PS 200 the next morning.

ANOTHER FEW WEEKS went by. One night, I was in the middle of my PS 200 homework when I heard Mom pick up the ringing phone and scream. Yando and I rushed into the living room. Mom had collapsed into a heap on the couch, screaming and crying so hard it scared us. I held her as she sobbed.

"Your abuelo Memo," she said, "is dead."

The phone rang all evening as each of Mom's five sisters called to reminisce about their father. Mom's tears spilled out in a steady stream. Memo had been ill with cancer for several years, but his deterioration and death had been sudden. Every one of his daughters had gotten to see him in person in the months before his death—except Mom. She'd been restricted to phone conversations, which grew shorter and less frequent as his health declined.

"I can't even go to his funeral," Mom cried into the phone.

I wanted to know why we couldn't go. I knew we didn't have much money, but Mom always found a way with money, so that couldn't be the problem. When she finally got off the phone, I asked why.

"Our passports are expired and we don't have *papeles,*" she said, fighting back a fresh wave of tears. "If we leave, we won't be able to come back."

Alone late that night, I tried to put together the puzzle of our *papeles.* It was the same problem that had kept Dad and Mom up arguing at night before he left us and returned to Santo Domingo. It was the same problem that made Yando the only person in our family eligible for food stamps.

I didn't fully understand what *papeles* were, but I decided we had to get them.

Two weeks later, Tía Mercedes came back from Puerto Plata with a lithograph of Memo for Mom. Mom installed it over the makeshift shrine in her bedroom where we prayed to Saint Michael and *los santos.* Every morning, we stood across from him as Mom led us in prayer. In the evenings, she told us stories about him. How Memo had taken her to his neighborhood baseball team's games; how he and his friends had taught a teenage girl how to swing a bat and field a ball. How he'd stepped in whenever Abuela was on the verge of delivering one of her *pelas*. How he'd tell Abuela to stop playing favorites and love Maria Elena just like she loved her other daughters. How he gave her money for sweets and made her feel special.

Mom allowed herself to dream out loud. One day we were going to fly back to Puerto Plata as a family. We'd be welcomed and embraced by all of her sisters. We'd visit Abuelo's grave.

I listened closely, and I fleshed out her dreams in my own mind. I was going to be the son who made her dreams come true. I would get my *papeles* first, get Mom hers, and before long we would be bound for Puerto Plata.

THE LAST WEEKEND OF FEBRUARY, Jeff rang to say he was coming over with presents. He arrived at our apartment with a small bag and pulled out two blue-and-orange Collegiate gym shirts—one for me and one for Yando. We tried them on and thanked him. Mom beamed. Jeff asked us all how we were doing. Mom replied that she was doing well, thank God, and that church activities were keeping her extremely busy. Yando said a few words about liking his first-grade teacher. I told him about the new set of books I'd checked out of the public library.

Then I sighed.

"I really hope I get into Collegiate. It has such a nice library."

Jeff's face opened into an enormous smile.

"You're in!" he exclaimed. "You've been admitted to Collegiate with a full scholarship!"

The admissions director had called him with the news. The letter and financial aid offer were on their way to our apartment.

I was almost speechless with shock, but I had to compose myself to translate for Mom. She started to cry. I cried, too.

WHEN THE ADMISSION and financial aid letters finally came in the mail a few days later, I inspected the Collegiate watermark on each and scrutinized the signatures to make sure they were real. At the top of each letter was the school seal in blue and white, and around it were the words COLLEGIATE SCHOOL • FOUNDED A.D. 1628. When I told Mom how old Collegiate was, she had jokes.

"Sixteen twenty-eight? It's almost as old as Santo Domingo!"

For her, the letters and their promise of a better future were God's gift to our family. She photocopied them and showed them off to her church friends.

Later that same month, a second set of letters arrived—from Prep, offering me admission to its new cohort of students. Since I'd read that the purpose of Prep was getting inner-city kids into elite schools, I wasn't sure the program would want me now that I'd been admitted to Collegiate. But I'd become very excited about the idea of summer classes, which seemed a much cooler way of spending the summer than sitting at home doing nothing. So I rang the number in the Prep admissions letter, explained my situation, and told them that I still wanted to come. The voice on the other end replied:

"Absolutely no problem! We'll figure something out. Welcome to Prep."

— CHAPTER 5 —

ON A JUNE EVENING, Mom, Yando, and I took the subway down to Trinity for Prep's Orientation Night. At the entrance to the Trinity cafeteria, a Prep staff member greeted us with a smile and handed me a packet containing a booklet introduction to the program, a planner, and the first reading assignment for the summer: Conrad Richter's *The Light in the Forest*. My eyes briefly lingered on the design printed on the Prep materials: the Greek god Apollo holding the reins to the chariot of the Sun and urging his horses onward. For a moment I tried to figure out what Apollo had to do with Prep—but before long Mom was tugging at me.

We waded through a sea of new students and their families and took our seats. Prep's executive director, Mr. Simons, introduced himself and began praising us as the cream of the crop. I fell in and out of attentiveness as I took in the sight of 150 black, Hispanic, and Asian American kids my age. I wondered just how smart everyone else in the room was. I wondered what each of them knew and didn't know, had read or hadn't read. I wondered if any of them spent as much time reading as I did.

Mom and I and the other students and families sitting at our table were then introduced to our new advisers, James and Akobe. All Prep students, we learned, were grouped into one of twelve units. Each unit had two advisers, former Prep students who had completed the program successfully and gone on to private school and college. James and Akobe shook our hands and told us where they'd gone to school. When James said he'd graduated from Collegiate and was studying at Princeton, my ears perked up.

I knew that even Jeff hadn't gone to an Ivy League school: he'd attended Vassar. I'd read that the Ivy League was where you got to go if you aced all your classes in high school and got a high score on your SAT. But I'd never met an Ivy Leaguer in the flesh. Now, here was James telling us that he was a Puerto Rican from New York who'd gotten into Princeton. But he didn't speak in big words or long sentences, which was weird, because I was expecting Ivy Leaguers to ooze knowledge every time they opened their mouths. And he was tall and athletic; I'd expected Ivy Leaguers to be skinny hyper-nerds. I wanted to ask James what the Ivy League was like and how he'd gotten there. I wanted to get inside his head and make every fact and book it held mine.

I paid no attention to the rest of orientation.

PREP MADE ARRANGEMENTS for a bus service to pick up students and bring them to Trinity for summer classes. On the first day of the summer session, an hour or so before my bus was scheduled to pick me up, Mom and I argued over what I could wear. She insisted I wear my public school uniform. I reminded Mom that the other new students had worn T-shirts and jeans to Orientation Night. Eventually I won the argument. But there was a problem: I owned no new clothes or sneakers; my nicest outfit was the public school uniform that I was refusing to wear.

When I boarded my bus that morning, I noticed that all the other boys had fresh sneakers, Reeboks and Air Jordans; T-shirts with cool designs on them; loose-fitting, new-looking jeans. I felt too insecure about my hand-me-down gray jeans and beat-up shirt to try to make friends. I was relieved when the bus arrived at Trinity and emptied its students out at the front entrance.

There, Mr. Simons was waiting for me.

"Good morning, Dan-el. How are you?"

I looked up at his crease-lined face, a little shocked. How did this white man know my name? One hundred and fifty new students, and he knew who I was? Did he know everyone's name?

"I'm good, Mr. Simons."

"We have a new schedule for you. We'd like you to follow this schedule instead of the one that came in your Orientation Night packet. You're going to be taking classes with the second-summer students, okay?"

"Yes, Mr. Simons."

I took a closer look at my new schedule as I walked to my unit's table in the Trinity cafeteria: Beginners' Latin, Intensive Math, Honors Literature and Honors Writing Conference, PIMAS, and PIMAS TPR. I didn't know what PIMAS and TPR were, but I worried that it was something I should know and that I'd come across as a dummy if I asked. So I kept my ignorance to myself.

When I got to my unit's table, James came up to me.

"How are you feeling?"

I put on the biggest cheese smile I could. "I feel good! I can't wait for class!"

"Do you have your new schedule?"

I showed it to him. Maybe he'd tell me what PIMAS and TPR were?

"You're going to be in class with the second-summers," he said, patting me on the back. "We know you can do it."

Basically, I'd been skipped: no fourteen-month boot camp for me, just two months taking the advanced second-summer classes. But how hard would those classes be? I began to feel a little scared.

PIMAS, I FOUND OUT later that morning, stood for Problems and Issues in Modern American Society, and TPR for Term Paper Research. The class was designed to introduce Prep students to the basic principles of sociology and to teach us how to write a term paper on a sociological topic of our choosing. The teacher—Ms. Haynes, a tall black woman with an awesome Afro—assigned us readings that ranged from dense passages of Émile Durkheim, for which I had to use my dictionary, to newspaper articles on the pro-choice/pro-life debate.

I quickly came to enjoy the material and Ms. Haynes's way of presenting it, but PIMAS was not my favorite class. I was finally learning Latin! And Honors Literature and Writing Conference was my true jam. The instructor, a tall white man with the fullest head of fiery red hair I'd ever seen, taught at a private school called Horace Mann. His first assignment for us was to read all of Book 1 of *The Odyssey* and prepare a summary of the book's contents for the next class. That afternoon, I boarded the yellow bus back to Bradhurst confident in the expectation that *The Odyssey* would kick ass.

Homer delivered: I was captivated by the story of Odysseus. Nothing moved me as much as the figure of Telemachus, the son seized with longing for his absent father. Angered at the suitors who swarm his house, he allows himself a moment of hope:

What if his great father
came from the unknown world and drove these men
like dead leaves through the place, recovering
honor and lordship in his own domains?

I immediately identified with him. Yeah, my father was alive, I had memories of him, we still talked on the phone. But Telemachus's questioning hope captured my own growing anxiety: that without a dad at my side, I'd have to fight for honor, respect, and recognition all on my own.

I FOUGHT ALL SUMMER. I'd heard that Prep was a place for the nerdy kids like me to meet and make friends, but it turned out that even Prep's super-nerds were cooler than I was. I was the new kid with the hand-me-down clothes and forever ashy ankles—so perfect for dissing. And the dissing didn't involve just recycled *yo momma* jokes. Prep kids were more creative.

"Why you always gotta look like a broke-ass Marine!"

It was lunchtime, early in the second week of Prep, and I was rocking these splotchy gray-and-white jeans. My assailant was a second-summer from the unit that sat closest to us in the cafeteria. About ten feet away, my advisers were talking to his advisers; they couldn't hear the dissing over the din of the cafeteria. But I didn't dare turn in their direction; if the grown-ups saw my look of distress and came over to end the teasing, I'd just be teased more ferociously later. And I didn't respond: my assailant had nice clothes, there wasn't anything about his face or how he looked that cried out for dissing, and I couldn't even remember a single *yo momma* joke that would shut him up. And what if my diss wasn't strong enough? What if he came at me with something worse?

So I bit down harder on my sandwich.

"Wack-ass first-summer . . ." But now my assailant had piped up just a little too loudly. James heard him, saw my expression, and came over.

"Everything okay, Dan-el?"

I nodded, trying to fight down the tears. Yeah, the teasing was over now that James had arrived. But I knew I'd have to see my bully and his friends again at recreation later that day—we were all in the same afternoon dodgeball elective—and I didn't want them to think that I was just some punk-ass bitch who hid behind his adviser.

By the time I got to the gym that afternoon, the recreation supervisor was splitting the students into teams. I was on one team, assailant on another. When the whistle blew, he picked up a ball and threw it straight at me. I ducked, but on his second attempt he got me. I walked to the line of "hit" students snaking along the wall and waited until I could sub back into the game. My first moment back out on the court, I picked up a ball and threw it with all my strength. It grazed him. Flush with the momentary thrill of victory, I didn't see one of his friends winding up to unload on me. A whiz through the air and I was clocked straight in the face.

But it wasn't long before I was off the waiting line and back throwing balls, aiming where I knew it would hurt. Whenever I struck, other kids laughed, a teammate or two gave me daps, and I felt awesome.

PREP GAVE ME lots of homework, but that wasn't going to excuse me from having to attend Mass at Resurrection, where I was now an altar boy. On a hot morning in late July, I made my way over to Resurrection to serve the 11:00 A.M. English-language Mass. In the sacristy, I put the server vestments on over my button-down shirt: white surplice over a wool cassock. I dawdled in the sacristy, parking my face right in front of the solitary fan that was installed in a corner of the room. But when the choir launched into the opening hymn and Father Michael signaled from the vestibule, the other altar boys and I rushed out and met up with him to begin the long procession up the center aisle.

At the end of Mass, I took off my vestments in the sacristy and headed to the vestibule to look for my friends. Out of the corner of my eye, I saw Mom and Yando waiting outside the church's main entrance for the 12:30 P.M. Spanish-language Mass. Mom was deep in conversation with Carmen and a few of their mutual friends, and Yando was talking animatedly to her son Peter. I waved at them and uttered a silent prayer that Mom wouldn't ask me to attend Mass with her. She had a habit of asking me to come along for a second Sunday Mass even when I'd already served at the 11:00 A.M.

"But Mom, I'm tired," I'd tell her whenever she asked.

"Too tired to spend time with Jesus?"

I couldn't bring myself to say yes; but sometimes, if I looked tired enough, especially during the summertime, she'd let me go with my friends without demanding that I come back into the church for round two. I walked over to her and Yando, greeted my godmother, and awaited the verdict. Mom studied my face.

"Go buy yourself a drink at the bodega."

She handed me a few bucks. I found six or seven of the kids my age hanging out downstairs in the church cafeteria and headed with them to the store around the corner. Three quarter waters and a few pieces of candy later, I was rehydrated. We slowly walked back up the block toward church. One of my friends suggested basketball, but everyone else agreed it was way too hot. So we decided to kill an hour or so in the cafeteria until the second Mass let out.

I was talking to my friends and daydreaming aloud about the cute girls at the Spanish-language Mass when the older teenagers began arriving. The "Immatures"—that's what they called themselves— usually went to the Saturday-night Mass, because they didn't like waking up early for the 11:00 A.M. For them, Sundays were strictly about hanging out, and so they rolled through, two or three at a time, until the cafeteria was humming with their gossip, their stories, their pranks.

I couldn't resist the pull of wanting to mingle with them. Pauly's baggy jeans, Frank's project stories, Michael's flirting with every girl who trailed them: these dudes were mad cool. When the older guys stopped with their storytelling for a fraction of a second, I jumped right into their conversation with the joint I'd first heard from Vic at PS 200: the kid who got jumped and had to walk back to the projects naked. I wanted to be cool just like them.

"Ay, yoooo, you hear about how . . ."—and I dragged my "yoooo" just like I'd heard them do before launching into my saga of the beatdown that wasn't.

At first I thought everyone would laugh and appreciate my storytelling skills. Then I saw the boredom on the older teenagers' faces. I became anxious, I talked faster, I made up extra details, I tried my hardest to get some laughs: nothing. The cafeteria was silence. Suddenly someone shouted out:

"Yo, your story was wack."

All the older teenagers laughed. My friends, too. But I wasn't about to give up. Another round of stories and gossip later, I was ready to try again. Except this time, one of the older teenagers simply cut me off:

"Yo, why you gotta be such a thirst bucket?"

Everyone exploded into raucous laughter.

"Thirst bucket!"

"Dan-el's a thirst bucket!"

"Yeah, look at him so thirst to hang with us, that young buck!"

The teenagers turned back to their stories. I steamed with frustration. When I felt the tears coming, I moved away from the group and, with my back turned to the group, sat at another table by myself. I clenched my jaw tight in an effort to force the tears to stay inside me—and at that very moment Father Michael walked through the cafeteria doors. The Spanish Mass had just let out. He saw me and walked right up to my table.

"Are you okay, Dan-el? What's wrong?"

"Nothing," I grunted through my teeth.

But there was no holding back the tears now.

Father Michael wheeled around.

"Boys, were you teasing him?" he asked the older teenagers, who immediately fell silent. Then, to me:

"Come up to the rectory. I'll get you a glass of orange juice. It's hot."

I stood up, followed Father Michael upstairs to the rectory kitchen, and sat down on a stool next to the kitchen counter. Father poured me a glass of orange juice, pulled up another stool, and sat next to me.

"Were they teasing you?" he asked.

"I just want to hang out with them," I muttered, fighting to suppress a new wave of tears. "Why do they keep making fun of me? It's like I'm not cool enough, like I did something wrong. What am I doing wrong? Why can't they be my friends?"

"It's going to be just fine," he said, passing me a tissue. "They're teasing you because they see how easily you get upset. For them it's just a game. But they're a little jealous of you, too. Everyone at Resurrection knows you're very smart. Even the older guys among them, they're intimidated by that."

I didn't believe that. How could the teenagers be jealous of me? What did I have that they wanted? He's just saying that to make me feel good, I thought. But is he lying? Because he's a priest; priests aren't supposed to lie.

"In the future"—Father was still talking—"you're going to meet lots of people—different people, very unlike the kids here or the kids you go to public school with—and you're going to make wonderful friends. But you're also going to meet people who aren't going to like you, because they feel insecure around you. I can tell you're very smart, and not just because you use big words—although that's what scares them: they think you're speaking out of a dictionary. Your mother told me about the summer program you're in and the amazing school you're going to this fall! That brain of yours is going to take you far. Beyond Resurrection, beyond Harlem. Don't be intimidated. And remember: if they tease or mock you, they're just jealous. You don't need to change for them."

RESURRECTION'S PARKING LOT did double duty as a basketball court: two hoops on wheels, rim height adjustable depending on how old you were and/or how badly you wanted to dunk.

"Yo, Pops can shoot the J!"

This was a momentous discovery. Father Michael—whom we all called Pops—didn't come out to play all that often, but the first time my friends and I saw him shoot, my jaw dropped. The older teenagers knew about his game because they spent more time with him, but I didn't have a clue until I saw him pick up a ball and just drill it from distance. I'd been thinking he was just some tall white dude who was really nice to me. But he could ball, too? What?

Now, it made sense that Father Taylor could ball. Our parochial vicar was a proud black child of Harlem who'd let you know that he'd been playing ball longer than you'd been alive. He wasn't tall like Father Mike, wasn't young like Father Mike, but he was built strong and played hard. When he drove to the basket, he'd lower his shoulder, and he could catch you with the step-back or the crossover if you weren't paying enough attention. And he had a nice stroke.

But usually the priests didn't have time to shoot hoops: they were too busy running in and out of the rectory, meeting with parishioners, bringing Communion to elderly women in the Polo projects. So the lot was ours to do with as we pleased, so long as we didn't scuff the cars or set off any alarms. We played teams, threw up trick shots, tried to dunk, beasted one-on-one. The younger teenagers almost never played with or against the older teenagers: some of the older guys had really nice game, and you did not want to get crossed so hard that you fell face-first onto the asphalt while everyone else laughed. So if the older teenagers came up from the church cafeteria to play, you stepped aside and watched. The only young buck who was ever allowed to ball with the older teenagers was Ray. Everyone made fun of him because he pronounced "church" *turch,* but the older teenagers picked him for games because he had the ill jump shot and could run circles around people. If I tried to play with the older teenagers, they waved me away.

"No thirst buckets allowed."

One summer weeknight, I was shooting hoops with Jorge, my godmother's son. His brother and my brother were running around the parking lot. Jorge and I were working on our game when I noticed two dudes pushing the parking lot gate open. I couldn't make out their faces until they closed the gate behind them and made eye contact with me. The taller, muscular, older one in the puffy jacket was Geno, and the skinny younger one with the mousy face was his cousin. Geno was in high school, Mouseface in junior high somewhere. I'd seen them both down the block before, on the corner of 151st and Adam Clayton Powell, messing around with younger kids leaving the corner bodega or cracking up their friends with stories about loose chicks in the neighborhood. They weren't church teenagers. They were just your typical hoodrats. And now they were strolling right up to me.

My heart began to pound. See, I'd made a big mistake. Yeah, I was a thirst bucket and a wack-ass storyteller and a loser at Prep. But I still thought I had game—that off-the-court kind. I'd been crushing hard on Jorge's sister, and I was positive that she was feeling me. She was fifteen turning sixteen, and I was eleven turning twelve, but we both liked talking about books. Behind our parents' backs, we'd started writing each other letters. We'd even made out in her room at Madrina's house when our parents were too busy chomping down on that *concón* to pay any attention to us, and I'd told her in my most suave *telenovela* voice that age didn't matter.

The next week, Mom had found the letters stashed in my bedroom and given me the yelling of a lifetime. But I hadn't cared, because Joemy was teaching me how to tongue-kiss. I'd felt so grown up. I'd even started bragging about it. But one of my PS 200 friends had a warning for me.

"She with Geno, though, right? He don't fuck around."

Yeah, Joemy had told me she'd been seeing him. But if he was such hot shit, why was she still writing letters to me? I'd fronted like I was bold to my friend.

"He ain't shit."

And now Geno and Mouseface were in my grill. Yando and Jorge's brother had paused their hide-and-seek game to watch.

"Yo," Geno said, pointing at my chest, "I heard your bitch ass is talking to my girl."

I tried to sneak a peek in the direction of the rectory. Maybe Father Michael was looking out the window? It was my only way out of the beatdown that was coming.

"You ain't gonna talk, bitch?"

And he punched me in the face. Mouseface had the instant reaction:

"*Ha-ha!* Fam, you snuffed that nigga straight in his face!"

I burst into tears. Geno had some final words for me:

"Scared-ass pussy. Don't ever talk to my girl again."

He and Mouseface rolled out. Jorge came up to me.

"You okay?"

I felt the side of my face.

"Yeah."

I dried my tears, took the ball from Jorge, and squared up to shoot. Anger filled my eyes with fresh tears. I hated myself for not fighting. Maybe I would have gotten the crap kicked out of me; better that than taking a punch straight to the face like a bitch and doing nothing about it. I hated Geno, I hated Joemy, I hated myself. But I took comfort in one thing: I hadn't fallen down when Geno snuffed me.

---------------------- PART 2 ----------------------

BOYHOOD

Boys from the hood:
Tía Mercedes in the company of Resurrection's altar boys, fall 1999

—— CHAPTER 6 ——

MY SELF-ESTEEM WASN'T at its peak when I completed Prep. But I told myself so many times that summer that Collegiate would be different—I'd be so effortlessly cool, the undisputed boss—that before long I'd allowed myself to float away on daydreams of my pre-ordained popularity. When the first day of classes finally arrived, I woke up at 5:00 A.M. and couldn't fall back asleep. Two hours later, Mom and I left Bradhurst to take the subway down to 79th and Broadway. At Collegiate's entrance, she told me I looked wonderful in my blazer and tie and kissed me good-bye.

I walked into the school lobby and met the new classmate assigned to be my buddy for the day, Ted. When Ted extended his hand for a handshake, I took it and gave him a knuckle-grinder straight from the public school textbook. I did the same for every single one of the forty-something pasty white boys of the seventh grade I met that day. I was determined to squeeze my way to coolness.

On the second day of Collegiate classes, I was making small talk with another new classmate. George had asked me if I listened to rap.

"Yeah, son," I'd replied, deepening my voice.

"You like Wu-Tang?"

"Hells yeah, son. Wu-Tang Clan ain't nothin' to fuck with!"

George gave me dap out of respect.

I knew about Wu-Tang only through my classmates at PS 200 and at Prep. Mom would never, ever let me listen to that *música de tígueres* at home. I had no tapes and no tape player, I'd heard only snatches of Wu-Tang playing on the radio and recited admiringly by Prep friends, but here I was telling George that I was the biggest Wu-Tang fan ever. Soon I was telling all my new classmates that I listened to that new gangsta shit. Of course I did—I was from Harlem.

The more I squeezed my classmates' hands, and the more I talked about the new Wu-Tang shit, and the more I conjured up all the slang I knew, the more everyone seemed to want to talk to me.

But rap, I quickly discerned, didn't give you the keys to the kingdom. At Collegiate, you were really popular if you were smart—a very specific kind of fast-talking, highly literate, ever so slightly sarcastic smart. And so I became obsessed with making sure everyone knew just how smart I was. Over lunch and after school, whenever my new friends and I launched into stem-winding conversations about the American Civil War or the novels on our English syllabus, I used the biggest words I knew and spoke in the longest sentences I could construct. It turned out that communicating your intelligence while retaining your coolness was an art in itself. Say you were trying to let other people know that you'd begun reading a really hard book the other day, something way too advanced for any normal seventh grader—a Dostoevsky novel, or Plato's *Republic*. You couldn't just say, "You know, the other night I started reading Plato," because someone would be ready with a volley of derision.

Most of the time, that person was Juan, one of the new Prep arrivals, gifted with a singular aptitude for bruising mockery. "*Oohhh,* look at me," he'd say, "I read Plato," and chortle.

———————

THE OTHER ROUTE to instant popularity? Athleticism. Intelligence might get you far, but a little athleticism didn't hurt. The Head Boys whose names were recorded on the wooden plaques in the Platten Hall lobby had distinguished themselves academically *and* athletically. The school newspaper put out by the upper schoolers went into great detail about every basketball game, track meet, and soccer match. And the annual yearbooks were crammed with photos of Dutchmen crushing the private school competition.

So, a week into the fall, I tried out for the soccer team. It seemed more fun than regular phys ed; I was becoming self-conscious about my body and worrying about what would happen if I didn't get into good shape; but most of all I wanted to be a social badass. Sure, I'd never played organized soccer before. I'd kicked a ball around, played random matches on the PS 200 playground a few times, and learned pretty much everything else I knew about soccer from watching Copa México matches on Univision. But I was still convinced I'd make the team. It wasn't as if any of my classmates were on track to become FIFA player of the year.

About twenty students came to the tryouts in Riverside Park, two blocks from Collegiate. We began with running drills that had me sucking air after five minutes. Then came the kicking drills. Whenever it was my turn, the ball slid off the side of my foot and sliced in the wrong direction. All the other students hit the ball cleanly and effortlessly toward the goal from whichever angle the coach told them to strike.

During a water break, I struck up a conversation with a black kid new to Collegiate. Unlike me, he wasn't from Prep. He'd stood out even among the very best of the other seventh graders: playing goalie, he'd blocked almost every kick.

"Do you play soccer a lot?" I asked him.

"Yeah," he replied between gargles of water. "My parents sent me to soccer camp."

"Where was the camp?"

"Europe," he casually answered before jogging back to the net.

Two minutes later, we were back to running and striking. I couldn't get myself to stay focused on the drills. Instead I thought about soccer camp in Europe: how much it cost, what it must have been like to learn how to play in one of the countries where everyone lived and breathed soccer, how I'd have mad skills if I could go to one of those camps just once.

The drilling and kicking went on every weekday afternoon for two weeks. Then cut day arrived. As the team walked back to school from Riverside Park, Coach pulled me aside. He was tall, rail thin, and dour, with a raptor-like face dominated by a slightly hooked nose. Rumor had it that he'd been on the way to a professional career in soccer until a devastating knee injury.

"Dan-el," he began earnestly, his enormous Adam's apple gliding up and down his neck, "I want to commend you on your hard work and effort during tryouts . . ."

I nodded silently, he gave me a pat on the back, and that was the end of my brief flirtation with soccer.

NONE OF MY CLASSMATES talked about money, but many of them did talk about things they had or places they regularly went that seemed to cost a lot of money.

"My parents just got me a new computer."

"My family's going to our country house this weekend."

"We're going skiing in Colorado."

"My parents are taking me to France!"

My go-to reply every time was "Cool." I didn't want to ask them questions about where their parents got the money to do what they did, and I tried my hardest not to think too much about how baller their lives seemed in comparison with mine. Instead I threw myself into studying for tests and writing and rewriting class papers. If I wasn't going to make it on the sports field, I was most certainly going to rock every single graded assignment. After a few early stumbles, I began to earn A's in almost all of my classes. I'd show off my report cards to Jeff, who was still coming over every other weekend or so to hang out on Bradhurst.

"Very proud of you, Dan-el!" he'd say, smiling and high-fiving me.

With Mom, things were a bit different. I was beginning to realize that my good grades were the only weapon at my disposal for countering and deflecting Mom's greatest fear: that Yando and I would grow up to be *tígueres*. She never explained what she meant by the word, but I gathered that she had in mind the slick-talking, good-for-nothing, disrespectful, foul-mouthed teenagers who paraded themselves daily on *Cristina,* her favorite Univision talk show. But even those *endemoniados* did not fully embody what *tíguere* meant to her. The *tíguere* was the realization of every single conceivable flaw in her children that would confirm her as a bad parent. In Mom's conception of the *tíguere,* the role of dress was paramount.

"Don't dress like that—you look like a *tíguere!*"

She practically worshipped the Collegiate dress code, because it forced me to wear a blazer and tie. But I didn't want to wear my blazer and tie on the walk to and from the subway every morning. So she'd try to guilt me:

"Why don't you want to look your best all the time, *mi'jo?*"

In response I wanted to shout, "I WILL GET JUMPED if I walk around Bradhurst in a blazer and tie! Already I get funny looks from the people sitting on the park benches!" But raising my voice at Mom would guarantee me either the *pela* or having to kneel in front of the *santos* for five hours. So I had to rely on passive resistance to get the point across. I came back home every afternoon with blazer in hand and tie removed. Eventually Mom yielded.

Emboldened, I pressed my luck. I hated on the jeans Mom had recently bought me. "Mom, I can't wear these tight jeans! They're embarrassing!"

Here Mom didn't budge, not for a while. My friends from Resurrection wore baggy jeans, some of my classmates at Collegiate wore them, but under no circumstances was I even to *think* about wearing them.

"A man doesn't dress like a *tíguere* with his pants falling on the ground!"

But then, to my shock, Mom relented again. She bought me a pair of relaxed-fit jeans, on the condition that I always wear them up to the belly button, *como un hombre.* I thought that was some Steve Urkel shit. Out of sight, I lowered them; in her presence, they came back up. But she'd sometimes catch me wearing them low, and when she did, she'd warn me that I was on the fast track to becoming a *tíguere.* In response, I'd whip out my Collegiate report card.

"Yes, Mom, I'll become a *tíguere,* all right—a *tíguere* who gets A's at school."

She wasn't buying that logic:

"You *should* be doing well in school!"

ON TUESDAYS AND THURSDAYS, I went straight to Resurrection after school and met Mom there. She was always at Resurrection for prayer group meetings, or adult catechetical instruction, or church cleanup before and after the weekday evening 7:00 P.M. Mass. To get to church from the subway, I'd usually walk up Adam Clayton Powell from the 148th Street terminal to 151st, then turn left.

But now I had a problem: Geno and Mouseface liked to hang out either on the corner of 151st or in the park across the street. About a month after I'd been snuffed for the first time, I saw Geno and Mouseface again. They were clowning around with their puffy-jacket crew on the north corner of 151st. Trying to avoid being spotted, I crossed Adam Clayton Powell and stayed on the south side of 151st. Too late.

Geno recognized me and started shouting: "Ay yo! Little nigga!"

I could hear Mouseface laughing.

"Keep walking, you scared-ass motherfucker!"

I kept walking. I justified it to myself: I was outnumbered, and Geno's friends were all bigger than me. But really, I knew the truth: I was a scared-ass motherfucker.

This continued every other week or so for a few months. If Geno or his crew made a move like they were going to cross the street and come after me, I would just sprint up 151st to church. But one day, I saw Mouseface with Geno's friends—and no Geno. Mouseface stared at me, but no one shouted, no one talked shit. Was the beef over?

I got some scoop from a PS 200 kid who was a cousin of a cousin of someone who knew Geno: Dude had been jammed up. Some juvie shit, theft or whatever. I felt so relieved. The beef *was* over.

So I thought. But later that week, when I stepped out of the public library on 152nd Street and Adam Clayton Powell, Mouseface saw me from a few feet away and rolled right up to my face. He and the puffy-jacket crew had moved off the corner bodega and into the open area of the housing development next door to the library, just up the block. I froze right where I was standing.

"Oh, this little nigga," he began taunting. "You scared, huh?"

He brought his fist up like he was about to punch me. I flinched.

"Ha-ha, you *scared,* nigga, you *scared!* Get the fuck out of my face."
I walked away. He and his boys exploded in laughter.

SPRINGTIME WAS APPROACHING when one of my Collegiate
friends asked me to come over to his apartment for a weekend sleepover.
I approached Mom very carefully, ready to promise to run every *diligencia* and perform every household chore for the next few months. She
was silent for a moment, taking the measure of my eagerness. Finally:

"I have to speak with your friend's parents. Otherwise, no. How
can I trust them and be sure that something bad won't happen to you
if I don't talk to them first?"

I beefed. She would have gotten to know them if she'd been
involved in the Collegiate Parents' Association—but she was too self-
conscious about her poor English to become involved. Whenever
she'd mentioned her anxiety about meeting the other Collegiate parents before, I'd understood; I didn't want her to feel embarrassed. But
right now I didn't have much sympathy for Mom's lack of confidence;
I just felt frustrated. I thought it was unfair of her to insist on speaking with my friend's parents first, not only because I was sure everything would be safe—what, I was going to be abducted by some kid's
rich-ass parents?—but because it meant that I would have to translate.
I didn't want to be a go-between. It was mad uncool, and I was willing to bet that my friend didn't have to do that.

This time, Mom wasn't caving in. So I decided not to relay her
request to my friend. When he called to ask me if I was coming over
that weekend, I played it off.

"Nah, man," I replied faux casually, "we're gonna see my aunt on
Saturday, then we got all this church stuff."

From that point on, my response to all sleepover invitations was a
variation on the same two themes: family obligations and church. But

I was eventually able to wring one concession from Mom: I could head over to my friends' apartments after school—if, and only if, I called in advance before leaving school to let her know where I was going and I returned home in time for dinner.

It was March when I visited my first Collegiate apartment. It belonged to the family of my classmate Steven, who lived on 83rd and East End. At the entrance of his building, a doorman greeted me, took my name, and showed me in. The lobby gleamed with metal and marble, and the elevators were spotless. But it was when I arrived on Steven's floor that the magnitude of the difference between his apartment and every other apartment I'd ever been inside hit me flush in the face. See, Steven's family owned the entire floor.

I chatted with Steven and our friends just as if we were chilling at school. But my eyes were straining to take everything in. When I noticed that there weren't many books around, for a hot moment I lorded it over Steven in my mind, priding myself on the bookcase back home where I had arranged my twenty or so books in alphabetical order. Then I saw that he and his siblings had separate bedrooms. Their own computers. CD and video game collections. A living room decorated with chandeliers and tapestries. A main bathroom that was almost the size of the bedroom Yando and I shared. And, a little removed from the hallway, a bedroom for Steven's old nanny that was half as large as my family's entire apartment.

At home that night, I breathlessly described Steven's apartment to Mom. I'd been bursting with the desire to tell Mom about it, but the longer I went on, the more her face tightened. Eventually I stopped talking, feeling guilty for taking up our dinner with all my talk of Steven's apartment. I didn't want Mom to think that because I'd gone to Steven's, I now hated our apartment. I was just hoping that she'd dream with me of what we could have one day, if everything broke right for us.

COLLEGIATE LET OUT for the summer. My classmates left the city for sleepaway camps with funny-sounding names in Massachusetts or Maine. I headed back to Bradhurst and passed the time reading books and watching baseball. Jeff and I made plans for Mom, Yando, and me to visit him at his family's country house in Connecticut. On the weekends, I saw my Resurrection friends, played basketball in the church parking lot, and tried my hardest to avoid Mouseface.

By the middle of August, I was praying for the summer to end, I was so bored. The next school year couldn't begin soon enough. When it finally did, though, I realized a lot had changed from the year before. The new jump-off at Collegiate was teasing the fuck out of each other.

Singly or in groups, everyone was in attack mode, all the time. Were you cool with that person? Yes? Then you shat on them even harder. Take my friend and Math A classmate Nick. In our gentler moments, our other friends and I mocked him for looking like Fred Savage of *The Wonder Years* and called him La Femme Nikita when he told us to stop. What really got us going was his earnestness, how he wore his disappointments on his sleeve: he'd grow so visibly frustrated with himself for not getting the right answers in class or not earning the highest grade on a test. So in our meaner moments, when the teachers had their backs turned to us, we cracked suicide jokes. And if he so much as happened to look in the direction of the small group of bullies whose ranks I'd joined, we'd make slashing motions across our wrists. We knew that what we were doing was wrong. We didn't care.

It was just jokes, right?

I thought I'd be tease-proof. I'd been dissed so hard at PS 200 and at Prep that I fronted like I didn't give a fuck. No way these kids were gonna mess with my head. But one fall afternoon, a few of my class-mates happened to be browsing the eighth-grade family phone directory when they came across my mother's name.

"Your Mom's name is Maria?"

"Yeah, Maria Elena."

"Maria!"—and it was on. Ted and Teddy and Juan and Stephen-Has-No-Sperm, Micah and Mike and other Mike and loser Mike whose voice always cracked: all of them started joking on my mom every single day.

"For a good time, call Maria!"

"*Me llamo Maria.* I'm here to seeeervice you."

"I'm Maria, and I burn with hot passion for you. I cannot wait to touch you."

All delivered in a stupid-ass, high-pitched falsetto—or some im-provised husky faux-Spanish sultriness designed to evoke Caribbean sensuality and steamy, sweaty sex.

I didn't quite get why the name Maria had opened the door to their relentless fantasizing-cum-mockery. Yes, I got the joke: my mother was a Hispanic prostitute; they'd all boned her; my classmate Ted, a full year older than me, had swum to Santo Domingo right after being born and seduced Maria with his baby penis . . . It was so funny. Except it wasn't. Every day, the same shit, until it drove me almost out of my mind.

"My name is Maria, and I give you pleasssuuure."

"Shut up, you fucktard."

The more upset I got, the more they piled it on. But the more I ignored them, the more they went over the top. Their crowning achievement? Maria bucks.

These fools got together in the school library and used the photo-copier to make a hundred fake dollar bills, each with a drawing of my mom's face. I saw Juan and Ted and a few others clutching scores of them, giggling like little bitches in the hallway. "Legal tender," good for payment at Maria's house, was distributed to my classmates.

At that moment, my fury knew no bounds. I schemed vengeance.

JUAN WAS THE FIRST VICTIM. I'd thought he and I would be tight, since he was the one Prep cat at Collegiate I was cool with and the only other native Spanish speaker in our grade. But he had to be a dick, and now I was coming after that bony, bigheaded, *ese*-looking fucker. When he left his backpack unattended in the hallway during homeroom one morning, I pounced.

While he chuckled it up with Stephen-Has-No-Sperm, I stole his backpack, ran down the stairs, and hid it in the locker room—a building and several floors away. I came back to homeroom out of breath but smiling. Soon it was time for class. Juan walked out into the hallway, looked in vain, and came back in.

"Anyone seen my backpack?"

Grinning, I gave myself away.

"Dan-el, do you know where my backpack is?"

"No, man, why would I know where the fuck your backpack is?"

"This isn't cool. I need it for class. Where's my backpack?"

"Dude, I told you, I don't know."

I got up to head to first-period science. Juan stood in my way.

"I need my backpack for class. Where is it? Stop being an asshole."

Me the asshole? You eggheaded piece of shit, YOU printed fake money with my mom's name on it and now you're calling me an asshole?

"Kid, I told you, I don't know."

Juan stormed off. He checked homeroom, then the hallway, then the other classrooms and lockers on the floor. I saw him head down the staircase and then, a minute later, run back up the stairs. Enjoying the sight of Juan's misery, I took my sweet-ass time getting to science class, which was just down the hallway from homeroom. I was nearing the door of the classroom when he confronted me again.

"Stop being an asshole. Just stop. Where is my backpack?"

"Didn't I tell you I have no idea where it is?"

"I'm gonna go right now to Mrs. Hulse and tell her you stole my backpack."

I didn't want to deal with the Middle School head, but I kept fronting.

"Uh-huh. And I'm gonna tell her I had nothing to do with it."

"*Ugh!*"

He stormed off again, this time to check the bathrooms. I was so amused by the spectacle that I stood by the door of my science classroom and waited for him to come back to confront me. Which he did, face redder than ever.

"I'm going to Mrs. Hulse."

"Okay, okay, you shithead, it's in the second-floor locker room."

"Not cool."

Off he went to retrieve it. I waltzed into class with an enormous grin on my face. Vengeance had been served. To see that little bitch who thought his Maria jokes were oh so funny turn red with anger and frustration: glorious. Now he would know not to mess with me again.

Problem: he was back at it *the very next day.*

We were walking into the locker room to get ready for phys ed, and he just had to make a Maria joke. Some shit about her blowing all our friends. I'd had enough. I grabbed the bony idiot by the shoulders, slammed him right into a locker, and pinned him against it. For a moment some crazy-violent thoughts shot through me. Head-butting him and breaking his nose. Punching his head into the locker. Grabbing the motherfucker by the neck. He was so weak; I was much stronger than his Halloween skeleton ass.

"It was just a joke. You're so sensitive."

And there he was giving me that defiant so-what look, daring me to do some shit he knew I wouldn't do. I wasn't about to get myself expelled from Collegiate. I let him go.

"Shut the fuck up."

And like that, we forgot about it. We didn't talk about my almost beating the shit out of him. We kept hanging out with the same group of friends. He kept making fun of Mom. I started making fun of him. Slowly I began stockpiling jokes I could use to shut him up. Like this:

"Why are there no Mexicans in the Olympics?"

"Why?"

"Because all the ones who can run, jump, or swim are on this side of the border."

For much of eighth grade, Dr. Beall's English class was the only thing I could focus on that didn't involve plotting to crush my friends' confidence or having mine crushed in turn. One day early that year, Dr. Beall, who was my academic adviser as well as my English teacher, told me that he liked my writing. I was flattered—and hooked. I worked as hard as I could to keep impressing him.

That winter, our class read Elie Wiesel's *Night.* For the assigned paper, I tried to sort out Wiesel's thoughts on divine justice. At Resurrection I'd learned that in the end God would wipe away all our tears. That we would be showered with his grace if we lived righteously and honorably. But confronted with the suffering and death described in *Night,* how could anyone reasonably say that there was a just purpose behind it all?

Mom would always tell Yando and me that there was a purpose to every obstacle we'd faced. Our lives, she said, were *special:* God had tested us in the shelter and was testing us now on Bradhurst, all to endow us with extraordinary spiritual and mental gifts and to shower us with his grace. Now, I could accept the idea that my life experiences had made me different, maybe even stronger and wiser in some ways, but it didn't follow logically that there had to be some purpose or reason to those experiences. And it didn't give me much comfort to imagine a purpose behind what I'd gone through. Whose purpose? God's purpose, Mom would declare—but what good did it do him to see us or anyone else suffer?

I was a little skeptical of Mom's declarations, and I wasn't buying much of what I was learning in Sunday school, either: there was an Almighty God out there, his idea of instruction was to mess with our lives, and the only way we could access him was through prayer and sacraments? There didn't seem to be much room for contemplation or intellectual discovery in that. I just had to believe that Saint Michael and God were always at our side, no questions asked; I had to believe that the Act of Contrition and the million other prayers I was expected to memorize would earn me some kind of favorable audience with God.

I hadn't lived Wiesel's life, sure, and I knew full well that there was no sensible way of comparing what he'd experienced to what my family had gone through. But I still felt that what my family had endured in the shelters and after entitled me to think about the big questions of God and purpose and destiny.

In the paper I wrote for Dr. Beall, I didn't refer to my personal history or my own inner struggle. No one at Collegiate knew about my time in the shelters, and I wasn't going to share that in a written assignment. Instead I approached my own issues from a distance: I analyzed how Wiesel reconciled his experience of the Holocaust with the existence of a just God. And writing about Wiesel's struggle, I started to come to grips with the misgivings I had about my faith. I *liked* having the doubts I did, in part because their presence convinced me that I wasn't far from Wiesel's own spiritual path: *he* had doubts, yet he couldn't bring himself to renounce his faith completely because by doing so he would have given up questioning, interrogating, listening in anxious hope to the silence. I was proud to be a skeptical believer, or a believing skeptic—I couldn't quite figure out which label suited me best.

For the remainder of the school year, I tried to think big in every English assignment. The higher I flew in the realm of pure thought, the more I tried to wrestle with questions that haunted me outside of Collegiate. In his grading report, Dr. Beall warned me to stay closer to the text and avoid soaring too high into the cloud of ideas. But, he went on to say,

> I should emphasize how impressed I am with the scope and depth of Dan-el's passion for literature, for history, and for the spirit of his education.

It was the nicest compliment I'd ever received. He had a Ph.D. from Columbia, he knew Italian, and his comments on my papers seemed steeped in many years of reading and interpretation. I began to hope that one day I'd be as smart and well-read as he was.

—— CHAPTER 7 ——

JUST BECAUSE I was feeling really skeptical about God didn't mean I was going to stop hanging out at Resurrection. Once school let out for the summer, I chilled almost every day with the other altar boys my age: Pablo; Ray of the smooth jump shot; Josué from the Polo projects; Mack from Bradhurst. To reward us for coming to church and staying out of trouble, Father Michael took us out to video arcades and theme parks. He never stopped reminding us how proud of us he was for attending school, staying true to the faith, and being good to our parents. Grateful for his kindness, we behaved ourselves at church. Outside of church, however, we got up to unsaintly schemes.

On a slow summer afternoon, we were hanging out in the cafeteria when one of the guys suddenly asked, voice lowering to a husky whisper:

"Y'all know about the chick in Polo who gives head for five dollars? In building three?"

Everyone nodded. I hadn't heard of her, but I bluffed along.

"Yeah, man. Any of y'all get down with her?"

"Nah, kid," came back the response. "Let's get it later today, though."

We agreed to meet up at night. Mom let me out of the house only because I told her I was meeting up with the altar boys to play basketball. When I saw them waiting for me outside Polo Grounds building 3, I was nervous and amped at the same time. We dapped, rode in a urine-soaked elevator to the twentieth floor, and wandered around until we found the girl's apartment. We dared each other to knock on the door. Finally one of us did. It opened just a little, and a black chick poked her head out. She was maybe seventeen or eighteen and had no front teeth. Crackhead.

"Y'all coming in?" she slurred.

The strap of her dirty tank top dangled from her left shoulder. We looked at each other. We each had our five dollars. Mack went in first. He returned, glowing, ten minutes later.

"Man," he declared, "can she work it."

Josué went in and came back smiling, then Ray. After Ray came out, the girl poked her head out the door and smiled at me. I was so hype to do it until I saw that smile—toothless, ghastly. In a split second, this wave of disgust and fear swept over me. She was straight-up *narsty*. And you never knew—bitch could have some crazy STD. I'd watched mad sex-ed presentations at Collegiate.

"Nah, I'm good," I told her and the guys.

We walked back to the elevator.

"You wasn't feelin' it?" Josué asked. "She sucks a mean dick."

"Nah," I fired back defensively, "she ain't got no teeth! Shit is gross."

"But that's *why* she suck so nice, my nigga."

No one judged me or taunted me—at least to my face—for turning down blow-job crackhead. On my walk back home to Bradhurst, though, I began to worry. Maybe I'd failed a test; maybe our trip to the crackhead was the guys' way of seeing how far I was willing to go. But I hadn't wanted the crackhead to touch my thing: she was busted! I'd never been touched by a girl that way before, and now I was gonna get head for five dollars in the projects?

I still felt this overwhelming urge to impress the guys. Next time, I told myself, I'd impress them. Next time I'd come through.

ON ANOTHER DAY that summer, Jeff came by and asked Mom if he could take me to his studio in Chinatown. He'd been visiting us less and less, so I was excited to see him and pleaded with Mom to let me go with him. She would still not sign off on my sleeping over at a friend's place, but she said yes to my visiting Jeff's studio. We left Bradhurst and took the subway downtown. When he let me into his apartment, I was blown away by how packed his crib was: every corner was jam-packed with photographs, cameras and camera equipment, books on photography and Zen meditation. Then I saw—resting on a table surface—a freshly developed photo of a nude woman.

I turned to get a better look. Jeff winked at me and asked:

"Do you like it?"

"She's beautiful."

He gave me the grand tour of his photography. Dissidents in Romania, prostitutes in the Meatpacking District, and beautiful women in strong but guarded poses were sprawled all over the furniture and walls. He offered me succinct explanations of each photo—where and how and why he'd shot it. I was astonished by the way he made every photo vibrate with a sense of color despite working exclusively in black and white. I was also astonished at how small his studio was.

"Being an artist," he said, perhaps reading my mind, "hasn't paid much, but it's made me happy."

True, I thought. He always seemed happy. And he didn't seem as though he was ever worried about money, unlike Mom, who counted every single *chelito*.

"But sometimes," he continued, "you need a little help to pay the bills. You interested in making some money?"

He went on to explain. He'd lined up a moving job for that afternoon—he didn't say whether it was a one-time deal or a more regular side gig—and wouldn't mind some help. I gladly replied yes—I wasn't about to object to making a quick buck. So we walked over to an apartment a few blocks away and helped the tenants lift some boxes and furniture into a moving van. At the end of the hour, Jeff slipped me a twenty and took me out to lunch. Over burgers and french fries, we talked about my upcoming freshman year.

"What classes are you taking this fall?"

"Well," I replied, "I'll have the usual ninth-grade classes—math, English, world history, an arts elective. Plus second-year Latin. And I'm starting ancient Greek and French."

"Wow," he exclaimed. "That's a lot of classes, but I know you'll be fine. How's your brother?"

Mom and I had submitted Yando's name for a Catholic school scholarship. It was only a few thousand dollars a year, but more than enough to cover his tuition at Resurrection's parochial school. Starting in the fourth grade, no more PS 200 for him.

"That's so amazing. Give him and your mom my love. You'll stay in touch?"

I didn't want to ask him why he hadn't been coming around to Bradhurst. He seemed to have something on his mind, but I had no idea what it could be, and I didn't feel it was right of me to ask. Our conversations had always been about me, never about him. I didn't know how to convey to him how much I missed his regular visits. I sensed from his parting good-bye that we wouldn't be seeing each other for a while, but I couldn't find the courage or the words to tell him how thankful I was that he'd entered my life.

When I rang his phone number a few weeks later, no one picked up.

AT THE END OF AUGUST, a representative from the New York City Housing Authority knocked on our door. When Mom answered, the representative introduced himself and handed her a letter. Mom called me to the door and had me translate his summary of the contents of the letter. A recent inspection of our building had determined that it was structurally unsound. As a result of the inspection, our building had been condemned and we would have to be relocated. The City was offering us a new apartment in Spanish Harlem, on 119th Street and Second Avenue. The City would send movers; all we needed to do was pack.

Mom thanked the rep, who gave us a number to call if we had any questions and wished us a good day. Over dinner that night, we became a little nostalgic about the building we were going to leave behind.

"Do you remember, my sons, the time the lights were out for almost four full days? I went to the bodega and got us candles, and you both did your homework by candlelight."

"Or, Mom," I'd chime in, "that one time right after the big snowstorm when the *calefacción* stopped working and we had to wear, like, five layers each."

"That 'time'? That happens every winter!"

The week of the move, I packed the books, Yando packed our bedroom, and Mom packed all the kitchenware and all our clothes. Whenever Yando and I fell asleep, Mom would keep packing, right until the wee hours of the morning. There was always something more to pack. On the day of the big move, the movers were in awe of how much we'd managed to cram into our small apartment.

THE FIRST DAY of ninth grade, I arrived at Collegiate thinking that I'd stand out: I had facial hair, I'd grown two inches, and I had manly body odor. But I wasn't the only person rocking a scraggly beard—several of my classmates had sprouted over the summer, and we all stank to high heaven.

I still had an opportunity to stand out: I could run for office. On the second day of freshman orientation, I decided to run for class president. It seemed like a high-upside play: I'd represent my grade in meetings with the student body president, organize events, make a name for myself. And if I lost? It'd sting, but it was still a risk worth taking.

About ten of my classmates were also running. Our campaigning came down to promises spread through the rumor mill and speeches delivered before the entire grade at the Upper School student lounge. I rehearsed my speech until I had committed its contents to memory, then searched long and hard for a catchy campaign line. It came to me in a flash as my friends spoke excitedly in the school cafeteria one day about *Pulp Fiction,* a movie I'd caught snippets of on TV one night after Mom fell asleep. What better way to end my speech than with Samuel L. Jackson's perfectly thunderous biblical speechifying prior to shooting the frat boy Brett:

"FOR YOU WILL KNOW THAT I AM THE LORD, WHEN I LAY MY HANDS UPON THEE!"

At the end of my election speech, I delivered the line to loud and sustained applause. The clapping and hollering were enough to make me giddy with the thought that maybe, just maybe, I was the most popular guy in my grade.

A few days later, my election as class president was announced at Upper School morning assembly. I was beside myself with joy.

LATER THAT FALL, I joined the Collegiate Debate Team, coached by a recent Princeton graduate whose horn-rimmed glasses and very deliberate manner of enunciating stamped him as a grade-A nerd. But I admired his nerdiness, and the breadth and depth of his knowledge of philosophy, to the point that I began following up every single one of his frequent book recommendations.

Our first away tournament, scheduled for the first weekend of November, was hosted by the debate society at his alma mater. Permission slip in hand, I approached Mom at home one evening, filled with dread at the prospect of her saying no. She still wasn't letting me go on sleepovers; how was I going to get her to let me go on a three-day trip? Surprisingly, Mom didn't beef. Once I told her Collegiate was putting the team up in a hotel, she signed my consent form and immediately went about readying a small piece of luggage with my clothes and toiletries.

I was shocked that she was making so little fuss. Had the name Princeton been enough to dispel her fears? I had no clue, but I didn't want to press my luck by asking her any questions. I was bursting with anticipation at the thought of visiting my very first Ivy League school.

The following Friday afternoon, the debate team packed into the Collegiate van and motored down the New Jersey Turnpike. When we passed the security guard booth on Elm Drive and made our way onto Princeton's campus, I gawked at the buildings. I'd never been on a college campus, not even Columbia's, so I had no idea what to expect. The campus seemed vast and distinguished beyond my comprehension. But I worried that if I expressed so much as the most fleeting hint of emotion, I would only open myself up to the teasing of my teammates. *They* had parents and siblings and cousins who'd gone to Ivy League schools; Princeton was just some typical shit to them.

THAT WINTER, snow came early to the tristate area. I was on my way to church one afternoon when I saw Mouseface again. He was with the puffy-jackets and a few little kids on the corner of 151st. All of a sudden he shouted, "Ay yo, hit that nigga!" He and his friends made snowballs and started running at me. I turned around and ran as hard as I could all the way up to the Resurrection entrance. A snowball hit me in the head and left a nice juicy welt.

TWO MORNINGS A WEEK, I reported to Collegiate at 7:30 A.M. for Ancient Greek with Dr. Russell, my eighth- and ninth-grade Latin teacher. I'd signed up for Ancient Greek because it seemed like the logical next step: I loved her Latin class, I wanted to learn more about the ancient world, and I remembered reading in those *Reader's Digest* abridged biographies I'd been so fond of when I was younger that it was the study of Greek that really separated the wheat from the chaff. The great men, the biographies all seemed to insist, knew their Greek.

The class consisted of five sophomores and two freshmen: Nick and me. As we moved on to harder and harder material, I became increasingly jealous of how easily Nick mastered aspects of the Greek language that consistently eluded me. And Greek wasn't the only class we shared where he shined; in math, Nick seemed truly in his element. I was intrigued by his talent, but I was even more intrigued by his denial of it.

"That was cool, how you translated that," I'd sometimes tell him after Greek.

He'd immediately toss the compliment aside: "Nah, that was just luck. I'm not smart like you." And his face would narrow into a dismissive scowl.

First I was amused, then confused, and finally worried. Was this some new game I hadn't figured out yet? He couldn't possibly believe that he wasn't smart—and how could he think I was smarter?

I FELT SO ALIVE at Collegiate freshman year—so energized by books, conversations, the class presidency—that I didn't look forward to the arrival of summer. Yeah, I had basketball to play with the Resurrection guys and Yankees baseball to watch at night. But odds were it'd be just another lame-ass summer in the hood, and I still had Mouseface to avoid.

Everything changed when Father Michael approached the altar boys with an invitation one day after Sunday Mass: Would we like to come down to Florida with him for a few days? He'd pay for the trip; it would be his treat to us. Universal Studios and Disney were a manageable drive away from his family's house in Melbourne. The invitation immediately had the other altar boys and me bouncing off walls, images of Florida dancing around in our heads.

After Mass, I rushed to Mom to share the news of Father's invitation. She smiled and thanked God and Father Michael for the opportunity they were giving me to travel and see the world. It was all joy and gratitude—until we remembered that I didn't have any kind of government-issued identification.

"*Mi'jo,*" Mom said over dinner that night, "you're going to need an official ID at the airport. What are you going to show the airport security? And remember, we don't have *papeles.*"

I hadn't had any reason to dwell on not having *papeles* in the years after Abuelo Memo's death. I was determined to keep my vow that one day I'd help Mom get her *papeles* so we could all travel back to her hometown to visit his grave. When it came to everyday life, though, I lived in communities where my status wasn't an issue. No one at PS 200, Prep, Collegiate, or Resurrection had ever asked me about my legal status or for government-issued identification. Once a year at the renewal meetings for Yando's public assistance benefits, the caseworker assigned to Mom—we'd get a new one every few months—would *maybe* ask whether she and I had Social Security numbers, but when Mom replied no, there was usually no follow-up.

Now here was this opportunity to travel that I'd have to turn down if I couldn't find an answer to Mom's question. I desperately wanted to go to Florida, but what kind of ID could I possibly show at the airport? I thought hard for a few minutes, and then—

"Maybe I can show my Collegiate ID. I'm going to do some research and see if that's acceptable on a domestic flight."

I decided to go online to do my research. I made a trip to the Prep for Prep offices on 71st Street, where the program had a computer room for students and alumni. I didn't want to go to the Collegiate computer room because it was too risky: it was summertime, so the school and room might be closed; but even had it been open, I wanted to steer clear of any direct contact with a human being who might subject me to a line of questioning I'd so far been lucky to avoid.

The search results were music to my ears. On domestic flights, minors could fly with any form of identification, even school-issued. My bootleg-looking Collegiate ID, splattered with food from the school cafeteria, could be pressed into service. I reported my findings to Mom, who smiled, then launched into a lecture.

"You can't embarrass me by not showering. Shower! Clean behind your ears—you never do that. Don't embarrass me and behave like someone who hasn't been raised right! And wear your jeans up high like a man, *y no como un tíguere!*"

Three weeks later, Pablo, Ray, Josué, his sister Marlene, and I piled into Father Michael's minivan. At LaGuardia Airport, my school ID was accepted. In an hour we were on a flight to Melbourne. The next week flew by in a humid haze. We went to the beach and roamed around Universal Studios, all expenses paid for by Father Michael. We played marathon games of Monopoly in his family's living room, the competitive silence punctuated only by Josué's trash-talking. And we all took turns driving around Melbourne while

Father Michael and the Resurrection kids travel
to Florida: Melbourne, summer 1999

Father coached us on the basics of driving. On my first drive, I lost control of the wheel; the car veered right into the curb, and I only narrowly avoided running over a mailbox.

WHEN WE RETURNED to New York, I was a new shade of crispy black from the Florida sun. The other altar boys and I had stories to last us months. I'd had a vacation I could actually tell my Collegiate friends about that did not begin with the words "I chilled at home." And I'd traveled beyond the tristate area, even though I didn't have *papeles*. Maybe, I thought, not having *papeles* wouldn't be such a big deal after all.

But the moment the thought crossed my mind, I wanted to unthink it. It was hot bullshit. How could I even front? Mom was too scared to get a real job because she didn't have *papeles*! We were still living on Yando's welfare payments, supplemented by the little money Mom made on the side helping church friends with odd jobs: accompanying a friend to the hospital, babysitting another friend's children, asking me to translate a notice or a legal document for a friend. Mom never charged for anything, but her friends sometimes spun her a twenty or a fifty in gratitude. And Carlos helped, too, whenever he was around—which wasn't much, because he was running one auto shop in the Bronx and another in DR. But even so, we were chronically broke.

On the phone, Mom's sisters tried to give her some advice.

"*Muchacha,* stop worrying about those *papeles*. You know how easy it is to get fake ones? Just say the word. We know people."

"I don't want to work with fake papers and a fake Social Security number, only to get caught and deported. It's the wrong thing to do."

Mom and I both knew the stories from Univision: hardworking undocumented mothers, working fourteen-hour factory jobs, rounded up by immigration officers and deported back to DR or Mexico or Guatemala. Mom didn't want to head off to a job one morning and never come back to us. But I was always coming up to her—shyly at first, then with increasing confidence that she'd find a way—to ask for a few bucks so I could get pizza with my friends or go to the movies or buy a book at Barnes and Noble. And Mom could never bring herself to say no.

So, over dinner one late-summer night, Mom announced her new plan.

"I'm going to start cleaning for the family of one of my church friends. They're offering to pay me eighty dollars to go in to clean their place a few times a week. Good money."

I frowned.

"But, *mi'jo,* we need the money. And if I'm ever going to have an employer support me if and when I can finally apply for my papers, I need to start working. This is going to be safe. Don't worry."

"Mom, of course I'm going to worry."

I didn't really know the family, so safety was my first concern. Thanks (again) to Univision, I knew all about immigrant cleaning women and nannies who were taken advantage of, cheated of their wages, assaulted. But my deeper concerns stemmed from pride. In my mind's eye, I saw her as the professional, the career woman, the executive director of the pension fund. I didn't want her to clean for a family. And I knew she didn't really want to clean for them. So I began to regret all those times I'd ever asked her for money. How could I put that kind of pressure on her, to make her feel that she had to take this job?

"My son, it's going to be okay."

"If you say so, Mom."

But in my mind, I was taking new vows. I was determined to make sure Mom didn't work long. I had to get a job and start making money. There was no way Mom should ever have to come home smelling like Clorox and Pine-Sol.

MOM HAD A SECOND SURPRISE for us at dinner a few weeks later.

"My sons, I received my GED!"

She brought out her certificate, newly arrived in the mail, and told us she'd been taking night classes for almost two years!

All that time, I thought she'd been heading to Resurrection for Mass or for meetings of one of the church groups; I'd listened only half-attentively to her as she readied to leave the apartment, heeding only her instructions for what to feed Yando if he got hungry. But it turned out that on many of those nights she'd been taking GED classes. And she'd finally passed the test. She was glowing with happiness.

"Me," she was now saying, "and I don't even really speak English."

Another surprise came along later that month.

For almost three years, Mom had volunteered as a Sunday school instructor at Resurrection; the work had convinced her that she needed formal catechetical training. So she'd enrolled in a degree program at the Institute for Catechetical Formation, run by the Archdiocese of New York, and was taking Wednesday-evening classes, hoping that when she finally got her *papeles* straightened out, a church or school could hire her to teach theology. Now Mom had a favor to ask:

"Could you type up this short paper I wrote for our first assignment? You're a quick typer, and I don't know how to use your computer."

(Collegiate had given me a used desktop for free, which I used to type my papers.)

"Mom, *¡claro que sí!*"

Beginning the following Tuesday, Mom stayed up late once a week to handwrite her papers. When she was done, I'd type them up. I didn't mind having to sacrifice some sleep. I wanted to do whatever I could to help her.

If any of my school or hood friends asked me what my parents did, I never mentioned that Mom was a cleaning lady or that she was studying to become a full-time catechist for the church. Instead I talked about her jobs back in DR. But at home, late at night, once Mom had dozed off and I was sure Yando had fallen asleep, I'd take a break from typing up Mom's papers and let my eyes fill up with tears. Not in frustration at having to type or from being exhausted, but out of pride in Mom's accomplishments that I didn't yet know how to brag about, couldn't bring myself to brag about, but that were more real and more genuinely impressive to me than any of the accolades she'd earned in her past.

── CHAPTER 8 ──

SOPHOMORE FALL, Dr. Russell's Latin and Greek classes finally began translating real ancient writers: first Caesar and then Ovid in Latin; snippets of archaic lyric poetry in Greek II.

Translation was trial by fire: you'd fumble and stagger for a bit, hopelessly mangle the first attempt, wilt in shame before your classmates as your attempt to make sense spun into incoherence. Then Dr. Russell would gently remind you, in the most measured and patient tone, "Read words."

It took me a while to figure out just what Dr. Russell meant. I got that she was reminding us to focus on each word, every individual word, until we'd extracted from those words alone—and not from some zone of anxiety-governed fantasy in our minds—the passage's meaning. After a while, it dawned on me that there was much more packed into her advice. Did translating really matter in the larger scheme of things? After all, you hadn't committed an unforgivable crime if an ablative in Caesar eluded you. Mistakes weren't a problem; it was fine to learn by making mistakes. But I began to understand that translation had to be approached with respect. You had to be loyal not to the smallness of your vanity—clawing desperately at any escape hatch to avoid the humiliation of being wrong in front of your peers—but to the bigness of the text. You had to give the text the fullest measure of your attention. You had to read its words.

As our introduction to the rhythms and forms of Latin poetry, Dr. Russell had us read Ovid's account of the Daedalus and Icarus myth, in the eighth book of the poet's *Metamorphoses,* and called our attention to the story's central lines, in which Daedalus addresses his son:

> *Instruit et natum "medio" que "ut limite curras,*
> *Icare," ait, "moneo, ne, si demissior ibis,*
> *unda grauet pennas, si celsior, ignis adurat.*
> *Inter utrumque uola. . . ."*

> He instructs his son, "I advise you to fly in the middle,
> Icarus, lest the waves push your wings down if you go lower,
> or the sun burn them if you go higher.
> Take your course between the two. . . ."

Once we were done translating for the day, Dr. Russell asked us to evaluate Daedalus's advice. We took our turns, speculating on what Daedalus might have said to better restrain his son. She weighed in, too—joining our ranks as a curious, probing student herself, face furrowed in thought:

"That encouragement to be mediocre, to fly in the middle: I'm not so sure I buy it. *Medio ut limite curras,* never aiming too high, always staying the middle course. Is it always too dangerous to aspire to something higher?"

I made a note of Ovid's lines, and of Dr. Russell's questioning response to them.

———

THROUGHOUT THE FALL and winter, I hung out with my Collegiate friends on weekdays and the Resurrection guys on weekends. I didn't want my Collegiate friends to come to my hood, and I didn't want to bring the guys down to the Upper West or the Upper East. But I found myself making one exception to my policy of segregating friend groups by time and space: Nick. It all began with a harmless enough invitation over the phone one February night.

"You wanna come see this play at Chapin?"

Chapin was one of our sister schools. Nick and some of our classmates regularly hung out with Chapin girls they'd met at private school parties or knew through mutual friends. Whenever they invited me along, I usually replied, "Nah, it's not my scene." I didn't want to put moves on a white chick only to get deaded. I thought the Chapin and Spence and Brearley girls only went for white guys—unless you played sports, like the other Prep and non-Prep minority guys my year. I didn't play sports; I wasn't anything close to athletic; I was just your typical, slightly chubby bookworm. Now here was Nick on the phone asking me to come to a Chapin play. The girl he was into had a lead role.

"Come on, kid," he urged. "Sarah has hot friends . . ."

"Fine, fine," I replied in mock exasperation.

The Saturday of the play, I met up with him at his place and we cabbed over to Chapin. Once the play ended, we went up to his girl and her friends. Nick introduced me. She was beautiful—hotter, far hotter, than any girl I'd ever dared talk to in my life. Her friends were hot, too. I was struck dumb with shyness. In embarrassment, I excused myself and took the bus back home.

On the phone the next night, I thanked Nick for inviting me.

"You gotta hang out more," he replied. "The girls thought you were cool."

I was certain he was lying—I hadn't been able to speak in coherent English to any of them. But I pretended not to notice.

"Oh yeah? No doubt, I'll be down again for sure. You and Sarah official?"

"Nah, man, we're just hanging out and stuff."

"She is banging, kid. You getting the hotties, big baller?"

"Shut up."

There was something about the nature of his personality and the nature of our friendship that made me feel comfortable with the idea of bringing him along to hang out with the Resurrection guys. Plus I wanted to reciprocate his gesture. So, three weeks later, I approached him with an invitation of my own:

"You wanna come to this party at my church?"

Several times a year, Mom and her friends organized and threw fund-raisers for Resurrection in the church cafeteria. The parties were community productions: lots of food, all prepared by Mom and her friends; lots of merengue and bachata, set up to blast all night long on the church's sound system; lots of neighborhood girls. The other altar boys and I would rotate from the front-door ticket desk to DJing to (least glamorously) serving food. Every party was a hit: the church would raise several thousand dollars; Mom and her friends would compete to see who could prepare the most and the best *pastelitos;* and the guys and I would try to talk to the neighborhood girls, a dicey proposition if any of them happened to be the shorty of an older hood-rat who might track you down after the party for some throwdown.

"Sure, man," Nick said. "I'm in. How do I get up there?"

Party night, I was working the ticket desk when Nick finally made it to Resurrection. After Mom brought him a plate of food, we headed down to the party, sat down with my guys, and drank Cokes. Nick was the only *blanquito* in the whole spot, but he seemed very at ease. Soon we relocated to the rectory basement, where the other teenagers were dancing at a safe distance from the grown-ups. Josué's sister Marlene and a few of the other church girls came over. I was standing next to Nick and trading jokes when my friend Monique materialized in front of us and dragged Nick to the dance floor before he could even say a word. In no time, she was shaking and gyrating, making Nick work his white-boy hips.

Pablo, Josué, and I doubled over in laughter.

At the end of the night, I walked Nick to the 148th Street terminal, then returned to Resurrection. There, the guys handed down their verdict:

"You see how Monique gave it to him? Your boy is cool. When you gonna bring him around again?"

And the girls could not stop talking about Nick's all-American looks:

"Is he with someone right now? Bring that white boy again!"

When I saw him at school on Monday, Nick didn't even sweat the divide between Private School World and HarlemWorld. He insisted I invite him to future parties. "No doubt," I told him. He'd made it seem so effortless.

WHILE I WAS BUSY with my tenth-grade social juggling act, my little brother was growing into a jumble of bones and curly hair. Yando talked all the time now, usually to make it very clear to Mom that he was not *me*. The Resurrection report cards were perfect: his classes were easy, and the threat of Mom's nagging discipline was always effective whenever his grades showed any sign of dipping.

But he was determined to stake his claim to difference in as many ways as he could. If Mom asked him, "*Mi'jo,* why don't you read for a bit?" he'd screech in reply, "That's what Dan-el likes. *I hate books!*"— hitting that intermediate decibel range just loud enough to convey aggressiveness but not loud enough to bring down Mom's anger on his head. Mom would shake her head and return to cooking, while Yando chilled on the living room couch watching cartoons.

I judged Yando for his unwillingness to read and Mom for indulging him. I ascribed it to her soft spot for him, the beloved younger son. I didn't understand why he had to object to books because of me—and I definitely didn't understand why he had to beef so hard whenever the subject of his following in my footsteps came up. Mom asked him one night over dinner:

"Wouldn't you like to attend Prep and go to a school like Collegiate?"

"I don't want to do something just because Dan-el did it!" he answered.

His words hurt—I wanted my younger brother to follow me. But I acted like I didn't care. Yando had tactics for breaking through that front, though. While I was reading in the living room one afternoon a few days later, he came around to offer a prediction:

"You're gonna be broke. I'm going to be rich. I'm not gonna waste my time reading all these books. I'm going to do something with my life."

"Sure" was my bemused response.

"I'm not smart like you," he continued. "But I'll make much more money."

"You *are* smart!" I insisted.

He blew me off. And now I was mad.

He had a gift Mom and I had seen in action at church: a musical ear and a precociously powerful singing voice. Yando enjoyed singing and wanted to do more of it. Thrilled at the discovery that my brother actually *liked* something, Mom tried her hardest to humor him. When she learned that the Young People's Chorus of New York was having tryouts for new junior singers at the 92nd Street Y, she brought him along to audition. Once he was accepted, Mom rejoiced to no end, bragging to her church friends that her younger son was singing for a citywide chorus. At home in the evenings, she'd play recordings of Andrea Bocelli songs on our cassette player and imagine, out loud, a future for Yando as a second Bocelli.

Yando was even happier.

"I don't *need* to study like you," he'd tell me. "I'm gonna become an artist."

He knew I couldn't sing for shit, couldn't even carry a tune.

ONE EARLY-SPRING AFTERNOON, I was walking from the 148th Street terminal to Resurrection when I ran into Mouseface. He'd been chilling in front of the corner bodega on 151st until he saw me passing the used-car dealership on Adam Clayton. Right then he made a straight line for me, all by himself.

I hadn't seen him in over a year. As he approached, I slowed down and tried to figure out what I had to do. I was fifteen—I wasn't about to be a bitch anymore. If he tried to do anything, I was swinging first. He was still taller than me, but maybe three or four inches at the most, plus he was real skinny. I had to be stronger—I was taking Advanced Weight Training at school. All I had to do was get him on the asphalt and slam his head into the concrete. He'd regret every single time he'd punked me out.

I clenched my fist. Within a minute he was an arm's length away from me. But instead of calling me "little nigga," "scared-ass mother-fucker," or "punk bitch," he just smiled and held out his hand.

"Nah, fam, we cool."

I wasn't sure. I didn't move.

"For real, we cool."

I didn't know what to do with his hand. Shake it? Dap it? I held out my hand. Half shake, half dap.

"Peace, nigga."

And he walked away.

A LETTER FROM PREP was waiting for me when I got home. The subject line: APPLY TO BE A SUMMER ADVISER.

Lately I'd been reminiscing about Prep. I was becoming closer to the other Prep students at Collegiate, and even Juan, the never-ending hater, was now my boy. Sure, Prep had been hard, but when I thought back on my time there, it was mostly the positives that came to mind. The mountains of Prep homework had prepared me to do well at Collegiate; James had inspired me to begin seeing myself as a future Ivy League Latino; I'd discovered the *Odyssey* and felt it speak to me. Maybe I owed it to the program to come back and mentor for them? Besides, it was a job for the summer, a job that paid. Finally I could help Mom out with the situation at home, and I'd definitely no longer have to ask her for money.

I filled out the application enclosed with the letter as quickly as I could and posted it back to the program offices. A month later, I was summoned to Prep's offices on 71st Street for an interview with the head of the advisory system. For three-quarters of an hour, the questions came at me in steady succession:

"What makes you want to be an adviser?"

"What qualities of character would you bring to your work as an adviser?"

"How do you see yourself relating to other advisers?"

The entire time, my interviewer's facial expressions were completely indecipherable. I grew nervous. Toward the end of the interview, I heard myself stumble into a muddle of semi-articulate rambling. The anxiety had won. On the way home, I reproached myself for the mess I'd made of my very first job interview. I regretted applying for the job in the first place. But two weeks later, I received a call offering me a position. Surprised, I immediately accepted. When Collegiate let out for the summer, I reported to Prep adviser orientation.

WELL INTO ORIENTATION, I was still so consumed with happiness at being offered a job as an adviser that I didn't see the major obstacle standing in the way of my legal employment. But this happiness vanished the moment we were plied with W-2 and payroll forms that required a Social Security number. While the other new advisers around me whipped through the paperwork, I sank into disappointment.

Of *course* I couldn't work for Prep, I angrily realized. All I wanted was to be a mentor, but I needed *papeles* even for that. I couldn't even hold a summer job mentoring students, all because I didn't have a stupid Social Security number!

I stepped out of orientation, took a deep breath, and tried to go over my options in silence. I couldn't just make up an SSN—what if Prep had a way of checking for fake ones, and what if they asked me to hand in a copy of the SSN card that I didn't have? I couldn't leave the forms blank, because we'd been told that no adviser could be paid until his W-2 and his payroll paperwork were on file. And I couldn't just quit the job right then and there: everyone—other advisers, my bosses, staff—would start asking questions until my secret came out;

and I'd be leaving Prep in a bind, because they'd have to hire a new adviser on the fly.

I made up my mind: I'd go to my bosses and explain my problem.

And that's what I did. I didn't go into all the details of my family's lack of status; I simply said that I didn't have a Social Security number because my mom and I were in an unusual immigration situation.

My bosses had me meet with one of Prep's senior administrators that same afternoon. I told him that neither Mom nor I had Social Security numbers and that our immigration status "was up in the air." A few days of discussion followed. At the end, we came to an arrangement. I would not be salaried or added to the payroll, but I would be allowed to advise. And if I ever needed money to help Mom with bills or for any Collegiate-related expenses not covered by my tuition, Prep would support me from a special fund they set aside for financially distressed students.

I was delighted. I immersed myself in the world of Prep. I was captivated by the dynamics of the advisory system office, an exhilarating environment of twenty-five black, Hispanic, and Asian Prepsters whom I could bond with about private-school life, hoodrat music, and—when we were actually doing our jobs—best practices in mentoring. But more than anything else, I loved apprenticing as an assistant unit leader under the guidance of my senior partner, Tim, and working with my group of twenty-two students. During the long summer days, I advised my new eleven- and twelve-year-old charges on everything from writing papers to making friends.

MY COLLEAGUES TOLD ME that I had well-behaved kids. It was their misfortune, they constantly griped, to deal with students failing every single class, indifferent and inattentive parents, chaotic units. In reply I'd tell them I had my own *necio* advisee, this kid Greg who simply refused to do the Shakespeare readings for his English class. Whenever I asked Greg why he wasn't completing his Shakespeare assignments, his response was real simple:

"It's boring!"

I amped myself up to go after him and pontificate about the Importance of Reading Shakespeare. Then I thought about it for a quick second. He sounded just like I did when I grew all petulant and annoyed at having to do my math or chemistry homework, which I had a habit of putting off—or simply not doing—for as long as possible until my faculty adviser at Collegiate yelled at me. I asked Tim for some advice. Maybe, he suggested, you'll get through to him if you find ways of making Shakespeare just a little more interesting to him. So, at my daily meetings with Greg, I started switching it up.

"Look at this," I'd say, taking his copy of Shakespeare's Sonnet 18. "Easy mack material: 'So long as men can breathe or eyes can see / So long lives this, and this gives life to thee.' You know how fly you'd make a chick feel with that?"

Shakespeare, the original mack: the idea was enough to make Greg laugh—and focus. I didn't have to worry too much about him after that.

For most of the summer, I thought of myself as just another fifteen-year-old working a fun summer job—but when payday came, I was the only person not receiving a check and taking a dreamy, languid stroll to the bank to cash it. By the time summer drew to a close, I was worrying more and more about not having *papeles*. Sure, I'd worked out something with Prep, but what would happen when I tried to get a job in the real world?

FALL OF JUNIOR YEAR, I signed up to take an elective with Dr. Russell: "Death of Socrates." The class kicked off with the pre-Socratic philosophers, then moved on to four Platonic dialogues: the *Euthyphro, Apology, Crito,* and *Phaedo.*

The *Euthyphro*'s examination of piety and morality brought back memories of reading Elie Wiesel and taking those first tentative steps in thinking through what my faith meant to me. But it was the *Crito* that really grabbed my attention from the opening sentence. In the dialogue, an imprisoned Socrates explains to his friend Crito why he plans to abide by the wishes of the Athenians who have condemned him to die. Crito is baffled. *We can spirit you out of Athens,* he keeps insisting. *Why are you submitting so meekly to the laws of the Athenians, unjust as they are?*

Because, Socrates tells his friend, *if the laws could speak, they'd tell me that they brought me into the world and nurtured me, oversaw my growth from youth to manhood; that I am their child and slave, that I was never and could never be on equal terms with them. And they'd add:*

Any of you who does not like us and the city, and who wants to go to a colony or to any other city, may go where he likes, and take his gods with him. But he who has experience of the manner in which we order justice and administer the State, and still remains, has entered into an implied contract that he will do as we command him.

The our-way-or-the-highway attitude of Socrates's personified laws angered me. In our class discussions, I tried to argue that the correct call was for Socrates to leave Athens; I didn't see anything redemptive or glorious in dying at the hands of a community whose laws treated you unjustly.

But my beef with Socrates's speaking laws quickly got more personal. Whenever I was sure no one else was around to read over my shoulder, I'd been consuming newspaper articles on immigration in the computer room. I kept coming across the fulminating rants of

anti-immigrant zealots who invoked the law as cover for their xeno-
phobia, saying that since the good-for-nothing illegals didn't follow
the law and didn't wait their turn in line, they had to be kicked out. I
wanted to ask them: What if the laws don't make sense? What if they
don't take into account the kinds of experiences my family had gone
through? What if the rules are simply wrong?

"Get out," I heard the laws shout back at me.

ON A THURSDAY EVENING that fall, Mom and Yando came down
from Harlem for the most anticipated event of junior year: College
Night. I met them in the school lobby and took them downstairs to
the school auditorium, where we mingled with other juniors and
their families until our college counselor appeared onstage and asked
us to take a seat.

My classmates and I had seen Bruce Breimer—a large, slightly
unkempt man with a perennial five o'clock shadow and the raspy voice
of a heavy smoker—prowling the Upper School halls before. Some of
us had even taken a history class or two with him. But that night, we
were officially introduced to Boss Breimer as *the* college admissions
savant. For twenty-five minutes he lectured the assembled crowd on
the intricacies of college admission. He went over the statistics, stressed
that they were not predictive of our class's fate but did serve to high-
light Collegiate's history of excellence in college placement, and took
questions—all while projecting an aura of unsurpassed knowledge and
supreme confidence.

While I translated for Mom, my classmates' parents badgered the
Boss about the college process and their own children about whether
they were hitting their deadlines. Little by little, a new realization
began to sink in: Most everyone else in my class had a leg up on me
without being aware of it. They had knowledgeable parents, SAT

tutors, awareness of how the system worked. Mom knew practically nothing about American college admissions except for the names of some of the Ivy League schools she'd heard me mention from time to time. Plus my classmates all had the security of being U.S. citizens! How would a college admit me without *papeles*?

On the subway ride back up to 116th, I was quiet. Mom scrutinized my face.

"Everything okay, *mi'jo*?"

"I'm okay, Mom, just tired. It's been a long day."

Mom tried to get me talking again as our train pulled into 116th and Lenox.

"Are you going to apply to Harvard?"

"I don't know, Mom. I'm not sure I'll get in. I really want to apply to Princeton, but I'm not sure I'll get in there, either."

"*Si Dios lo quiere.* I'll be proud of you wherever you go."

I fought back every urge to hurl back that I felt royally fucked, that no one could possibly understand how frustrated I was that every word of praise and every good grade I had ever received would turn to dust the moment the secret of our not having *papeles* came out.

THE ANGRY THOUGHTS kept prancing around my head and draining my energy. Outside of Dr. Russell's classes, I fell into an academic rut for the first time in my life. BC Calculus and Physics were my undoing. I had to study practically around the clock for those two classes to even scratch the surface of a respectable grade; I wasn't getting much sleep as a result; and I was so anxious about what not having *papeles* meant for my future that I found it impossible to focus. And even in Dr. Russell's classes, I was just a little slower than usual, a little more prone to making mistakes. She noticed.

One morning that fall, I found a note from her in my school

pigeonhole. "Dear Dan-el," it began. "You've seemed very tired and worried lately. If you ever need to talk, I'll be glad to listen. Just remember: *Forsan et haec olim meminisse iuvabit.* Love, Dr. R."

The line of Latin verse came from Book I of Virgil's *Aeneid:* "Perhaps it'll be pleasing one day to remember even these things"—Aeneas's words to his dejected, storm-tossed men. Alone in the school mailroom, I squeezed the card tight. I wasn't ready to talk, not yet, but just the consideration and love Dr. Russell showed for me was enough to lift my flagging spirits.

—— CHAPTER 9 ——

AT RESURRECTION, the word was spreading that Pops was leaving.

It was just gossip at first. I told myself and the guys it couldn't be true. Then Father Michael confirmed it at a Sunday homily: He'd been chosen to serve as the new pastor of the Church of the Sacred Heart in the Bronx. He'd accepted the assignment reluctantly, at the request of the Archdiocese. After a transitional period, Father Taylor would become Resurrection's new pastor.

We pleaded with Pops not to leave. We were sad, and not only because Father Michael was leaving. Father Taylor did not take kindly to our hanging out in the rectory or the church cafeteria on weekday and weekend evenings. And he was definitely not down with our playing basketball in the parking lot.

"You need to spend more time at home," he'd grumble. "This is God's house."

When Pops left to take over Sacred Heart, we began to spend more time at the local video game arcades and the neighborhood basketball courts. That meant more interactions with the neighborhood hoodrats, who were happy to push you away from an arcade machine after you'd emptied out your quarters into it, or who'd steal your ball while you played hoops and threaten to fuck you up if you even thought about trying to get it back. Those hoodrats made Mouseface look weak. Mouseface had tried to punk me with his fists, but these grown-up hoodrats would get at you with a box cutter or worse. You did not want to rock a big-ass scar on your face or get shot over some dumb shit. So no fucking around with them.

One Tuesday night that winter, I went into the Resurrection sacristy to get ready for the 7:00 P.M. Mass. I'd been paired up with Josué to serve Mass. He came in just as I was putting on my cassock and filling up the cruets.

"Waddup, my nigga," he greeted me. "I'm'a be King."

"What?"

"I'm'a be Latin King, you know what I'm saying? *Amor de Rey.*"

"Why you gettin' down with a gang like that?"

"Cuz, bro, they take care of you like you family."

The things I knew about Josué's childhood—which no one ever, ever talked about—briefly flashed through my head: how one of his brothers had been shot and killed when he was small; how his mother had grieved; how the specter of that dead brother hung over his family.

"Do your own thing, kid," I said. "Be safe, though."

"You not down, though? They can protect you."

"Nah, fam, I'm good."

I was way too scared of Mom to even think about joining a gang. If word ever got to her that I'd gone all *tíguere,* she would take it upon herself to spirit me away to DR and make sure I never came back. But I also knew I didn't have to join a gang. I'd been inhabiting my two worlds, HarlemWorld and Collegiate, fully confident that I could be down at school and at home without missing a beat. If shit ever really popped off, though, I had my safe white-boy school, my safe white-boy friends, my safe Upper West Side. For my Resurrection friends, on the other hand, Harlem was the world. They had to live there, go to school there, grow up there. If they talked shit on the block and the next day someone was waiting for them in front of their high school, who would have their back?

WITH NOTHING FUN to do at Resurrection, the guys and I started going on weekend adventures. When winter gave way to spring, we'd jump on the subway and head downtown—but not before first buying lotion or lube at the store around the block from Resurrection and squirting it on every subway seat in every car of the 3 train as it pulled out of the 148th Street terminal. As passengers began to board, we'd nudge each other and whisper, giggling:

"Psssst, *mira loco,* the woman in the suit is gonna sit down!"

On every trip downtown, we stopped by the Tower Records on 66th and Broadway to stare at album covers and argue over which new rapper had dropped the hottest new track. But one afternoon, our conversation took a different turn.

"Yo, we could cop mad shit from here if we work as a team."

Honestly, I couldn't tell you whose idea it originally was, but I know I took the lead in planning. I suggested we scout the store first and locate all the CCTV cameras.

"That's why D-Man is the genius, kid!"

We decided to cop only things we could resell—Walkmans, head-phones, earbuds—and set a date for the heist: the second Saturday of March. That morning, the six of us met up at 148th and took the subway downtown. On the ride down, I tried to read my friends' faces. Pablo had the same relaxed look he always did: you'd think we were going to eat at McDonald's or see a movie, he seemed so calm. The other guys were hyped with excitement, laughing with each other as if all we were doing was jacking quarter waters from a local bodega.

I was nervous as fuck. If you get caught and arrested, a voice in my head kept saying, forget about punishment from Mom—immigration will deport your ass. I told the voice to shut up. No one was gonna catch us! Plus it was the wrong time to be a punk-ass bitch; I had to man up. And what was so wrong about stealing a little merchandise from some big-ass company? Nothing. So be easy.

We got off the subway, split up into two teams of three, and staggered our arrivals at the store. My team went to the second floor and began removing bar-code strips from five or six CD-player boxes as discreetly as we could. We'd talked about trying to demagnetize them, but on action day we had decided to simply peel them one by one in the surveillance blind spot I'd identified. The longer it took us to peel, the more I worried that a guard would notice. But finally we finished stuffing our backpacks with the bar-code-less CD players. I breathed a sigh of relief. It would all be good now.

We strolled down the rock and pop aisles, looked at the newest CDs, and cracked jokes—keeping our eyes peeled for the second group, which was supposed to have completed its job on the first floor. After a few minutes, we spotted them streaking to the exit. A guard chased them out the door and ran after them but quickly gave up. Our guys ran down the block, crossed to the other side of Broadway, and kept running, past Columbus, on their way to the meet-up spot on Central Park West we'd picked out beforehand.

Now my team had to take advantage of the distracted guard and make our exit. But right as we approached the front revolving door, one guard stepped in front of us, and two others blocked the exit.

Hands were placed on our shoulders; we were physically turned around to face a very angry-looking man in a suit who was coming toward us.

"This way," he gritted through his teeth, motioning to the back of the store.

With a guard behind each of us, we were escorted to a half-lit corridor, which terminated in a windowless room whose four walls were covered ceiling to floor with TV screens. There, our backpacks were taken and emptied, and their contents inspected for damage. The angry-looking man, who introduced himself to us as the store supervisor, began yelling at us.

"Did you really think," he said, his voice rising in anger, "you were going to outsmart us? We were paying attention to you the moment you walked in, idiots."

"Excuse me, sir," I interrupted, in a fit of faux courage, "I have the right to be addressed—"

"Oh," he exploded, "he wants to talk about his fucking rights! How about I call the police right now? You wanna talk about your fucking rights with them?"

That shut me up. Through the blur of the tears I desperately fought to hold back, papers were shoved at me to fill out and sign. The papers stated that I admitted to shoplifting at Tower Records, that I'd been informed of Tower's decision to ban me from its stores for five years as a consequence of my shoplifting, and that the police would be summoned and I'd be arrested if I violated the ban. A copy of my Collegiate School ID would be kept on file. In a few weeks' time I'd receive at my home address a bill for four hundred dollars, the cost of replacing the items I'd damaged.

"You're lucky you're sixteen, kid"—and now the supervisor, dropping his bad-cop routine, was speaking to me in a normal voice.

"You'd been under the age of sixteen, we woulda had to call your parents."

I was escorted to the store exit and released. The rest of my team and I walked up to Central Park West and 62nd, where the other guys were waiting. Their backpacks were loaded. They dapped me and slapped me on the back.

"You look shook, kid! We good, though! Look at all the stuff we got!"

"We sell this shit to some cats and we'll be real good."

By afternoon's end I was even laughing and joking with the rest of them. But on the inside I was silently terrified about the billing notice on its way to my apartment.

I HAD TO INTERCEPT IT. Every single weekday for two weeks, I rushed back home from Collegiate to check the mail before Mom returned from her cleaning job. Mom's English still wasn't good, but she was more than capable of puzzling out the letter and figuring out what the bill was for. When the letter finally came, I was relieved to have gotten to it first. The relief promptly evaporated the moment I read that if I did not send Tower the four hundred dollars within two weeks, they would take me to court.

Panicking, I ran down a mental checklist of people who might be able to spot me the money. Asking Mom was out of the question—she'd never let me out of the apartment again. I had friends of friends who I knew were in the smack game, but I wasn't about to compound my monumentally stupid decision to shoplift by dealing or messing with dealers. I couldn't ask my Collegiate friends; I'd have to explain why I needed the money, which I didn't want to do, and I had no way of paying them back. Jeff had been a ghost for ages, and I didn't have a new telephone number for him. And if I came to Prep and asked them for help, I was positive I'd lose my advising job. Which I deserved, because I'd been fucking stupid to get caught up in this mess in the first place.

There was only one person who could—and I thought *would*—help me. I got on the subway and went to see Pops at his new church in the Bronx. The rectory secretary buzzed me into the waiting room. Five minutes later, Father came down to see me.

"Wonderful to see you, Dan-el! To what do we owe your visit?"

He hugged me. I started shaking.

"What's wrong? Is everything all right?"

He led me by the shoulder to the kitchen and had me sit down.

"Father," I began, "I really messed up"—and I pulled out the bill.

Through tears, I told him what I'd done and asked for his help. I promised that one day I would pay it back to him and the church. I knew it was an enormous favor to ask, and I would completely understand if he did not want to help me out. I had to learn my lesson and was fully prepared to accept the consequences of my stupidity.

He frowned and was silent for about a minute. Finally:

"Dan-el, I am very disappointed in you. You have always been a mature young man, and I am extremely upset that you became involved in this. But I will take care of this"—he reached over for the envelope and the bill—"and it will be our secret, on the condition that you never, ever get involved in anything like this again. Remember the church when you're the successful adult I know you'll become."

"Thank you, Pops."

He smiled. I smiled.

"I can't believe," he was now saying, more to himself than to me, "that you're almost done with your junior year of high school! Yesterday you were just a little boy in CCD who knew the pope's Polish name."

I laughed. I thought about the day when he'd invited me up to the Resurrection rectory kitchen for orange juice and reassurance. I didn't know why he'd taken such a liking for me then, or why he still believed in me now, even after being presented with definitive proof of my stupidity.

Our conversation turned to college. He was full of questions. Was I going to apply to an Ivy? What was my college guidance counselor saying? When was I taking the SAT?

I'D BEEN FRANTICALLY trying to cram in SAT review in the midst of junior-year classes and extracurriculars. On the morning of the exam, I woke up afraid that I hadn't studied enough, and in my desperation to get in some final minutes of review, I ran late to my rendezvous with Nick. Together we took the subway downtown to Stuyvesant, the massive public high school where we'd both registered to take the test. At the school entrance, Nick and I were directed to separate classrooms. I walked into mine just as booklets were being handed out. Once the room proctor intoned, "You may begin," the race was on.

The math sections slowed me down. Just when I was really beginning to worry that I wasn't working quickly enough, my calculator stopped working. As time wound down and the proctor began making the rounds to collect booklets, I was seething—at the damn calculator, at myself. When I reunited with Nick outside Stuyvesant, I played it cool. But back home and alone with my thoughts, I quickly became a mess of worries.

I'd been doing some research into the college admissions prospects of undocumented immigrants, both in the Collegiate computer room and in the Prep computer cluster. Getting into schools would be one problem, but the major obstacle looked to be paying for my college education, since undocumented immigrants weren't eligible for federal financial aid. Which meant that I'd either have to win a private scholarship or obtain private, nonfederal financial aid from the college that accepted me—or both. So I absolutely had to be even better than perfect for the colleges I wanted to apply to. I *had* to do well on the SAT: borderline-perfect-score well.

The Score Report arrived a few weeks later. I snatched the letter from the mailbox, opened the door to our apartment, and called out to see if anyone was home. When no one replied—Mom was out taking Yando to chorus—I fiddled with the envelope for a minute before finally mustering the courage to rip it open. And there it was, in dark blue type on a white background, my SAT score: 1430 out of 1600. My eyes ran over the section breakdowns: strong verbal, mediocre math.

I stormed into my bedroom and kicked my desk.

The next morning, I headed to Breimer's office to break the news. I braced myself for a lecture on how I'd messed up and doomed my college prospects to everlasting perdition because of my 1430.

"Come in," he said when I knocked on his door.

"So I got a 1430. My calculator acted up. I just didn't have time to finish one of the math sections. I'm so sorry. I really should have done better."

"Sorry?" he rasped. "So you didn't do as well as you'd hoped. You have time to study for the next session. The glory of Score Choice. You'll take it again and do great. *Study.* Work on the math. Got it?"

"Yes."

"We'll meet next week to talk about schools. You're very competitive."

He waved me out of his office. I left happy, but confused. Competitive for the schools I wanted with a 1430? And what would he say if I told him I didn't have *papeles*?

OUR NEXT MEETING began with his taking a pen and scribbling down in almost illegible handwriting a list of schools on a notepad. The very first school on the list was Princeton.

"I am told," he began, "that you have a promising future in the study of the Latin and Greek classics. Princeton has an excellent classics department. We will not"—he paused, feeling for the right metaphor—"put all your eggs in one basket by any means." He resumed scribbling down names. "Nevertheless, it is appropriate in your case to aim high."

Eventually, his hand stopped moving. On the list, I counted fifteen colleges, sorted into three categories. I figured that the top category—Princeton, Harvard, Yale—consisted of reaches, the next of matches, the third of safeties. But I wasn't about to press for clarification, not yet. He turned to me.

"Will you be visiting any colleges soon?"

I replied that I'd be going on one of the college trips Prep was arranging for high school juniors who'd graduated from the program. And I'd have a chance to visit some colleges with the debate team in the fall, since we had a few university tournaments scheduled.

"Good. You have a plan."

He scrutinized the list one final time, then placed it flat on his desk.

"Now, then," he resumed, "do you have any questions about the college process? Any concerns?"

The words started coming out of me at breakneck speed. I didn't even fully realize until I was well over halfway into the explanation of my family's circumstances that I was telling him I didn't have *papeles*.

"Let me get this straight," he interrupted. "You're not a citizen?"

"No."

He thought to himself for a moment. I searched his face for clues to his reaction. He seemed intrigued—that was about all I could make out. Did he understand the scope of my problem? Was there something else I needed to say to make things clearer? I was certain he'd never had a student in my situation before, but what did I know? Everyone said the Boss was a college admissions wizard.

Finally, the gruff smoker's voice cut through the silence.

"We'll see how Collegiate can help. Is it a problem? Yes. But we'll find a way to make sure it doesn't affect your college admission prospects. And *you*"—he pointed at me—"stay focused. Keep doing what you've been doing and you'll be fine."

"Thank you, Mr. Breimer."

I walked out of his office feeling light as a feather. I hadn't told him the full story: how long my family had been out of status, how unlikely it was that we'd be able to acquire legal status anytime soon. I didn't tell him about the anxiety that had been eating at me and distracting me from schoolwork. But I was happy to know the Boss and Collegiate would stand behind me.

LATER THAT DAY, I was hanging out with Nick in the student lounge. He wanted to know why I wasn't absolutely confident that an Ivy League school would admit me.

"When a college looks at your grades, you're going to be fine," he was saying. "You're set. What could possibly stand in the way of your going to Harvard or Princeton? I just don't see it."

I blurted out the secret again. Twice in one day? I was on a roll.

"There's one thing that can definitely hold me back. My family and I came over to the U.S. legally, but our paperwork expired. It's not clear that colleges will admit me if they know I'm not legal. It's my fault—I should have done something earlier to make sure this wasn't a problem."

Rationally, I knew there was nothing I could have done. But for months I'd been tormented by this irrational guilt that kept telling me I could have controlled what had happened to my family but had somehow fucked up.

Nick didn't understand how I could be blaming myself.

"What could you have done otherwise? Stop being so hard on yourself. This is such bullshit"—his face was now turning red with indignation. "*Bullshit,* unfair bullshit, that you have to deal with this."

I shrugged. "I mean, it's just something I'm gonna have to face, unfair or not. Nothing I can do to change things now, not with the way the laws are set up."

"It's so fucked up." His face was still red.

"Do you want me to talk to my dad?" he asked. Nick's dad was a prosecutor in the district attorney's office. "Maybe he'll know someone who can help."

I was perplexed at how worked up he was getting over something that didn't even affect him. But another part of me was moved by the depth and sincerity of his concern. Yeah, he was my friend; but he was also an Upper West Side white boy, and I hadn't *expected* him to see the unfairness of my situation and empathize with my frustration, let alone try to do something about it.

"Don't worry about it, man. If there's any way you or he can help, I'll let you know, but I'm just not sure there's anything anyone can do right now."

"You know I'll do whatever I can for you. Did you tell Breimer?"

"Yeah. He was supportive."

"Of course. He loves you. It's ridiculous that you have to deal with this. Promise you'll keep me posted, whatever happens."

"No doubt."

I didn't want to tell Nick how emotional it made me to think that I had the best friend I could ask for, and the very best school I ever could have dreamed of, on my side. I cracked a joke, changed the subject.

— CHAPTER 10 —

WITH SUMMER on the horizon, Mom put her foot down:

"Yando, you're going to apply to *Pre' fo' Pre'*."

"I don't want to!" was his first response. But when he saw the you-better-not-disagree-with-me look on Mom's face, he went for a different form of protest: glum and unrelenting silence.

After his teachers at Resurrection recommended him for the program, I helped Mom fill out the parental materials and accompanied Yando, angry scowl and all, to his test battery. Although Mom and I were sure he wouldn't bomb the tests intentionally, we stressed about his face-to-face interviews. Would he be rude? Or would he simply not talk?

But late in the spring, an admissions letter welcomed Yando to Prep. Mom kissed him on the forehead and thanked God for his mercy to our family. I tried to pump him up about the program:

"You excited about going to Prep this summer?"

He was underwhelmed. "Eh, not really."

When June came around and school let out for the summer, Akim—a newly hired adviser and one of the few friends I'd made during my summer at Prep—was assigned to my brother. I crossed my fingers that Akim would get Yando to buy into Prep and focused on my new crop of advisees. Before long, Prep summer session was in full swing.

ONE SCORCHING JULY AFTERNOON, Yando and I were just getting back home from Prep when we noticed a very familiar-looking man standing in front of our apartment building. I squinted. He began to smile as our eyes made contact with his.

It was Dad.

"I wanted to surprise you!" he exclaimed, sweeping us up in his arms. He was wearing slacks, a dress shirt, and a blazer, and was carrying a tagged suitcase; he'd come directly from the airport. A mild scent of cologne wafted from his face.

"*Bendición, Papá,*" I said.

Yando hesitated; I coaxed him with a nudge. Dad didn't seem to mind.

"How are my *triunfadores* doing?"

We led him into our apartment and sat with him in the kitchen. I glanced at the note Mom had left on the dinner table: she was at Resurrection and would be back in a while. I had no clue how she'd react to the sight of Dad.

Dad barraged Yando and me with questions about school, books, plans for the future, the New York Yankees. I quickly warmed to him and everything about him: the suave voice that sounded so much richer in person than on the phone, his arresting handsomeness, the erectness of his posture, the wit and cadence of his speech. At the same time, I kept thinking that he was lucky Carlos wasn't around. Did he know Carlos was back in DR on a trip to check up on his auto shop there? I'd recently overheard Mom mention Carlos to Dad over the phone. She'd told Dad, in no uncertain terms, that Carlos was the man of her life now: they were living together.

An hour passed. Then I heard the rustle of Mom's keys and the clang of the apartment door.

"¡*Muchacha!*" And Dad bounded to the door to hug Mom. Her face changed colors—I'd never seen her look so shocked. They hugged, stiffly. She dropped her purse off in the living room and returned to the kitchen to begin preparing dinner. I took Yando to the bedroom, set him up to do his homework, and came back into the kitchen for a glass of juice. Mom was questioning Dad, who was sitting on one of the kitchen chairs.

"How long will you be in New York?"

"Five days."

"What brought you back?"

"I wanted to see you and the kids. And I have some business with a friend."

The nature of this business was not specified.

"Where are you staying?"

"How would you feel"—Dad flashed his hustler smile—"if I . . ."

Mom was silent for a few seconds before nodding.

"You can sleep on the couch in the living room."

Dinner was served. Over *arroz con habichuelas,* Dad tried to make conversation. After dinner, Yando headed back to our bedroom to finish his homework. I followed, to keep an eye on him and to work on the reports I had to file for each of my Prep advisees. Dad lingered in the kitchen with Mom. From the other end of the corridor joining the bedroom to the kitchen, I had an unobstructed view of them as Dad joked, teased, flirted. She was polite, and she laughed once or twice at his stories—but after an hour of Dad's game, she excused herself and went to bed.

The Yankees were on TV; my advisee reports were on my desk. I was typing up notes with one hand and holding a small bag of ice on my chest with the other: my improvised A/C. Dad ambled over from the kitchen and sat down next to me.

"My *triunfador,* what have you been studying in school?"

"Latin and Greek!"

I showed him my Hansen and Quinn Greek textbook. I told him about the writers I'd been reading for my Latin and Greek junior-year classes: *Cicerón en latín, Platón en griego.* Cicero had bored me stiff, but Plato's *Ion* was fascinating.

"And in Latin we've been reading much more poetry lately, first Catullus and Horace and now Virgil"—and I pulled out my backpack. I'd tagged it with Latin verse, one line each from Catullus and Virgil. Some of my school friends had teased me about it, but I didn't really care.

"*¡Triunfador!*" Dad praised me. "A *triunfador* of languages!"

WHEN I GOT UP at six the next morning to wake up Yando and get ready for Prep, Dad was in the kitchen frying *platanos.* By the time Mom woke up to the smell and walked into the kitchen, he'd made us all *tostones* for breakfast, which we ate together. Then Yando and I got ready to catch the Prep bus. On our way out, Dad hugged us at the apartment door. When we returned home in the evening, he was in the kitchen helping Mom with dinner.

Every day that week, Yando and I came home from Prep to Mom and Dad. Every night, he stayed up with us, offering to help Yando with his homework and me with my teenage love life.

"How are the *novias?*" he asked.

I told him about a few Resurrection girls I'd briefly dated. I told him I wasn't sure how to make moves. Whenever I'd really liked a girl, another guy had swooped in. And I didn't think it was really worth it to get too worked up about girls—not since this one time in the ninth grade when I'd made a poetry portfolio for one of the Resurrection girls and handed it to her in the church cafeteria, only to have her laugh in my face.

"*Muchacho,*" he replied, looking at me earnestly, "*ponte serio.*"

Get serious: the way he said it, I immediately gathered (or made myself believe?) that there was a deeper meaning. He was telling me to be more aggressive, to impose my will on the situation. I vowed to be *serio.* And I delighted at the opportunity to receive real advice from him—to feel myself a true son to a physically present dad.

IT WAS FRIDAY, and our week together was up. When Yando and I came back home from Prep that afternoon, Dad was packing his suitcase to catch a late-afternoon flight. When he was done packing, he dialed a cab service from our home phone, then sat down with us in the living room. We watched TV in silence until we heard the honk of the cab. Dad rose from the couch, kissed Yando and me on our foreheads, wrapped his arms around Mom, and picked up his suitcase. He noticed the downcast expression on my face and tried to cheer me up.

"We'll see each other next summer! I'm coming for your Collegiate graduation. You're my *triunfador.*"

The cab honked again. Dad ran down the stairs to the curb. I went to the window of my bedroom and watched the cab take off on its long journey to JFK.

Mom turned on the stove and began preparing dinner. Yando came into the bedroom and spread out his Prep books on the desk. Heading back down the hall, I took a seat in front of the living room

TV, tried to read, gave up, and simply stared into space for a while. When I was sure no one was looking, I cried.

I'd had him for five days! Now it was back to that distant voice that came on the phone every other week. We hadn't even had a chance to talk about college! We hadn't talked about what not having *papeles* meant for my future! I hadn't wanted to ruin the serenity of our time spent bonding. And now I didn't feel like explaining the whole mess over the phone, either.

He called early the following week. I told Mom to say I was too busy to talk.

AT PREP ONE AFTERNOON, I took a lunch break and went to the computer room to check my e-mail. I was relatively new to e-mail and didn't have much of an opportunity to write or read it: since Mom couldn't afford a home dial-up connection for my desktop, the only chances I had to browse the Internet and check my Collegiate and Hotmail accounts were at school or at Prep.

When I logged into my Hotmail that afternoon, I found an e-mail from the Princeton dean of undergraduate admissions, addressed directly to me. Dean Fred Hargadon was writing to ask whether I was interested in coming down to campus the last weekend of September for a three-day event: the Humanities Symposium. The symposium brought together prospective undergraduate applicants and professors from various departments to study and discuss a specific topic in the humanities. I'd been recommended to Princeton as a promising future major in the humanities and was being invited down to sample the university's humanistic riches. This year's topic was the culture and literature of Weimar Germany. Would I like to participate?

I was so hyped, I did a little dance in my seat while I replied to confirm my desire to attend. But doubt soon set in, and my mind flooded with questions. Was I sure, absolutely sure, I wasn't being punked by one of my Collegiate or Prep friends?

When I met up with some Collegiate heads later that week, I accused them of trying to mind-fuck me with this Humanities Symposium nonsense—it just seemed like one more plot cooked up by a classmate to make fun of me. But they responded to my allegations with looks of confusion. Fine, so maybe the e-mail had been real, but how had Princeton gotten my e-mail address? And *Princeton* wanted *me*? Please.

THE SUMMER HEAT broke just in time for the school year. The first day of senior year, I found a two-word note from the Boss in my pigeonhole: "See me." I made straight for his office. He greeted me with a slightly mischievous grin.

"Did you receive an e-mail from Dean Hargadon regarding the Humanities Symposium?"

"Yes. I was wondering—"

He cut me off. "Did you RSVP?"

"Yes. But how—"

He anticipated my question. "I gave Dean Hargadon your e-mail address. We have the privilege of nominating two prospective applicants a year to attend. We nominated you and your classmate G.J. I'm glad you replied promptly. The students we've sent in the past have greatly enjoyed the symposium. Most went on to apply to Princeton early and were admitted. You'll be an impressive humanities applicant. We were pleased to nominate you."

"Thank you. This is such an honor. I'm so honored."

"Blow 'em away! You'll be a star. Now, did you register to retake the SAT?"

"Yes."

I lied. Registration had completely escaped my mind during the summer. I didn't want to tell the truth and have Breimer turn on me for an easily correctable oversight. I made a mental note to re-register the moment I stepped out of his office.

"Thank you again so much, Mr. Breimer—"

"You're welcome," he said, returning his attention to the pile on his desk.

I was ecstatic at my good fortune. True, my classmate G.J. was the presumptive class valedictorian, and I could think of at least three or four other students, Nick included, who were as qualified if not more qualified for nomination to the Humanities Symposium. But I wasn't going to let that self-doubt stop me from relishing the sweetness of the moment. Thanks to Breimer, I was going to spend three days of my senior fall at Princeton! And I knew from my research on the Internet that if I did get into Princeton, financial aid would be very generous, so I wouldn't have to worry about paying for my ride. Now I had to make it work; I had to blow everyone away at the symposium, then submit a bomb-ass application with fly board scores.

TWO WEEKS LATER, I was summoned into Breimer's office to review my college admissions profile. At his request, I'd drafted the list of extracurriculars to be included with my applications: I'd been elected co-captain of the Collegiate Debate Team together with Nick; I was the new copy editor of the Collegiate student newspaper; I was an adviser for Prep.

"How does that sound?" I asked Breimer.

"Competitive."

Breimer was in an especially laconic mood that day. The silence was punctuated with occasional grunts as he studied a printout listing my College Board and AP exam scores and a printout of my transcript. Grunts of approval for the five SAT II's in the 770-to-800 range and seven over 700; the AP 5's in U.S. History and English and the 4 in French. Then the grunting stopped: he was looking at my SAT I score.

"Did you study over the summer?"

"Yes."

I was fibbing again. I couldn't and didn't want to say that I hadn't had all that much time to study because of Prep. I was confident that the second time around I wouldn't struggle as much on the math. But I swore in my mind that I would study before retaking. And since I was going to study, I reasoned, it wasn't as bad a fib.

"I'm taking it again this Saturday."

"Good." He closed my file. "Call to obtain your score when it becomes available. Now go and study math!"

The week after I retook the SAT, Mr. Breimer had me excused from Friday classes so I could attend the Humanities Symposium. I boarded New Jersey Transit at Penn Station, got off at Princeton Junction, transferred to the Dinky shuttle, and wandered all over campus until I found West College and met my student host.

My debate coach had rattled off the names of prominent professors to be on the lookout for at the symposium: Anthony Grafton from the history department, Michael Jennings from German language and literature, Alexander Nehamas from philosophy, John McPhee in creative writing. Grafton, one of the world's foremost authorities on the history of humanistic learning, led the opening session of the symposium. Nehamas taught my Saturday-morning seminar on twentieth-century German philosophy, Jennings my after-noon seminar on German literature. At the symposium's conclud-ing dinner Saturday night, McPhee read to us from "Crossing the Craton," the final installment of his four-part work on the geology of the American continent. With his gravelly voice, he made even rocks come to life, though to be honest, I was so hooked by the splendor of the occasion and the intellectual possibilities of a future at Princeton that he could have been reading from the white pages and I still would have been enraptured.

My host for the Humanities Symposium was a hard-partying soph-omore who didn't give two shits about the no-serving-minors warn-ings repeatedly issued to the hosts. On the last night of the symposium, he took me on a tour of Princeton's eating clubs, the mansions on Prospect Avenue that dominate the university social scene. Cheap beer was poured everywhere, and female students in skimpy outfits danced all night long. I loitered at one club with G.J. and another symposium participant until we'd had our fill of Milwaukee's Best. When the parties started dying down, we walked over to the student campus center, which was open late for the students streaming in from Prospect. At the student café, we couldn't stop talking about the eat-ing clubs, the drinking, the dancing, the general awesomeness of the symposium.

"So are we all applying early?" one of us asked the others.

"Yeah!"

"To early decision at Princeton, then!"

We toasted with coffee. I lost track of my host. At night's end, I had to clamber back into his dorm room through a half-open win-dow. At eight the next morning, I boarded NJ Transit back to New York. I was ready to tell anyone and everyone who asked that Prince-ton had been awesome.

———

A DAY LATER, I met with Breimer and immediately started gushing.

"The symposium was fantastic. I had an absolutely wonderful time. Thank you so much again for nominating me. The symposium classes were amazing—"

Smiling ever so slightly, he cut me off. "Early decision to Princeton, then?"

"Yes!"

I threw myself into drafting essays for the Princeton application. I worked hardest on the essay prompt that asked me to write about the future I saw for myself. In response, I sketched the story of my life in Harlem and tried to explain how important books had been to me.

I grew up (and still live in) one of New York City's most impoverished regions, and confronted with the day-to-day reality of poverty I promised myself that I would find a way to transcend the squalor around me. All I had as a little child were books, and I fell in love with them because they offered glimpses into a life so much richer, so much more fulfilling, than the intolerable crudeness of the ghetto. Beginning with my days at Prep for Prep and extending into my years at Collegiate, education has become a safe haven of sorts: for a few hours I can forget the uncertainties that face me. . . .

In the classroom I can explore the concerns of the mind and spirit and not be overwhelmed by the pessimism and the despair of the faces that greet me every morning as I step out of my apartment, or every night as I walk back home from the train station. I am convinced that education is my faith and hope, because I truly have nothing else to fall back on. . . . My chief expectation is that my college experience will provide me with a very clear understanding of who I am, where I am headed, and what I can contribute to the society I live in.

Finished, draft in hand, I second-guessed myself. Hadn't the hood brought me richness of a nonacademic kind, friends who I knew would be loyal to me no matter what divergent paths our lives took? But Josué was running with the Kings, some of my other guys were also throwing down with gangs, and the Resurrection girls were getting knocked up, popping out babies, dropping out of school. Yeah, I loved them and my memories with them, but I hated the poverty that had forced my family to live in buildings where the lights went out and the tap water ran brown, where the crack addicts stumbled down the staircases and the dice rollers didn't budge from the front entrance. I hated getting punched on a basketball court, running away from hoodrats, riding urine-soaked elevators in the projects. Hated all that shit. Wanted better, so much better.

Through books and Collegiate, I'd imagined a way out of poverty. Admission to Princeton would be the final step in transforming my imagination into reality. I'd have full financial aid, I'd get a great education, and I'd earn a Princeton degree. Not having *papeles* wouldn't mean a thing by the time I became an adult: who could turn me down with a Princeton B.A.? I'd leave the hood and take Mom and Yando with me.

I RETURNED to Breimer's office a few days later with the drafts of my essays. He handed me a copy of the secondary-school reference he'd prepared, to submit on Collegiate's behalf.

The product of East Harlem's blighted El Barrio, Dan-el Padilla is one of the most remarkable success stories that Collegiate has witnessed since our venerable institution became truly inclusive with the advent of students of color in the mid-1960s. Raised in the most problematic of surroundings by his heroic single parent mother, this memorable lad of Dominican extraction has somehow managed to transcend the squalor and despair of his neighborhood to emerge as a refined and articulate young gentleman, and a ranking scholar of the first order. Watching this purposeful and cheerfully optimistic young boy attack Collegiate's accelerated curriculum with such unbridled gusto, one is provided with a first-hand encounter of the indomitability of the human spirit. Plucked out of his marginal environment by a Collegiate alumnus who has made his life's work assisting inner city youth, Dan-el joined our fast-paced community of budding scholars and high profile personalities at the beginning of the seventh grade, and there has been no looking back for him ever since.

I knew of students and parents who objected to the self-congratulatory prolixity of Breimer's references, but reading mine, I didn't care about their criticisms of his style. The more I read and reread, the easier it became not to give a fuck about the whispering ghost of race/survivor guilt that had haunted me as I drafted my essays. Seeing myself through Breimer's eyes, I felt baller as hell: he'd composed my life story to read like the Dominican American *Ragged Dick,* and I wasn't about to let anyone say I didn't deserve the props, especially some stupid voice in my head.

HALF A MONTH before the November 1 early-decision deadline, Breimer called me back into his office to give me marching orders for the Princeton open house for prospective New York City applicants.

"At the conclusion of the open house, you will approach the admissions officer running it and explain your immigration predicament.

You will ask whether your predicament will be factored into the assessment of your application."

For a moment I was speechless: Breimer wanted me to do *what*?

He went on: honesty was the best policy; better a straight answer now from admissions than applying, receiving a rejection, and never knowing whether the rejection had to do with my status or not. It sounded crazy, but it made sense.

I went to the open house, took a seat in the back of a large room filled with about fifty or sixty prospective applicants, and prepared myself to approach the associate dean of admissions. When she'd wrapped up her overview of the many opportunities in store for those of us who chose to apply to the university, I joined the swarm of students streaming toward the front of the room with questions for her. I waited in line, listened to the conversations of other students, and tried to relax. Before long, we were face-to-face. I introduced myself, took a deep breath, and launched into my story.

"So my family fell out of legal immigration status when I was a child. We haven't had an opportunity to rectify our situation. I'm currently out of status." I cut straight to the chase: "Will that be a factor in the admissions office's decision on my application? Should I be worried?"

Her eyebrow went up slightly as I spoke, but by the time I had finished my question she was smiling.

"We will evaluate your application only on its merits," she said. "Your legal status isn't our concern."

I thanked her, shook her hand, and danced out of the open house.

I sent in my application the following week and clowned around in the student lounge with my six classmates who'd also applied early. Together we entertained hopes of that magical word from our college of choice that would liberate us from having to pay any attention in class during second semester of senior year.

Privately, I allowed myself to dream of a future in which going to Princeton freed me from ever having to think about being broke in the hood and not having *papeles*. I crossed my fingers and prayed hard. I couldn't have even told you whom I was praying to: God, Saint Michael, Olympian Zeus. I was pleading with all of them to make my dream come true.

— CHAPTER 11 —

FOR MY BIRTHDAY earlier that fall, Mom had bought me a cell phone. I used it mostly to prank-call my friends while we were in class. The afternoon of Thursday, December 13, I was up to my usual shenanigans in AP Euro when Mom's number appeared on my caller ID. The moment Dr. Maglione let us out of class, I ran into the hallway to listen to her voice mail.

"Hello, Dan-el. I just got back from cleaning and found a letter from Princeton in the mail. Call me back when you can, *mi'jo*."

A letter? Not a big envelope? My classmates and I had all learned the formula: big envelope = admission; small envelope = deferral or rejection. My heart began beating violently as I dialed back. When Mom picked up, I didn't even greet her.

"Is it a small envelope or a big one?"

"*Sí, sí,* it's a big envelope. Should I open it?"

"Yes, open it!"

My friends gathered around me. Through the blaze of Spanish words, they'd figured out what the call was about. In a group we walked to the auditorium for Upper School assembly. Their attention was on me. Now Mom was back on the phone.

"There's a letter and some materials."

"Can you read the letter to me?"

Mom's English wasn't great, but I needed to know what was in that letter.

"*Sí, claro*"—and she began reading the very first sentence, carefully enunciating every single syllable: "Dear Dan-el, YES! We are delighted to admit you to the Princeton Class of 2006."

I jumped into the air and whooped into the phone. My friends cheered.

"*¡Muchacho!*" Mom lowered her voice in half-serious reproach. "*Mi'jo*, this is wonderful, but why are you making so much noise?"

"Mom, can you bring the envelope to Collegiate? I want to see the letter."

"*Claro*. I'm so happy for you. Thank God for this blessing."

Then a sound I couldn't make out—a sob? Mom's first and last giggle?

We hung up. I walked into the Collegiate auditorium, where the word had spread to my other classmates. They applauded and cheered. Nick high-fived me.

"I knew it, kid," he whispered. "You were a lock."

My high school adviser hugged me. My teachers waved and smiled as my friends and I took our seats in the auditorium.

The hour-long guest lecture for the day's assembly began, peaked, and concluded. The entire time, I was lost in happiness, thinking only of the moment when I'd have the letter to touch—the tangible proof I needed to convince myself that this wasn't simply some ridiculous dream. And just as assembly was letting out, Mom arrived in the school lobby with the letter. I gave her the mightiest of bear hugs.

"*¡Muchacho!*"

I spotted Breimer making his way across the lobby and walked up to him, letter in hand.

"So I hear there's been some good news. Congratulations."

"Thank you, Mr. Breimer! Thank you, thank you!"

"You have only to thank yourself, Dan-el."

He offered his hand; I nearly yanked it off, I shook it so hard.

THE HOLIDAYS SKATED BY. I started chilling more and more with Derrick, one of my friends from Prep, former bus companion from our time in the boot camp and now a fellow mentor. My dude had grown up ten blocks away from me in Spanish Harlem and knew what it was like to live in our hood. He and I had become tight over the previous two summers. Derrick was back home from boarding school and had college admissions news of his own: early action to Brown. We celebrated by wearing our hot new Princeton and Brown hoodies all over the place.

One night, we were walking around the Upper East Side, bored out of our minds and doing absolutely nothing. In the distance, we spotted a middle-aged white man getting his late-night jogging in. He was wearing an NYU shirt. We hated on him *hard*.

"Look at dude repping NYU. NYU! That's some weak shit. Ivy and black all day, biiitches."

We kept the hate among ourselves—we weren't about to heckle him. He was still probably worth more than we'd ever be worth, and we weren't about to put a premature end to our Ivy careers by having the cops called on us for harassment. But it felt so good to bump that Ivy League name—and to hate on this random white, no-doubt-in-our-minds privileged dude for his NYU pride.

AFTER THE NEW YEAR, it was back to school and schoolwork. Early the second week of January, I happened to be riding the elevator up to AP Bio with my classmate Damien when he began ranting about college admissions. He'd applied to six schools, regular decision, and was in full freak-out mode. A whole summer of tutoring for the SAT I, all that studying for SAT II's, writing stupid college essay after college essay—what if he didn't get in anywhere? And he couldn't let his grades drop even for a moment: Breimer would have his head. His parents were breathing down his neck. The pressure was killing him. It was all so unfair.

I wasn't really listening, and I wasn't in a particularly sympathetic mood. I wasn't close with that fool. For much of high school, he'd never stopped bragging about sleeping with his old nanny, having anal sex with his girlfriend, having a big dick. My friends and I had mostly ignored him or made fun of him behind his back. And now he was talking about how unfair the whole college admission process was. Unfair? I could give a shit about his Upper East Side ass, tutors at his beck and call. Unfair? Try being a poor immigrant. I tuned him out. But then he tugged at the skin on his wrist and said:

"It must have been so easy for you because of this."

I snapped back into focus. Did this motherfucker just say that I got into Princeton because of my skin color?

"Yeah, it helped, all right," I muttered angrily, glaring at him.

We got off the elevator and walked to class. Every minute of AP Bio that morning, I wanted to shout at this clown until his ears bled: *I'm more qualified than you! My grades are better. My SAT II's and APs are better. My extracurriculars are better. You couldn't accomplish half the shit I have!*

From fury at him, I turned to self-questioning. Was it because I fronted like I was hood that he'd made that remark to me? Yeah, I dropped the N-word from time to time, and I still dropped rap lyrics on the regular. Maybe he thought that was all there was to me, since we hadn't had many classes together. So he'd underestimated me.

Word, though: that was because he was too dumb to be in most of my classes. Fuck him. I wasn't going to change. I thought long and hard about retaliation before deciding to use my column in the school newspaper to tell the story of how one of my classmates had insinuated I was an affirmative action admit to Princeton. And when the column came out, friends rallied to my side, none more firmly than Nick:

"Who was it? I'll punch him in his face."

And I knew he was dead serious. Which was funny, because no one actually threw down at Collegiate. Nick's seriousness calmed me down a bit. In the larger scheme of things, was it really worth beefing with Damien?

"It's cool, man. It's not that serious."

But it was serious enough for me to keep dwelling on it. In and out of class, on the subway rides to and from school, Damien's words tugged at me. I reminded myself that I'd deserved to get into Princeton on the basis of my grades and my boards—*and* that my skin was part of the story of what I'd had to overcome to get those grades and high board scores in the first place. Sure, college admissions was a hustle. With Breimer's help, I'd sold myself as the poor Harlem Latino humanist. But I wasn't about to accept the idea that it was all hustle. If Damien couldn't spin the drama of overcoming that I could, that was on him—he'd never had to overcome shit.

I decided I had to take precautions to ensure that the dumbness that had come out of Damien's mouth wouldn't come my away again in the future, because the next time it did I'd slap somebody. Hence my New Year's resolution: at Princeton, my achievements would speak for me, and I would kick so much ass in all of my classes that not one person would have the audacity to say to my face or whisper behind my back that I'd gotten in just because of the color of my skin.

Then I remembered my night stroll with Derrick. Hadn't it been fucked up of me to make fun of NYU Dude? Did I—the sucker who was super-sensitive to any accusation that I hadn't properly earned my place—really want to play that pulling-rank game?

WEDNESDAYS AND SATURDAYS that winter, I'd head up to Trinity to mentor Prep students taking school-year classes and check in on my brother. Yando was approaching the program's halfway mark, acing his classes and making plenty of new friends. Mom and I thought it was time to get him thinking seriously about Collegiate. Over dinner one night, she tried to get the ball rolling.

"*Mi'jo,* don't you think it'd be great to go to Collegiate?"

I chipped in:

"You'll have people there who know us. It'll be easy for you to make the transition. I can give you pointers on the teachers, the social life, everything."

Frowning, Yando stared down at his dinner plate.

"All those people know *you,*" he said through clenched teeth.

One Wednesday, I was coming out of a meeting at Prep when my friend and Yando's adviser, Akim, pulled me aside. "Playa," he said, "your brother is really feeling the pressure of following in your footsteps. Maybe it's not a bad idea if he goes somewhere else for school?"

"So long as he's happy," I nonchalantly replied, "I don't care."

Bold-faced lie.

With Prep's help, Yando applied to three schools. The day after his final school visit, he told us that he wanted to go to Riverdale Country, in the Bronx. A few weeks later, I was making my mentoring rounds at Prep when the director of the Preparatory Component asked me to step into her office for a quick chat.

"Riverdale is very, very excited about Yando," she began, winking just in case I didn't grasp the full import of her words. "Are you and your mother excited about Riverdale? We know you both had your hearts set on having him go to Collegiate. But Yando absolutely loved his visit to Riverdale, and they loved him, too."

"Absolutely!" I smiled. "Thank you so much for sharing this, Mrs. Duffy."

"Now remember, Dan-el, not a word until the letter comes."

When the official letter came, I was home to see Yando open it. He didn't cry, he didn't dance up and down with joy; he just smiled, long enough for me to believe that he wasn't going to hate Mom and me forever for having twisted his arm into applying to Prep. Then he returned to his usual business, with the same slightly underwhelmed look on his face.

Mom? She was radiating happiness. Now her younger son, she

Collegiate commencement: Nick (center) and Dan-el
with their classmate Steve, spring 2002

rhapsodized, was going to attend an elite private school with a *beca*—a massive *beca*! And Riverdale wasn't like Collegiate—it was an actual campus, with all these buildings and all this open space!

The moment she said that, Yando frowned again. She'd dropped the naughty word—Collegiate. It was his moment, and he still wasn't free of the burden of comparison. I felt bad for him. Kinda.

SENIOR WINTER and spring lazily streamed by. After telling anyone who would listen that no school would ever take him, Nick was admitted to Yale. I dapped him up and promised to take Metro-North up to visit. Everything was coming together so perfectly.

Soon it was mid-May and Dad was on the phone, asking what I was planning to do for my summer before college. I updated him—Prep advising, nothing new there—and then the line went silent for a moment. I could hear him breathing, so I knew he was still there. It sounded like he was composing himself.

"I'm sorry"—he was speaking fast now, very unlike him—"but I don't think I'll be able to come to your graduation. Things over here, you know, and the cash situation, not so great."

Also very unlike him to be so vague. I played it cool.

"I understand, Dad. It's not a problem. I hope you're back in New York soon."

"Yes, for your graduation from Princeton. I promise."

"*Sí. Bendición.*"

"May the Supreme Maker take care of you, my *triunfador.*"

We hung up. I tried to console myself. Mom and Yando were coming to graduation, Father Michael and Carlos, too; I'd have my classmates to cheer me on, plus I was meeting up with two of the Resurrection guys after commencement to go see *Undercover Brother,* which had just come out in the theaters. The whole day was going to be butters. But then the little voice inside my head began to scream: How much was it to ask for a father to show up for his son's graduation? How unreasonable was it of me to expect him to be there just this once?

COLLEGIATE COMMENCEMENT turned out to be a blast without Dad. But the realization that high school was *over* had me bummed out for a few weeks. Little by little, though, excitement about college kicked in. When my full financial aid offer from Princeton finally came in the mail, I was thrilled—right until I noticed that one of the components of my offer was a Federal Work Study allotment.

I didn't have *papeles* or an SSN—how the hell could I do work-study?

In panic, I called the financial aid office, which passed me on to the office of the undergraduate dean for international students. From them I learned that for the purposes of the university's paperwork I'd been classified as an international student. I was also informed that my immigration situation could be resolved very quickly—which was news to me. When I explained to the office that I didn't have proper visa status in the United States and was therefore ineligible for work-study, one of the office's representatives asked:

"Why don't you apply for a student visa from the Dominican Republic?"

The representative made the process seem very simple. The university would provide me with the I-20 form I needed in order to file a student visa application, I would fly to Santo Domingo and submit the application, the visa would be approved, and I would reenter the United States in good standing.

Except I knew it wasn't quite that straightforward. I'd done research on my own and discovered that I probably wouldn't be able to secure a student visa. But just to make sure I wasn't wrong, I asked Prep for help, and they set up a series of free phone consultations with an immigration expert they trusted. Over the first two weeks of July, the expert and I went over my options.

If I chose to return to the Dominican Republic, she explained, I ran the risk of having my student visa application denied, for two reasons. First, I'd been residing in the United States illegally for years. Second, with next of kin continuing to reside in the States, I would have a hard time meeting one of the immigration service's core requirements for the issuance of a student visa: nonimmigrant intent. In other words, to qualify for the student visa, I needed to prove to a consular official that I had no intention of immigrating permanently to the United States—a tough task, given my history of residence and the stateside presence of my mom and brother.

"You would be better served," she concluded after reviewing my options, "by remaining in the United States and hoping that legislation to normalize the status of undocumented students is passed soon."

Mom and I had been following the news about this legislation for a while, she on Univision and I on the Internet. In 2001, a bill offering a path to legalization for undocumented students, the DREAM Act, had been introduced in Congress. But after 9/11, the passage of the Patriot Act, together with the increasingly negative perception of the undocumented immigrant community, had ensured that the bill didn't make it through Congress. There wasn't much of a chance that it would be voted on and passed anytime soon, but at least we could hope. Hope wasn't much to live on; but there wasn't much else I could do.

"Now," the lawyer went on, "should you happen to have a loving U.S. citizen girlfriend ready to commit to you in marriage . . ."

She trailed off. In my heart, I dismissed the option as unappealing.

But there was also a practical impediment to even entertaining that as a possibility.

"Unfortunately," I replied, "I don't even have a girlfriend."

"Then cross your fingers that the DREAM Act comes up before Congress soon! In the meantime, talk to Princeton again and see if they come around. You don't have to be in legal status to enroll for classes."

She wished me good luck. I thanked her for the advice. Before calling the point person at Princeton, I gave Breimer a ring. After commencement, he'd given me his cell phone number and told me to call if anything came up.

"Hello?" Over the phone, his voice sounded as gruff as always.

I quickly outlined my situation and summarized the lawyer's advice. "It's a bad idea to return to the Dominican Republic. But I'm worried that Princeton won't let me matriculate in the fall if I remain out of status."

As the last few words came out of my mouth, my voice cracked. I was starting to get emotional. I knew how Collegiate worked, I knew how Prep worked, but I had no idea how Princeton worked. No one there knew me personally. No one there had any reason to be supportive of me.

Breimer was back on the phone.

"You get back on the phone with them," he commanded me, "and remind them that you had a conversation with an admissions officer back in October! They knew the student they were admitting! You're going to be fine. But call me again if they keep giving you trouble, okay?"

I composed myself enough to say "Yes."

That same day, I called Princeton and reminded the representative in the international students office of what the admissions officer had told me: that to Princeton my status would be a nonissue. As for work-study, I wondered, I'd read in the aid materials that the financial aid office made nonfederal loans available to students; couldn't I take out one to cover my books and expenses?

"We'll see you in September" came back the reply.

PART 3

YOUTH

Yando and Dan-el dancing at the Princeton Senior Prom,
spring 2006

— CHAPTER 12 —

AT 6:30 A.M. ON THE FIRST SUNDAY of September, the moving
caravan—Mom, Yando, Carlos, Tía Mercedes, Tío José, and one of
my cousins—came together to move me into Princeton. First we
ate *mangú* for breakfast. Then Mom marched me to the makeshift
shrine in her room with a reminder: "Don't forget to say good-bye to
the *santos!*"

I made my prayers. Mom stood next to me and called on the protection of the Virgin Mary and Saint Michael. Then it was time to
load up and roll out. In five minutes we were on the Harlem River
Drive going past PS 200 and the 3 train terminal at 148th Street; flying by the Macombs Dam Bridge, Polo Grounds, the Rangel projects, and Washington Heights; crossing over to the New Jersey side of
the George Washington Bridge. We burned down the Jersey Turnpike, reaching the New Brunswick exit in half an hour. From there
we took the overpass that joins the turnpike to Route 1, then drove
on Route 1 until we hit Alexander Road. We turned off Route 1 and
followed Alexander Road up to the signs for the Princeton University entrance. One final right, another left, and we'd arrived at the
Elm Drive traffic circle.

In the near distance rose tennis courts and the Butler and Wilson dorms; farther up, Dillon Gym and the superstructure of Blair Arch; and at the very top of Elm Drive, immediately to the left of Richardson Auditorium, Holder Hall, my ultimate destination. But before heading up there, I had to stop by the housing office on Elm Drive to pick up keys and a housing packet. When we arrived, a line of freshmen and parents was waiting for the housing doors to open. At the sight, Mom turned to me, exulting in self-vindication:

"*Te dije,* we should have left New York earlier."

But we had to wait only a few minutes for the doors to open. After a smiling middle-aged woman handed me my freshman packet and room keys, my family caravan started up again on its way up Elm Drive to Holder. When we pulled into the parking lot right behind Richardson Auditorium, Mom stirred Yando awake and we all got out. While the adults strolled around Richardson and admired the architecture, I walked into Holder Courtyard, swiped my new proximity card on the door to entryway 7, and climbed up a flight of stairs to room 75. There, I met my three new roommates, already moved in, who offered to help unload the car trunks. A few trips later, we were done. As we stood by the entryway door catching our breath, Mom came up to me.

"We're leaving."

Carlos and Tío José had work that day, Mom had Mass and church activities, and no one wanted to be a nuisance to me by sticking around any longer. Carlos and Tío slipped me some twenties. We exchanged good-byes. The cars started up again. Soon Mom was waving to me and reminding me to call home in a week's time. My caravan pulled out of the parking lot.

IN THE AFTERNOON, I reported to freshman registration in Dillon Gym and was issued an identifying number with the same number of digits as an SSN. It was strictly for use within the university, but it had the virtue of sparing me the awkwardness of having to recite my tale of SSN-less undocumented woe whenever I had to stop by a campus office to file paperwork.

The next morning, I took a trip to the financial aid office and explained that, while the university grant in my aid package met most of my needs, my ineligibility for Federal Work Study left me about two thousand dollars short for covering book expenses and incidentals. The financial aid officer on duty took a look at my package and confirmed what I'd learned earlier that summer: although I wasn't eligible for any federally backed loans or grants, I was eligible for an unsubsidized loan directly from the university. I filled out the paperwork, signed the forms, and waited to hear how the loan would be delivered to me.

"We'll process your paperwork and send a check to your campus address in about two weeks," the officer said. "Do you have a bank account?"

It hadn't crossed my mind to open one. Somewhere in my mind I'd thought it perfectly reasonable to try to cash the check and keep the money in a desk drawer. Seeing the look of surprise on my face, the officer clarified:

"It's easiest for you to deposit the check in a bank account."

At first I worried that without a proper Social Security number or government-issued form of ID, I wouldn't be able to open a bank account, and I'd be back in the financial aid office within a few days begging them to get the money to me in a different way. But then it hit me that I might be able to use the pseudo-SSN to open a bank account. A few hours after my trip to financial aid, I wandered over to PNC Bank on Nassau Street, armed with my new college ID, my dorm address, and the pseudo-SSN. The bank, a stone's throw from my dorm, had been recommended in the orientation literature. Within five minutes I was set up with a matronly personal banking representative who outlined the bank's checking account offers and plied me with sheet after sheet of papers to sign. When she asked for my Social Security number, I shuffled through my papers for the relevant sheet with my Princeton 999 number and said:

"This is what I have for now."

"Ah," she exclaimed, "you're an international student! Where are you from?"

"The Dominican Republic."

"Ah, yes, a beautiful country! Your English is very good."

I nodded in silent agreement and signed more forms; she congratulated me for opening a bank account with PNC and thanked me for my business. Two and a half weeks later, I deposited the loan check.

I THUMBED THROUGH the undergraduate course catalog and drew up a list of six courses. But before officially enrolling, I had to meet with my faculty adviser and obtain her signature for my course selection sheet. Three days after move-in, I went to see her at her office in the philosophy department.

Professor Bennett was young, probably in her mid- to late thirties, and stylish—very different from the imposing if somewhat scruffy white men I'd taken seminars with at the Humanities Symposium. She had a no-nonsense directness about her that reminded me a little of Dr. Russell.

"You can't sign up for six courses, Dan-el," she said after reviewing my course selection sheet. "Four is standard for freshmen, five is stretching it, and six is a no."

I politely asked why.

"Princeton coursework is very demanding," she answered, "even for someone who's had the kind of background preparation you had in high school."

I argued that I could complete the coursework for every single one of the classes I'd picked, that I'd carried a heavy academic load for all of high school, that I had the AP scores to demonstrate I could handle college-level work, that—

She cut me off. "Tell you what"—she was smiling, I couldn't tell whether out of bemusement or exasperation—"you can shop the classes, see which ones are your favorites. I'll sign off on five. I will not sign off on six, so pare down your list."

My freshman seminar on Ovid's *Metamorphoses* met in a basement classroom at Forbes College, where the sunlight came in slantways and the ambient temperature was just warm enough to lull me into closing my eyes for a second. Before long, I'd feel the nudge of a classmate, take a look at the clock positioned above the door, and realize that five or ten or fifteen minutes had passed.

Our professor was razor sharp, fully in command of the material, and always ready with a crisply articulated insight to help us along in our interpretive fumblings. The readings were exciting and challenging: selections from Ovid's *Metamorphoses* in translation, Book II of Spenser's *Faerie Queene,* Shakespeare's *Titus Andronicus,* Ben Jonson's *Volpone,* Virginia Woolf's *Orlando.* And my classmates seemed cool, with the exception of the seersucker-wearing clown who got into an argument with me one afternoon about the ekphrasis that opens the second book of the *Metamorphoses:* the scene embossed on the doors of the Sun's palace.

Materiam superabat opus, just like my argument overcame his that day. I knew I was being a jackass going after him the way I did, but I had to set things straight. *Read words.* Dude's tangential musings had no grounding in the actual text. So I targeted Seersucker Boy for making a silly point. But if I wasn't going after him or scribbling some notes to myself about something clever our professor had said, I had an impossible time staying awake.

The seminar was three hours long. At the halfway mark, Professor Dolven would let us out for ten minutes. We'd get up, stretch our legs, walk across the hallway to the Forbes College office, and pick at the candy and chocolate bowls set on top of the waiting area's two coffee tables. At first we were islands of freshman shyness. But little by little, we began to make conversation.

"Are you in Forbes?"

"No, Rocky. And did you say the first day of class that you're from San Diego?"

"Yes!"

Her name was Rachel and, unlike Seersucker Boy, she definitely knew her shit. With her and the other girls in our class, Seersucker Boy tried to play it like a country club gentleman: holding the door open for them whenever we came back from break; ever so gently and graciously "correcting" her or the others whenever his unfailingly astute literary judgment indicated to him that his adversary in class discussion had wandered off the true path; talking some pseudogame to one or two of them before or after class with his laughably affected patrician inflections. I chuckled. Soon I was chilling with not just Rachel but our other classmates as well. We'd get lunch in Forbes dining hall before class—and Seersucker Boy was most certainly not invited.

RACHEL WAS A TALL, long-limbed, and long-haired Jewish Californian who could recite "Jabberwocky" from memory—which earned her an A-plus in my book. A few weeks into the fall, I introduced her to Juan, my old Prep and Collegiate quasi-nemesis, now at Princeton, and to Amanda, a Latina New Yorker who'd done Prep with Juan and me back in the day. Rachel introduced us to two of her new freshman friends: Judnefera, a D.C. girl who'd taken the International Baccalaureate curriculum at her high school, spoke French, and in the most understated and chill way possible talked about experiencing and changing the world; and Christine, a Staten Island native, half Irish and half Italian American, who, like Judnefera, was interested in public policy issues and, like me, was Catholic by upbringing.

At first, we were hype with freshman-year excitement, but by the time end-of-term exams came around, we were a hot mess of exhaustion. Our morale-boosting solution was to "study" together. In the evenings and on weekends, we piled into Cafe Vivian, on the ground floor of Frist Campus Center, to watch music videos, rap to 50 Cent, and pretend to read until we were kicked out. Then it was off to another study lair elsewhere on campus. Eventually the caffeine highs would wear off, the guilt of not having finished readings for the next day's classes would come knocking, and finally we'd all trudge back to our dorms.

Rinse and repeat, Sunday through Wednesday. Thursday, Friday, and Saturday nights were the holy nights of dancing and partying at the Princeton eating clubs.

Little by little, Juan started hanging out with us less—he was rushing for a fraternity—and so by the three-quarter mark of freshman year it was just me and the ladies. This made me an object of curiosity among the few dudes I did hang out with on campus: my roommates, the guys in my writing seminar, Juan in his reincarnation as frat-boy homie. The perpetual question:

"Look at *this* guy with his groupies. Are you trying to bone any of them?"

"Nah."

Product of an all-boys education that I was, I knew my tribe well enough to read between the lines of guy questioning. If dudes looked at me suspect when I swore up and down that I wasn't trying to scheme on any of the homegirls, there was a basic reason why—and I was never under any illusions about what it was. Guys and girls couldn't be best friends; scientific confirmation was available through *When Harry Met Sally,* "ladder theory," or straight-up common sense. If a guy was best friends with girls and didn't get the raging hard-on of lust for any of them, he had to be gay. It would all make sense, too: kid went to an all-boys school *and* was (notionally) Catholic? Plenty of room for all kinds of self-suppression.

But I wasn't sweating that—I felt pretty confident in my sexuality. No doubt, I lusted hard on the girls I tried to mack to at the eating clubs every weekend, and initially I lusted after the homegirls, too. It just didn't take that much mental energy to set the lust aside and become normal friends with them. Plus, as the weeks and months went by, I realized that little by little I was thinking less and less of them *that way.* Like caring sisters, they looked after me. They reminded me that I couldn't spend all day in the library reading and then just head straight to the eating clubs to get my mack on. I had to eat, you know—and occasionally take a full shower that was not of the Febreze variety, because otherwise no one would come close to me.

I WENT FOR COFFEE early one winter night with one of the five New York Dominican girls at Princeton. On my way to Cafe Viv, I laughed at the thought that I couldn't ever tell Mom I'd gone on anything even vaguely approximating a date with *una cibaeña bien educada*—Mom's ensuing euphoria would know no bounds. I mean, I thought Shorty was fly as hell, hence coffee; but I didn't need any maternal overhyped reinforcement of that idea, not yet.

Fly Girl and I got our coffees and jumped straight into conversation. It was all going so well . . . and then Amanda walked up to our table, her face streaked with tears.

"What's wrong?" I asked.

The tears started spilling again. I excused myself and told Dominican shorty we'd catch up another time. Amanda and I went on a long walk while she tried to unburden herself.

She and her boyfriend were having problems. Amanda had been all about this guy Salim for two months, and they were starting to get serious. He was a biracial dude our year who lived around the corner from Amanda's dorm. The drama: She had hang-ups about physical intimacy. Salim wanted to smash, but she just didn't feel ready yet. And now he was being an ass, letting her know—not even that subtly—that there were some other chicks in their dorm who were down to fuck. Which didn't surprise me: Salim's floppy hair got some girls our year very excited.

"You can't let him manipulate you like this," I told her. "You deserve better, and fuck him if he's pressuring you and making you feel like shit."

"But—I really think I love him," and the tears came again.

"How much does he really care about you if he's doing this to you?"

I told Amanda jokes to make her laugh, walked her to her dorm, and went back to Cafe Viv to get my laptop and go home. On the stroll up campus to Holder, I wondered why Amanda, sweet and wholesome—easily the most wholesome of my new friends—was so smitten with this Salim loser, who just wanted to hit it and quit it. But a part of me was jealous of Salim. I didn't have anyone head over heels like that for me. Shit, I wasn't even close. What was my lame ass even doing going on coffee dates?

———

MY BOY DERRICK would call or message me to give me the scoop on his new life at Brown. Then he'd tease me whenever I told him stories about the freshman girls I was feeling. His question every single time:

"What, another white chick?"

See, Dominican *chula* had been an exception. Usually I had holla thoughts about *this* chick in my Latin class or *that* chick in my Greek class or *that other* chick in my European history precept—and, wouldn't you believe it, I was the only melanin-tinted person in those classes.

Derrick and Nick were among the few non-Princeton dudes I stayed in touch with. The Resurrection guys had all scattered to the four winds, and I wasn't back in the hood often enough to chill with them. The few times I did run into any of them, we had jack shit to talk about. I had new stories of eating clubs and scheming on white girls and reading Dostoevsky—real hotness in the hood. But Nick and I could talk Collegiate and Ivy League gossip, and Derrick and I could talk Prep and Ivy League gossip. The conversations with Derrick always turned into an ordeal, though, because he came at me on the same topic whenever we talked.

"Why aren't you dating black or Latina chicks?"

"My nig, there are like five at Princeton, and they are all wifed up."

And then I'd be treated to some lecture about how I wasn't trying hard enough, how I had a responsibility to keep my dating game black or Latino. I'd audibly snore at Derrick over the phone. Clearly my dude had gone to Brown and hopped on the militant bandwagon after taking, like, five ethnic studies classes. Since when did my dating choices make me complicit in some kind of socialized and institutionalized marginalization of black and Latina women? If he wanted to get at me because I still dropped the N-word in conversation with him and my black and Latino friends, that was one thing. But this? Accusing me of being neck deep in some larger structural perversity because I was trying to make out with white girls? Blame the socio-economic structures that make Princeton the landscape of whiteness it is! Don't hate on me.

Oh, he hated.

"It's like you're scared of black chicks. All I hear whenever you tell me about a shorty is *blanquita, blanquita, blanquita.* You're not thinking about what your choices *signify* and shit."

"Yeah, the Ivy League is swimming in black chicks. How's that jumping off for you at Brown? Nigga, I cannot *wait* until you call me and say that some white liberal progressive girl from Portland is trying to jump your bones."

I fronted real hard like I was in the right and Derrick was undeniably in the wrong. But a tiny part of me did wonder whether Derrick had a point. Did I really have some obligation to *la raza*? Let's say I dated Judnefera, the only black girl among my close friends. How was that advancing the cause? What cause, exactly? Derrick was tripping and tripping hard. But I still felt like I had to justify myself.

One weekend during freshman spring, I made out with Brittany, this chick from Florida who happened to be friends with a friend, and went back with her to her dorm. It was a magical encounter, but not because of the chemistry of the hookup or anything like that. Shorty was black. I hadn't even really intended it—or had I? We were at a party drinking some awful Everclear punch when the sloppiness popped off. The day after the magic went down, I hit Derrick up just to boast.

"So, good sir, have I discharged my obligations to *la raza* now?"

"Aight, you hooked up. But are you going to date her? Is she some shorty for you to holla at until the next *blanquita* comes along?"

I didn't even have game like that—to keep her fiending after me while I deliberated which white girl to mack to next. For all I knew, Brittany would simply ignore me the next time I ran into her, if I even did.

"That's just . . . ridiculous. Shut up."

"You know I'm right. Maybe you just can't handle a black or Latina chick. Shit is too real for you. You like being a fetish for these white girls you mack to and for those white-girl friends of yours. Hood kid who knows rap lyrics and reads books—you are *that* played-out stereotype."

"What the fuck are you even talking about?"

Derrick burst into laughter when he sensed the hint of anger in my voice.

"Kid, I'm just messing with you."

So we let it drop. But I couldn't shake what he was insinuating: that even my new cherished friendships were erected on this quicksand of racial politics and that I had to be careful not to be *that* Negro, that totem. Derrick's hectoring had a way of sticking with you.

CATCHING UP WITH Nick was much less stressful: our phone conversations almost always started with tall tales of guy-girl schemes before transitioning into Yankees–Mets banter and discussions of Derek Jeter's fielding ineptitude. Occasionally, though, he'd ask:

"Anything new on the immigration front?"

"Nah."

"Do any of your new friends know?"

"Nah. Why would I tell them?"

But I didn't tell *him* that a simple reminder of my problem happened to be woven into the very fabric of my social life: the name of the student campus center that housed Cafe Viv. *Frist.* I tried desperately not to think about it, but it stared me in the face: *Frist, Frist, Frist.* Named after the family of Senator Bill Frist, who was Senate majority leader at the time. His son was in my class, and word was that he was quite the bro. But I was more interested in the father, maker or breaker of my future. The DREAM Act was up for consideration again.

The act had failed in the 2002 session of Congress. For the first few months of 2003, though, there were whispers of a potential bipartisan agreement, of a Republican president and his party finally grasping the urgency of DREAM. So, on late nights and weekends apart from the homegirls, I loaded up my Internet browser to read about the latest legislative maneuverings. I read about the opposition to the bill: all the CNN and Fox News pundits, cable talking heads, and conservative politicians screaming, *Don't give those illegal aliens amnesty! They've invaded the country. If they're breaking the law to get here, they don't belong here. They take away jobs that belong to good, hardworking Americans. Deport them . . .*

I'd be alone with my laptop and thoughts when the anger washed over me and I felt the strong urge to snuff Lou Dobbs in the face. The anger was interrupted by flights of fantasy. I imagined myself in the guise of a classical orator, mocking and shaming the flimsy rhetoric of the DREAM Act opponents with the most perfectly timed *supplosio pedis* to put the figurative and literal stamp on my argument.

But the fantasies quickly veered into nightmares of powerlessness: of Mom getting picked up by immigration, of a knock on my college bedroom door, of immigration officers storming into one of my classes to arrest me. How embarrassing *that* would be. Fuck being deported; I'd just die of shame.

I didn't dare open up to anyone. I made sure no one knew that my spirits were rising and falling with every update on the DREAM Act's progress through the Senate. And my friends never got to see how emotional I became when I saw—buried in an online article about congressional developments—mention of Senator Bill Frist's decision not to allow the bill to come up for a floor vote. In front of them, I was just another freshman working frantically to finish his papers before the second-semester Dean's Date deadline.

WHENEVER I CAME BACK home from Princeton, Yando and I would go shoot hoops at the neighborhood courts. Over games of 21 we'd catch up: I'd tell him about my new college friends, he'd tell me about his Riverdale classmates and their entitled-as-hell lives.

Most of the time, I was dumb casual with my game—slow dribbles, lazy jumpers, lots of posting up to overpower my skinny competition. Yando was anything but casual: hard dribble, running layups from every angle, three-pointers with a lazy hand in his face, and a decent imitation of an ankle-breaking crossover that he would whip out as if he were the second coming of Allen Iverson. He was also dead serious, which made me laugh.

"You ain't got nothing on me," I taunted him.

He really couldn't stop me if I just kept posting him up. I mean, on my way to the "freshman fifteen," I'd become two of him, plus I had three or four inches on him. But he kept talking mess.

"I'm gonna beat you, just watch. *One day* I'm gonna beat you."

"Talk is cheap."

And then I'd teach him a lesson or two in the post.

I was back home for the summer when we dusted off the ball for the Padilla Peralta best-of-three. As we walked over to the courts, Yando kept yapping about how he'd worked on some moves during the school year. He was going to school me this time.

To the hype talk, I fake-yawned. We got to the court and shot for first possession. I bricked mine, he drained his. All good: I figured I could spot him a few points and still come back to win. I checked him the ball. He picked up his dribble, jab-stepped me, and drained a jumper. I still wasn't stressing. He'd hit that shot before; what was so new? I checked him the ball. He picked up his dribble and flew by me so quickly I barely had time to react. I turned around to block his attempt. He went under the rim for the reverse, using the basket to protect himself as he launched a twisting layup. I hit him on the forearm as he released the ball.

"That's a *foul,* dude." But he was smiling at the and-one; despite my forearm check, he'd still gotten enough on the damn ball to get it in. Next three possessions: swished three-pointer; missed jump shot that he recovered for an easy layup; and dribble sequence where he tricked me into thinking he was going left (his strong side) before crossing hard to his right, pump-faking me, and nailing a long two-pointer. The score was 12–0.

Fortunately, I reminded myself, we were playing to 21. I had a comeback in me. This was my *younger brother,* after all, not fucking Vince Carter or Tracy McGrady. I blocked his next shot, took up position in the post, and was immediately stripped by the whirling dervish. Three-pointer, three-pointer, bank-shot two-pointer, and I was now staring at a 20–0 deficit. I had to storm back. I was not losing to him.

I hounded him whenever he picked up his dribble, draped myself all over him. I discarded my crap jumper and focused on the easy high-percentage post-up shots I'd always tormented him with. Soon I had six quick points. But when he checked me the ball and I charged at him to make it eight, he stripped me, ran to the three-point line, and bombed away before I could get in front of him. Game over.

"*Told you* I'd beat you one day!"

Outwardly, I was very chill. "It was just a game, my dude. You want a rematch? I'll floss on you."

"You're just some crusty old dude with bad knees."

"Shut up."

The rematch started out in my favor, but within ten minutes I was too winded to put up much of a fight on defense. He rained shots on me. In the blink of an eye it was game point again. He calmly drained the last shot, came up to me, and did his best imitation of P. Diddy's voice:

"Take that, take that."

SUMMER OOZED ALONG. Soon it was too hot to ball. One late July afternoon, I came home from Prep mentoring, poured myself a glass of water, and sat down in front of the kitchen fan. Suddenly Mom called out from the living room:

"*Mi'jo,* there's a letter from Princeton on the table."

I picked up the envelope and studied it before opening. OFFICE OF THE DEAN OF THE COLLEGE. Worried thoughts swept through me: What the hell could this be about?

I fought down the anxiety and opened the envelope.

The letter bore the signature of Nancy Malkiel, the dean of the undergraduate college, and had been copied to the president of the university and the master and dean of my residential college. It informed me that I was the winner of the Freshman First Honor Prize for the Class of 2006, awarded to one student for exceptional academic achievement during freshman year. I'd be presented with the award at the fall's Opening Exercises.

By the time I'd finished reading the letter, Mom was in the kitchen and her eyes were trained on me.

"What's it about?"

"It says that I'm receiving an award for academic performance."

But before I could even get another word out, I melted into tears.

"That's wonderful!" Mom exclaimed. "But, *mi amor,* why are you crying?"

I didn't really know why I was crying. I stuttered my way through an answer.

"I just think about everything we've gone through . . . and for me to win this . . . I won it for you, Mom."

"You won this for yourself, my son," she said, kissing me on the cheek.

—— CHAPTER 13 ——

THE WEEK AFTER I returned to campus for sophomore year, Mom, Carlos, and Yando came down to Princeton for Opening Exercises. I picked them up at the train station. Mom was wearing her trademark black blazer, white blouse, and long black skirt; Carlos and Yando were rocking fresh haircuts and dark navy suits. We strolled around campus until it was time to report for the academic awards luncheon hosted by Dean Malkiel and President Shirley Tilghman at Prospect House. My family and I sat at a table with the dean, a kind-faced senior academic who was very interested to learn more about my family. When it came out that Yando sang for a New York City youth chorus, she was intrigued. Did he see a future for himself as a singer?

"Yes!" he insisted confidently. "I have a great voice."

After lunch, we made our way to the chapel for Opening Exercises. The prizewinners lined up for the academic procession. Mom, Yando, and Carlos joined the families of the other prizewinners at the seats reserved for them. My friends walked in and sat as close to the front as they could. Then the processional struck up, and drummers and flag bearers swept down the center aisle. Dean Malkiel stepped to the podium and presented the prizewinners to the audience: the recipient of the award for highest academic standing entering senior year; the co-recipients of the award for junior-year academic performance; and the recipient of the award for sophomore academic performance. Then it was my turn.

"The recipient of the Freshman First Honor Prize, Dan-el Padilla Peralta."

When Dean Malkiel finished reading from the bio I'd been asked to prepare for the occasion, I could make out Carlos, Mom, and Yando cheering and, behind them, the homegirls hooting and hollering. Despite the warmth of their applause, I didn't really feel *there;* I was hovering outside of myself, chuckling at the spectacle of the beer-bellied Dominican kid who'd briefly become the focus of everyone's attention.

In thirty minutes, it was all over. Students and faculty poured out into McCosh Courtyard; I greeted my friends; I walked my family to the Dinky station and kissed them good-bye.

Later that day, I caught up with my friends at Frist and tried to relax into sophomore-year normalcy. But I wasn't anonymous anymore. From time to time, classmates would come up to me to congratulate me on the prize, make small talk, and then attack me with questions about the classes I'd taken and the grades I'd earned in them. I didn't mind the questioning too much, but it struck me as so bizarre that people were all of a sudden trying to be cool with me so they could be initiated into the mysteries of high achievement at Princeton. It was the Ivy League equivalent of star fucking.

THAT FALL, Rachel began bringing along a cute San Diego girl to dinner at Frist. San Diego and I hit it off. She picked up on my slang and started greeting me with:

"Waddup, *son?*"

True story: white girl saying that made me laugh. She and I flirted. A few months into the school year, we began dating. Of course, when I told Derrick that I was hollering at this San Diego chick—

"Let me guess: another *blanquita*."

"'It don't matter if you're—'"

"Date a black chick, then."

"Come on."

But I didn't care. I had a shorty, and she was feeling me.

Well, until she wasn't. Two weeks into the dating, San Diego asked me if we could bring our relationship back to friend status, "to get to know each other better." She was worried that our personalities and temperaments weren't ideally aligned, some joint like that. She was the relaxed SoCal girl, I was the fast-talking New Yorker; I was driven and ambitious, she was still trying to figure out what she wanted out of college and life.

I didn't understand why she'd suddenly gotten cold feet about dating, but I kept it cool. So she wasn't feeling me quite as much as I thought—no big deal.

The real truth, the next-level truth, spilled out of her a few weeks later. I can't even remember where we were: walking around the Mathey College courtyard, maybe, or at Frist late lunch while I stuffed my face. Wherever it was, she began talking with a rawness I hadn't heard before in her voice. Turns out San Diego had told her parents about me a little before we'd both gone home for break, and they'd deaded the prospect of an interracial relationship instantly: under no circumstances was a black man going to date their daughter, not if they had any power to prevent it. And with admonishments came threats: they would sooner not pay her way through Princeton than allow her to entertain anything beyond a simple friendship with me. She'd decided to yield to them.

And I still kept it cool. In front of her, I was all understanding, like her parents had not clowned me on some real *You are a nigger* tip.

Later that same day, Nick called me to catch up. I dropped my newly acquired intelligence on him; he was caught off guard by my facade of casualness about the whole episode and went ballistic with indignation on my behalf; I maintained the ill stoic front. On the inside, though? I judged her for being weak. Here the San Diego JAP, faced for the first time in her comfortable life with a high-stakes decision, had caved to the racism of her parents.

With judgment came revisionist history. I told myself that she actually hadn't come close to understanding me or what I was about. That her humor about the slang I spoke and about the few ghetto experiences I was willing to confide to her seemed a little too uninhibited, in the manner of those white boys I'd known from Collegiate—beginning with my Wu-Tang–aficionado seventh-grade classmate—who wanted to be down with the streets because it was, in the end, a big appropriate joke. That she'd categorized me as just an exotic Harlem boy who fit very tidily into a small descriptive box: poor, black, Dominican—*but he's smart, you know, and funny, someone to entertain myself with.* Fuck that.

One morning a few weeks earlier, we'd watched the sun rise over campus from Blair Arch and gotten into this far-ranging policy discussion that touched on immigration. I'd spoken in general terms about the need for immigration reform, but something had cautioned me against mentioning my own lack of *papeles*. Now that the truth about her parents and her unwillingness to fight them was out, I felt vindicated. She didn't deserve that kind of trust.

San Diego and I still hung out and studied together, but I didn't let myself get worked up about the relationship that had been stifled before it could progress much further. And when she wrote me an e-mail saying she felt so bad about what had happened that she'd been crying to the same Kelly Clarkson song on loop? I didn't sweat that, either.

ONE WINTER NIGHT, my friend Daniella led me from study break to study break: muffins at Frist, subs at Wilson College, Thai food at Forbes College—Princeton was just one never-ending study break, and the game that night was to see how much we could gorge ourselves. At Forbes, we caught up with mutual friends over noodles. I began debating U.S. immigration policy with an attractive girl from D.C. whom I'd crushed on briefly back in freshman year. Her position on immigration was crystal clear and unbending.

"Those illegals shouldn't be in this country. They entered illegally, and we should throw them out. They don't contribute anything to our society, they're a drain on our economy, and they definitely don't belong here."

I deployed the arguments I'd formed in my mind in my parallel existence of secret research and reading: that the term "illegal," as wielded by the contemporary talking-head discourse, is deceiving and distortive. That U.S. labor demand drives undocumented immigration. That the hands and feet of the undocumented contribute significantly to the American economy. She was unimpressed.

"But it's only the right and legal thing for us to police our borders. Those illegals are lawbreakers who don't contribute to our society and take away jobs from other Americans."

I started to get twitchy. I wanted to yell that she had no idea who we were, or what our lives were like, or how far we were willing to travel and how much we were willing to endure in pursuit of the dreams that mattered to us. What did I actually do? I said diddly-squat about my own status. I still hadn't summoned the courage to tell my new friends, and among my old friends, Nick alone remained the guardian of my secret. Hell, I hadn't even broken it down for Derrick. So why would I tell her? Instead of going gangbusters with some emotional disclosure, I returned to listing the contributions of illegal immigrants to the economy and questioning the sense and logic of the term "illegal."

Neither of us was yielding. We agreed to disagree, and I took off.

On the walk back to Holder, I got heated with myself for not confronting her with my own story. I knew I was scared to open up, and I hated myself for being afraid. But even as a voice told me that invoking my own story would be the socially responsible thing to do, another told me that it had been fine of me not to make it so personal. Better to move in the world of disembodied arguments. And why did I have to enlighten D.C. *blanquita* by reintroducing myself to her as an undocumented immigrant? Like she would care.

FOR A FEW MONTHS, I kept myself so busy with classes and sophomore-year drama that it became relatively easy to pretend nothing else existed outside of the Princeton bubble. It wasn't until the passing of Mr. Broquet, Collegiate's longtime French teacher, that I woke up to the world beyond the FitzRandolph Gates. I'd never taken French with him, but I had fond memories of my hallway interactions with him, and my Collegiate classmates used to tell countless stories of his Gallic mannerisms. He was a Collegiate legend.

Many of his former students traveled to Paris for the funeral. Among the travelers was my friend Victor, a year my senior at Prep and at Collegiate. At the funeral, Victor ran into a much older former student of Mr. Broquet's. They began to talk and quickly discovered they had someone in common. A few days later, Victor sent me a message with Jeff's contact information.

I immediately banged out an e-mail. That same day, Jeff wrote back to say how thrilled he was to hear from me. He'd read about my Princeton award in the Collegiate alumni magazine. He was now living in Paris, but he missed Yando and me enormously. He'd put up a photo of us on his apartment wall.

For about a month, we called each other once a week. He wanted to know all about my last few years at Collegiate, my freshman- and sophomore-year experiences at Princeton, about Mom and Yando. When it was his turn to update me, I found out he'd moved to Paris permanently. He didn't say why he'd moved there—and I didn't want to ask—but he told me he'd become a very successful photographer.

"Oh, it's so wonderful to hear your voice, Dan-el. You have no idea. Tell me more about Princeton. What's your major? How's the social life?"

Classics was in lead position, but I had another month to make up my mind before I officially declared; I had cool friends; I had occasional girl drama, but nothing to write home about. What was Paris like?

"Amazing. Life-changing. I've been living here for the past few years and have this great apartment. A gallery on Rue de Seine is exhibiting my photos. I just feel so glad to be living here. You'll have to visit sometime."

I promised I would.

Soon the mad panic of e-mails and phone calls calmed down; we went another stretch without communicating. I didn't mind the return of silence too much: it had been a bit tiring to catch up at the breakneck pace of those first few phone calls, and I had school and a social life to focus on. But I was happy beyond words to have Jeff back in my life.

It was two weeks before the final deadline for declaring majors (or "concentrations," in Princeton-speak). Amanda and I were dawdling in front of Frist. Neither of us really felt like going to class.

"So I just don't know," she was saying. "Some days I think French, other days comp lit. Or politics?"

From the dean's office on down, the official message was that Princeton students should major in something they loved and stop worrying about what might look "good" on a résumé or in the eyes of a prospective employer. But my friends and I were all having a bit of a hard time internalizing this message. It just seemed a little preposterous to think that you could major in classics or comp lit or philosophy or Romance languages and literature and then land a high-paying job in finance or consulting, or apply successfully to law school or med school or whatever. And having to explain to your parents that you were majoring in something so impractical . . . Oy. But this was so much privileged neurosing, and we all knew it: at day's end, we'd all be sporting Princeton degrees, so what was the big deal?

Amanda and I had taken classes together, so I thought I had a pretty good handle on the kinds of subjects she liked most.

"You like reading and talking about French novels, right? Do French or comp lit. Politics—meh."

"But I've been thinking a lot about something Juan José said to me the other day."

A Chicano classmate of ours, Juan José—everyone called him Juan Jo—was beginning to make a name for himself as the über-Latino. At the beginning of the year, he'd chugged three-fourths of a bottle of tequila at a campus room party. There had been much vomiting afterward. Amanda hung out with him on the regular. Even though she was still with Salim, I suspected she had a side crush on Juan Jo, which, if true, was decisive confirmation of her bad taste in men: fool was a classic *mujeriego*.

"When I told him I was thinking of majoring in French or comp lit, he was like, 'Oh, that's that white-people nonsense.' He said that I had to stop acting like a white girl. That Ivy League minorities needed to stop pretending we were white people. That I had to major in something that would position me to make a real contribution to society after graduating."

"That is some BS. What the fuck is he majoring in?"

"Politics."

"So joining the hordes of sophomores declaring a concentration in politics is gonna prepare him to make a 'real contribution to society'?"

Amanda shrugged and threw up her hands.

I'd been giving my leanings toward classics a lot of thought. Sure, it *was* some white-people nonsense: there wasn't another Latino/a or black face in many of the Latin and Greek classes I'd taken. But the problem, I was beginning to notice, wasn't the majors themselves. It was that previous schooling and preparation really shaped major choice—if you managed to make it to college in the first place. Even for those of us black and Latino kids who were lucky enough to be at Princeton, how many had been exposed to the study of Latin and Greek or of Romance literature in high school? And there was another related problem: black and Latino kids who'd made it to Princeton were socialized to think that only by majoring in something "practical" could they properly honor their obligations to the betterment and advancement of *la raza*.

Juan Jo's words struck me as irresponsible—on the same tip as Derrick and his date-black-and-Latina-girls-or-else jump-off.

"He's on some dumb shit. Following his logic, no minority should ever major in the liberal arts. Forget that. Maybe we should pick our majors because we're excited about the classes we'll be taking. Maybe we *should* be like the white people who major in impractical shit because they can."

Decision day came. Amanda declared a major in French. I declared mine in classics—with a minor in public policy. See, I was committed to the humanistic lifestyle, but not so committed that I wouldn't draw up a contingency plan or two if for whatever reason I couldn't hack it as a classicist.

DERRICK AND I were still hitting each other up every few weeks or so, usually over e-mail or instant messenger. We didn't stop beefing over white girls—he was always ready to lecture me. But he was becoming my lifeline to the world outside the Princeton bubble when I needed a break from that bubble. Dude was the only cat I was close to who could understand how strange it felt—those times I allowed myself to feel it—to be a broke-ass Spanish Harlem kid at an Ivy League school. Yeah, we'd both had plenty of advance preparation for the experience: all those years of immersion in the prep-school world had provided ample instruction in what was to come. Even so, it amazed us how . . .

"Cats are just so *casual* with their privilege, right?"

We talked about white students making snide comments about affirmative action; the upper-middle-class jokers condescending to the black and Latino staff at my campus center or his dining halls; and the *bia-bia* who had the temerity to let everyone in my education-policy class know that if certain school districts happened to be chronically underfunded and their students routinely underserved:

"Well, *some people* have to become janitors."

"The bitch said *what?*" Derrick almost lost his marbles when he heard that.

He had fewer of these incidents to report. On the whole, Brown came off well in our conversations—like a liberal's wet dream—though Derrick was quick to decry the *fake* liberal vibe and the bougie-ass mind-set of all those well-meaning kids who agitated for some amorphous vision of social progress while clinging desperately to their lame upwardly mobile pretensions. You know, do the campuswide protest one minute, interview for a consulting job the next. As for Princeton? Well, my friends were very open-minded, but the more I thought about immigrant-hater chick from the fall and San Diego of the racist parents, the less I inclined toward a favorable view of my Princeton peers. Yeah, small-sample-size vagaries and all that, but maybe Derrick was right:

"Y'all are fucking up down there."

Most of the time, though, we trafficked in Prep gossip: Derrick was a *bochinche* maven. First there was the scoop about Derrick's former advising partner at Prep, Keith. Always telling jokes and never fussing about anything, Keith had gone to Wesleyan for college and was on that seven-year weed-enhanced graduation plan. One afternoon my man was back home in New York, chilling outside his building in LeFrak City and minding his own business, when this guy strolled up to him and—

"Slashed him across the throat?"

"Yup, cut him over some dumb shit."

"Where he at now?"

"Got out of hospital, at home recovering. Keith was lucky—cut wasn't deep, otherwise Keith woulda bled to death before the paramedics got there."

"Fuck."

Yeah, I was shook. But Keith lived, so I told myself everything was okay. And when I ran into him at a Prep event some time later, dude had the ill scar but was upbeat and relaxed like nothing had happened to him.

And then—well, Prep heads started to e-mail like crazy, and before long I was talking to Derrick again. It was about Tim, my advising partner from back in the day: Horace Mann kid who'd gone to Franklin & Marshall, then enrolled at the Institute of Audio Research. I hadn't stayed in touch with him after he finished his four-year run as a Prep adviser, but I'd bumped into him the summer before sophomore year and dapped with him. He was one of the friendliest, nicest guys we knew.

I'd recently gotten an e-mail and hadn't even fully processed its contents. Tim had been working as a manager at an Old Navy north of the city. When he left work one Saturday the second weekend of March, I told Derrick, "this guy followed him into the parking lot and dropped him. Shot him dead."

I mean, I couldn't even believe what was coming out of my mouth.

"What the fuck? Are you serious?"

"Yeah."

"Why?"

"No one knows. Heard this guy was jealous because Tim was friends at work with his girl, thought Tim was trying to talk to her. But you know Tim was never like that."

"Fuck."

The funeral was held in the Bronx, on a Wednesday in the third week of March. Derrick wasn't able to make it down from Brown, but most of the Prep advisers who'd worked with Tim were in attendance. There wasn't a dry eye in the audience. After the funeral, I caught up with a few Prep advisory friends. We hugged each other tightly and made small talk about the schools we were attending.

Back at Princeton the next morning, I had all this paper writing and exam taking staring me in the face. No comfort in the seclusion of the bubble, though, not this time: I dwelled on what had happened to Tim for weeks. Derrick and I started messaging more just to talk about it. One of us would say:

"It makes you feel like this shit we have, this education we're getting, is so fucking fragile. You try to make something of yourself, you go to these schools, everyone pats you on the back and tells you to keep grinding. And then some nigga shoots you over stupidness and that's it?"

"Yeah."

Eventually I told myself that I had to get over what had happened to Tim, that I couldn't let it fuck me up or detract from my focus. It wasn't long before Derrick and I were back to trivial gossiping and storytelling, pretending like real shit hadn't even happened. But sometimes my thoughts would stray, I'd think of Tim, and for the most fleeting moment I'd fear that no matter how hard I worked and no matter what I achieved, I'd always be one angry motherfucker away from getting popped.

WHILE I RACED to write second-semester papers, I became friendly with one of my classics professors, Joshua Katz. In the fall he'd allowed me to enroll in one of his graduate seminars. Ever since, we'd been meeting once or twice a month for dinner at Forbes College, where he was an academic adviser. Since Katz was also the faculty adviser to all undergraduate classics majors, he became my first port of call for guidance on professors and classes once I officially declared my major. One afternoon in early May, we were in his office finishing up a conversation about my course selection for junior year.

"Dan-el," he was asking, "have you thought about studying abroad? You've missed the deadlines for junior-year study abroad, obviously, but you'd be a great candidate for one of the postgraduate fellowships."

My heart began to pound. I'd been trying so very hard not to think about the likely future consequences of not having *papeles*. Now Katz was putting me on the spot. Within seconds I felt what I never felt around my college friends: the compulsion to spill the beans on my undocumented woe.

"I can't leave the United States, because"—and boom! The story dropped like a ton of bricks in his East Pyne office.

Katz was indignant.

"These laws make absolutely no sense! This situation must be so stressful for you. There has to be something the university can do for you! Do Dean Malkiel or President Tilghman know? They're big fans of yours."

"No," I replied, "I don't think so."

"You really should write to them. Please. I'm sure they'll be glad to help. Just write to them. Promise me you will. If you'd like me to, I'll be glad to put in a word for you."

"Sure. I promise."

But even as I walked out of his office that afternoon, I hadn't fully committed to the idea of reaching out to them. I didn't know what, if anything, they or the university could do. Legislation still seemed the only realistic avenue for legalizing my status, and the DREAM Act showed no signs of being resurrected in Congress. So I put off writing the e-mail to the dean and the president until the summer. Once final exams were over and I was back mentoring at Prep, then—maybe then—I'd take time out to draft an e-mail.

In the middle of June, I finally composed the e-mail. I edited and reedited it for about a week before hitting Send to Dean Malkiel and President Tilghman. Once the secret of my status made its way over the Internet, I was captive to my in-box for what seemed like an eternity until Dean Malkiel replied.

"I don't know what we can do," she wrote, "but we'll do our best to help."

—— CHAPTER 14 ——

WITHIN A FEW DAYS, I was put in touch with Stephen Yale-Loehr, an attorney at Miller Mayer, in Ithaca, New York. I'd heard he was one of the leading experts on U.S. immigration law. Surely he would know some way, however arcane, for me to regularize my status? I wanted to pick his brain, but I was worried about how expensive the consultation would be—outside of my Princeton financial aid, I didn't have a dime to my name.

My first week back on campus junior year, I went to see Dean Malkiel at her offices in West College. When she offered to arrange a consultation with Steve free of charge, I gratefully took her up on it.

Over the phone, Steve and I reviewed my family's immigration history and the possible remedies I could pursue. "Your options," he told me—in my mind's eye I saw him ticking them off on his fingers—"are: marriage, if there's a significant other in your life and you are prepared for the next step; the passage of the DREAM Act, presently stalled in Congress, as you know; or a private bill, if a congressman should be willing to take up your case."

The last of these options looked to have some potential, at first. Discreet inquiries were made and fielded, and my story was relayed to a friend of the university who arranged for me to chat with the deputy chief of staff of a member of Congress. I marveled at the well-connectedness of the university, but I also found myself fighting off a creeping guilt about tapping into those connections. I knew the other undocumented kids I read about online didn't have a Princeton going to bat for them. But whenever I called home to update Mom, I reminded myself that I wasn't doing this just for myself, but for Mom, too. She needed her *papeles* as much as if not more than I did.

Carlos was a permanent resident, which meant that if they chose to marry, her status problem could go away; but Mom wanted Carlos to obtain an official annulment of his first marriage so that they could get married in church. She'd remind Carlos from time to time that *she* was good, since she and my dad had never actually gotten married; it was *Carlos* who had to take care of that *asunto* before they could stand before the Lord as husband and wife. And Mom definitely wanted to become official in the eyes of the Lord before, not after, they got married in City Hall.

Her position didn't make much sense to me, but Mom's ways were her ways. Until they got married and he filed a spousal petition on her behalf, the door was always open to Mom's being picked up by immigration officers and placed in deportation proceedings. So I needed the contacts I was establishing to work on Mom's behalf as well as mine; no way I could allow her to continue running the risk of getting deported.

For about a week or two, my hopes ran wild: the contacts would work out, Mom and I would regularize, and everything would be perfectly fine. But a follow-up call strangled the little optimism I'd allowed myself.

"At the present moment," the chief of staff informed me, enunciating every single syllable with such perfect crispness, "it doesn't look like a private bill sponsored by the member would make it through Congress. There would be very serious resistance. The likelihood of your being exposed, with serious ramifications for you and your family, would be unconscionably high. We're sorry."

"I completely understand," I replied. "Thank you so much for your hard work, and please thank the congressman for the interest in my case. I sincerely hope that the DREAM Act passes sometime soon."

"We hope it works out for you, Dan-el. Best of luck."

I returned to Dean Malkiel's office later that day to report the news. She asked me to take a seat on her couch and summarize the latest developments. Once I was done, she asked:

"How are you feeling about all of this?"

I couldn't even begin to explain how, in spite of my best efforts at self-discipline, my hopes had spun out of control—only then to be extinguished. In response, I simply said something about having steeled myself for the outcome. She studied my face closely for a moment, then reiterated her support and asked me to stay in touch. For her own part, she added, she'd keep looking and exploring. And if I ever needed to talk, the door to her office was always open.

MOST JUNIORS on campus joined upperclassman eating clubs. My friends and I were no different: we all joined Terrace (unofficial motto: food = love), home to an ethnically diverse assortment of potheads, Baudrillard-spouting intellectuals, and die-hard fans of Le Tigre. We'd meet up there to eat and hang out whenever we didn't want to pretend to be doing work at Frist.

Come mealtime or cocktail hour or Saturday night at Terrace, I went out to champagne and campaign. Otherwise, I reduced to the absolute minimum any free moments I might have where the anxiety of not having *papeles* could take over my mind by taking as many classes as I could and sleeping as little as humanly possible.

From time to time, Dean Malkiel wrote to check in. I'd drop by her office and reassure her that I was doing fine: I wasn't sweating the uncertainty, it was just another obstacle to deal with, I was sure a solution would come along sooner or later. Until then, I'd just enjoy my undergraduate years as best I could. That was my story—and I wasn't being entirely fake about it. On most days, I did manage to convince myself that everything was or would be fine. And whenever revisiting the drama of not having *papeles* at my "checkups" with Dean Malkiel left me feeling dispirited, I had only to walk over to Terrace to feel normal again. Mealtime conversations almost invariably revolved around the classes my friends and I were taking, the books we were reading, and new morsels or well-chewed scraps of hookup gossip. And if Amanda or another friend happened to ask, "Why are you seeing Dean Malkiel so much these days?" I'd successfully improvise some answer: my grad school plans, the dean's new grade-inflation initiative, or just the first plausible-sounding excuse that came to mind.

For the first few months of junior year, everything was all good—and then my in-box exploded, all because of some immigration beef.

It all started with Juan Jo, onetime humanities hater and now a Terrace fixture himself. He'd been hanging out in one of the residential-college dining halls when he spotted a flyer for an event being organized by the International Festival Committee. Staffed by foreign undergraduate and graduate students at Princeton—some of whom were Latin American residents whose first experience of life in the United States was Princeton—the IFC was responsible for putting on an annual celebration of our campus's multicultural diversity. That year, the committee had chosen what seemed to them like a perfectly witty slogan for the annual celebration:

"Meet the Aliens—the Legal Ones."

The moment Juan Jo saw the flyer, he banged out a mass e-mail urging as many people as possible to show their displeasure at the IFC's insensitivity by boycotting the event. Replies came in bunches, three or four belligerent or conciliatory e-mails at a time. The IFC students were incredulous that their cutesy slogan could be misconstrued as offensive. Ah, but then it was revealed that there was a backstory to the drama. A few weeks before Juan Jo's sighting of the flyer, his successor as president of our campus Chicano Caucus had learned of the proposed slogan and asked the IFC students to reconsider. The IFC students had insisted that it was just a joke designed to riff on the word *alien* and had stuck with their decision to print flyers with the slogan—even after a Princeton library employee brought the possibly offensive construal of the flyers to the attention of the IFC. And so the debate over unintended meanings swiftly metastasized into a big Latino-on-Latino throwdown over e-mail.

Those of us who found the slogan offensive started *chismorreando* over lunch at Terrace that the IFC members who were Latino came from affluent and cosseted backgrounds: *they* were the cream of the Latin American political elite, sent off to receive their high-prestige American educations before they returned home to assume their preordained positions of *liderazgo*. How much did they personally have invested in the debates roiling the United States over illegal immigration? Nothing. That's why they kept blithely saying over e-mail that people shouldn't get so worked up over a *malentendido,* that they shouldn't let "politics" stand in the way of "culture." *Cabezas duras:* politics *is* culture!

They were not us. *We* were first-generation immigrants or the children of immigrants, and more than a few of us were close to people who were "illegal aliens." And this is where Juan Jo spit hot fire: he wasn't afraid to let everyone know that *his* parents had been illegal aliens. He'd dropped that autobiographical bit right in his first e-mail, said he wasn't going to let anyone talk down to him because of it, and vowed not to let the IFC get away with a slogan that basically amounted to a diss.

For the briefest moment, I thought about firing away an e-mail in which I let everyone know that *I* was an "illegal alien" and that *I* took the slogan very personally. But when the moment of reckoning came and I sat in front of my own laptop with an e-mail draft ready, I couldn't bring myself to open up like that. I realized that it took real courage to do what Juan Jo had done—and I didn't have that kind of courage. So instead I wrote and sent along some platitudinous, "make peace, people" missive. When I reread it some hours later, I felt the stirrings of self-loathing.

THE CHAIN E-MAILS, and my spineless response to them, shattered the illusion I had worked so doggedly to sustain. For much of the spring, I wrestled with the frustration of not having *papeles*.

Now it began to truly hurt when I saw my people taking advantage of those travel- and study-abroad opportunities that were closed off to me. Rachel and Christine had already been abroad the previous summer to study in Spain; now Amanda was chilling in France for a whole term and writing to me about how boss Paris was. Nick, whom I still talked to on the phone once a month, had studied abroad in St. Petersburg the summer before and had gone on a trip with the Yale rugby team to Ireland earlier in the year. And Derrick? Abroad *for the year* in London, at the School of Oriental and African Studies, sending me dispatches studded with pearls of self-conscious enlightenment:

"The world is so much bigger and more interesting than the United States."

I wanted to confirm that for myself, but how could I?

As spring semester threatened to come apart at the seams from the pressure of my swelling frustration, I tried refocusing myself by formulating a new set of personal goals. I told Prep I wouldn't be coming back to mentor and made plans to study German at Middlebury College's summer immersion program. The hope was that becoming good enough at German to read some Kafka and Rilke in the original would enable me to conjure up my own fantasy of Europe in small-town Vermont. Plus I'd been told that having some German on my transcript would look good if I ended up applying to grad school in classics. Once the plans came together—Princeton classics and the dean's office agreed to hook me up with some aid to foot Middlebury's steep tuition—I allowed myself to get just a little excited about the thrills of studying German and fighting off Vermont mosquitoes. Not as fly as Spain or the UK or Russia, but it was something.

MY MIDDLEBURY SOJOURN, abundant in *Hören Sie gut zu*'s, wrapped up at the beginning of August, and by month's end I was back on Princeton's campus with two weeks to kill until senior year started up in earnest. Already my in-box was beginning to fill up with e-mails from the university's fellowship and career development offices, each offering to open the door to a world of first-rate graduate degrees, life-altering travel, gainful employment. The e-mails all had this slightly breathless quality to them, this "You are a Princeton student and the world is your oyster" subtext. I could apply for fellowships to Oxford, to Cambridge, to Trinity College Dublin. I could apply to fellowships for study or work in Latin America or Asia or Africa. I could work in finance or in tech. I could teach.

Slowly filtering back onto campus, all my friends seemed to be fretting about applying to jobs or grad school or law school or med school. In front of them, I shared in the general collective privileged angst; alone in my dorm room, I was mad jealous. *They* could work or study or teach, or do whatever they pleased, no problem—but what about me?

Briefly, I played along with the world-of-infinite-possibilities jump-off and attended a Teach for America event on campus. The TFA e-mails that went out to juniors and seniors struck me as corny and pretentious beyond belief—"Change things," read each subject line; "change *what* things?" I wanted to reply—but between the years of mentoring work at Prep and my public policy minor, I was beginning to believe that I might have a future teaching black and Latino kids in the inner city.

A few days after the event, I was e-mailed by a recruiter who flattered me with surprisingly detailed references to my accomplishments and offered to set me up with a TFA alum for coffee. On the appointed date and hour, I showed up at Viv, got a latte, and sat down with the alum. I decided to bring up my special problem, just to see what—if anything—TFA might be able to do. I wasn't optimistic, but I figured it was pointless to string the recruiter and the alum along if TFA wouldn't even hire me in the end.

The alum's face dropped.

"I'm not sure TFA can do anything about that," he replied after a moment of silence. "So you can't work?"

"Not now, not legally," I replied.

"I wish you the best of luck with resolving your situation," he said, draining his coffee cup. "Please let me know if it gets sorted out!"

After that encounter, I decided that seeking employment right after graduation was probably pointless. Anything more high-profile than working as a *mesero* for tips would probably not fly, since any prospective employer was likely to take one look at my situation and shun me. Yeah, there was a shortage of elementary and secondary teachers, but no teaching-fellows program and no school district in the country would want to mess with my legally unemployable behind. Grad school in the United States? I imagined I'd have to be legal to be employed as a teaching assistant, so that was out of the question. Sure, I could lie or try to hustle some fake *papeles,* but hadn't Mom made the choice not to lie? And I'd be screwed beyond redemption if I got caught. So what choices did I have?

A WEEK INTO FALL TERM, I met with Princeton's fellowships dean, Frank Ordiway. A postgraduate fellowship to study at Oxford or Cambridge was starting to seem like a pretty cool idea, even though I had no idea how I'd be able to leave the country and return successfully. Still, if I didn't have any realistic opportunities in the States, why not just bounce?

I explained my status problem to Dean Ordiway in full—not that I had to, as it turned out; he'd heard through the grapevine. Then I picked his brain about specific scholarships. He was worried about my applying either to the Rhodes or to the Marshall: my legal status seemed to stand in the way of eligibility, and you never knew who on a Rhodes or Marshall committee would be inclined to "out" me as undocumented to the immigration authorities.

"But," he insisted, "you'd make a great candidate for the Sachs."

I read on the university's fellowships Web site about the Daniel M. Sachs Class of 1960 Graduating Scholarship, which had been instituted in memory of a highly accomplished student athlete and Rhodes Scholar who'd been cut down in the prime of his life by cancer. Every year since 1970, a committee consisting of the trustees of the scholarship—and, in time, the elected scholars themselves—met to select a new holder of the fellowship, which provided two years of funding for study at Worcester College, Oxford. The fellowship was open to all Princeton seniors; there was no stipulation that the applicant be a U.S. citizen or permanent resident.

The second week of October, I set myself the goal of explaining in my application letter why the classics in particular, and humanistic education more broadly, had come to mean so much to me. The words didn't come easily at first; everything I typed struck me on a second read as the musings of a blowhard. On the fourth or fifth try, I (sort of) found my groove. I wrote about how, for the younger me growing up in Harlem,

> reading about the Classics was an immensely relieving escape, a way of erecting in my imagination some kind of bulwark against everything that I found so threatening.

And how, for the older me now studying Greek and Latin literature and history, it was not only at the academic but at the most deeply personal level

> where I have felt most enriched and vitalized. I think often of Helen Vendler's remarks in a *Paris Review* issue about the importance of poetry: lyric and verse can be faithful and lifelong companions, personal resources, aids in times of anxiety and distress. Latin and Greek poetry have left an indelible impression on me precisely for these reasons; they are embedded in how I have come to frame my personal responses to the world and have taken root in a kind of secondary consciousness I have of myself.

I was invited to interview with the Sachs Scholarship Selection Committee on the Saturday morning of the first weekend in December. The interview flew by; at its conclusion, I wasn't sure I'd acquitted myself well, but the committee members had given me a chance to go on and on at great length about why I enjoyed humanistic study so much, and for that opportunity alone I felt thankful.

Early the following morning, I was packing up for my daily pilgrimage to the library when the chair of the selection committee called me. He wanted to know if I was free for a second interview, to be held at the campus student center in an hour. From my desk I grabbed the notes I'd taken during the first interview and ran out the door into a flurry of snowflakes. I met the chair and another member of the committee in front of Frist. We shook hands, walked into the building, and took seats outside Cafe Viv. I steeled myself for a second round of questions. They broke out in smiles.

"Congratulations," the chair said, "on being chosen this year's Sachs Scholar!"

"What?"

I thanked them and the committee profusely, shook their hands, and walked back into the falling snow. I was bound for Terrace, to gorge myself on breakfast pancakes. I told myself I'd earned them. Oxford, Oxford! I'd dreamed of Europe for so long, and now I'd be spending two years there!

On the walk to Terrace, I called Mom.

"*Mi'jo,* what a blessing! This is wonderful!"

THERE WAS JUST one problem: the ten-year ban on reentering the country if I left the United States to study abroad. I knew from my consultation with Steve the year before and from my own research that the ten-year ban—the punishment levied on visa overstays—would kick in if and when I left the country. But I wasn't going to let that knowledge get me down, not yet. I basked in the glow of being chosen a Sachs Scholar and tried to live it up senior-year style. There were classes to take and senior theses to write and professors to meet before graduation hurled us into the great abyss.

There was also the hookup hustle: you looked to your left and to your right, saw that hot girl you'd been thinking about from time to time, and said to yourself, What the hell, I'm graduating in six months—isn't now the time? Senior-year romance was in the air. In a moment of weakness—so I thought the instant the words flew out of my mouth—I told Nick on our monthly phone catch-up that I was feeling Amanda.

Over the phone I tried to break it down to him—and to myself—why I should not swing any game. Yeah, I knew she was sorta single: her relationship with Salim was on its last legs, or so she kept saying. But she and I had been tight for so long, which was part of the problem: we were a little too close for the mack to be easy. We'd become such good friends that we'd picked adjacent dorm rooms for senior year. Now I saw her every day, not just at our dorm but over Terrace lunch and dinner with our other friends. So if I tried and bombed, it would be an awkward final few months of senior year, for sure. And I wasn't positive I was feeling her on that serious-relationship tip. I'd been single for so long; maybe it was the *mentula* speaking?

"Dude, who cares?" Nick replied. "I think you're being chicken. Just go for it."

I wasn't the go-getter Nick was. As fall and early winter of senior year roared by, I fell into a rut of indecision. First, I'd decide that I was into Amanda and declare to myself that I would make "it" happen; then I'd doubt myself; finally, I'd go after one of her friends or someone on the periphery of our Terrace friend group.

Yup, I was on some weird tip, and I didn't need Nick or anyone else to tell me that. But she was on that weird tip, too! She was still hooking up with Salim. All these years, she'd spent so much time getting worked up about him, complaining about him, basically saying he was an asshole who'd used her for play and cheated on her—and then I'd spot her on the walk of shame back from his room. I'd get mad at her, and no amount of debriefing with Nick would make the anger go away.

I SPENT THE WINTER holidays playing basketball against Yando, who, despite his braces-wearing, acne-spotted gangliness, had evolved into a much superior basketball player. Our games of 21 were victory laps for him, ordeals of shame for me.

Only when I returned to campus in January for exams and papers did I begin to obsess with finding a way around the ten-year ban. I sat down with the chair of the Sachs, who promised his and the fellowship's support and assistance. I sought guidance from the professors who'd written my references for the Sachs. I dropped by Dean Malkiel's office to seek her advice again. The emergent consensus from all of those conversations was that I had two choices: either defer taking the Sachs and hope against hope that the DREAM Act would be passed, or take the Sachs, leave the USA of my own free will, and subject myself to the ban against reentry—on the hope and the prayer that the ban would somehow be lifted.

But when I got back in touch with Steve, the lawyer I'd consulted with the year before, he opened my eyes to a third and more attractive possibility. He'd done some research on the possibility of filing a retroactive change of status. We'd build an application around a clause in the immigration statutes that held open the prospect of a status adjustment if the applicant could demonstrate that extraordinary circumstances had prevented him from adjusting at the time he initially fell out of status. The ultimate aim would be to have me adjusted to F-1 student visa status. On its own, Steve explained, the application would not be likely to compel an immigration officer to rule in my favor; we'd need supporting letters, from close friends and mentors familiar with the circumstances of my life and from highly influential and visible players in government and public life. If successful, the application would reg-ularize my immigration status before I headed off to the United King-dom and enable me to travel without fear of the ten-year ban.

We couldn't be confident of success, but this option was better than nothing.

With Steve's encouragement, I began canvassing for letters of sup-port. Starting the third week of January, I spent an hour or two each day sending out e-mails and making phone calls. The letters began to come together. From Sacred Heart, Father Michael wrote one prais-ing Mom and vouching for my character. Jeff e-mailed in an account of our earliest days together at Bushwick. A senior administrator at Prep for Prep wrote about my maturation in the program and my con-tributions as an adviser. Dr. Beall, Dr. Russell, and Mr. Breimer wrote about my time at Collegiate. Four of my college professors spoke of my love of the humanities and my engagement with education policy. Dean Malkiel told the story of my admissions file and related her impressions of me from our many conversations. The chair of the Sachs discussed my application for the fellowship and affirmed the interviewing committee's support for my goals.

Many of the letter writers also reached out through contacts to local congressmen and elicited letters of support from them as well. Results trickled in a few weeks later: letters from Representatives Charles Rangel, Carolyn Maloney, and Rush Holt; Senators Hillary Clinton, Chuck Schumer, Ted Kennedy, and Mark Dayton.

As Steve and his assistant coordinated the support letters and prepared my final application for submission, I came to feel so massively indebted to my supporters that for a brief period at the beginning of February I couldn't even bring myself to write thank-you notes. I just didn't know how to express my gratitude.

I WAS STILL convinced that none of my friends apart from Nick would ever have to learn about my lack of *papeles*. If the application Steve was putting together did its magic, I'd adjust status before Princeton commencement and not have to worry about any postgraduation drama. It would all be so gravy. Secure in that hope, I decked myself out in the trappings of normalcy. Most weekdays and weeknights, I focused all my attention on research for my senior theses, with breaks to spend time at Terrace.

This thesis-and-Terrace idyll proved to be very short-lived. In late February, a *Wall Street Journal* reporter e-mailed me out of the blue to ask if she could write a feature-length article on my life. Miriam Jordan had found out about me from Jeff's sister and was convinced my story could make a difference in the public debate over immigration.

I read and reread her e-mail, not sure of what to do. I wasn't that optimistic about the capacity of my story to make a meaningful difference, and in any case I had some concerns to address before I could embrace that kind of publicity. Yeah, publicity would certainly insert my story into the public conversation; it might provide a boost to other undocumented high school and college-age students; it might bring enough pressure to bear on the immigration service to induce them to approve my change of status. But it could also blow up in my face if the service decided to make a public example of me or

Mom by deporting us. And publicity would bring an end to the multiple-identity game and the side hustle: every student on campus, every classmate at Collegiate, every old friend at Prep and Resurrection would know that I didn't have *papeles.*

I talked through the pros and cons with Steve and Dean Malkiel. Then I called Mom and asked for her advice. She laughed.

"*Ay, mi'jo,* I always told you when we were going through our hard times that one day people would write about us."

Only when Mom gave her blessing did I begin exchanging e-mails with Miriam. Within a few days we were talking on the phone, and I gave her permission to go ahead with the piece. But even then I allowed a new fantasy to take hold: I wouldn't *have* to talk to my friends about anything until the story broke, and once it did, I'd let the profile speak for me. I wouldn't have to face any hard questions from them beforehand, and if the profile was as thorough as Miriam had promised, I wouldn't have to deal with any after.

Miriam quickly put a stop to that dream.

"When can I come down to visit you on campus?" she asked one day over the phone. "I'd love to interview your friends for the piece."

"They don't know I'm undocumented."

"They don't know? Anything?"

"No, I haven't told them."

"Why?"

For the longest time, I'd been so confident about my ability to compartmentalize the hustle, but lately it had become fatiguing to keep spinning bullshit. The more Amanda and our other friends kept pressing me on my furtive doings and wanderings, the more I spotted cracks in my inner resolve. There were days when I'd feared that in response to their questioning I'd cave—but when the questions did come, I was always ready with some evasive answer. Now that I'd agreed to have a newspaper profile done on me, though, why the hell was I keeping my guard up?

"I've never wanted to burden them with that knowledge," I heard myself tell Miriam. "I never wanted to involve them in this other part of my life. I don't want them to worry about me."

"Would you be ready to tell them now?"

I sighed. It was time. Better from my lips than from a reporter's.

ONE AFTERNOON later that week, my Terrace friends and I took a break from thesis work and ventured into town for some ice cream. Spring was in the air. We dropped by the Bent Spoon ice cream shop and then walked over to a newly paved open-air court on Witherspoon Street, where we sat down.

I told them what I had to say.

Immediately they wanted to know how they could help and what they could do. So I asked: Did they mind being interviewed for the *Wall Street Journal* profile? No, but they wanted to know what else they could do. There had to be something else. Marriage?

"Every lawyer I've talked to has brought up marriage, but you all know I don't have that love-boo in my life yet."

They laughed. Soon they were telling stories and I was laughing my head off, just like any other day. Then we scattered to our respective study locations on campus, with promises to reconvene for dinner at Terrace.

It had been that easy to tell them. I had some kick-ass friends.

BEFORE LONG, it was the first week of April, and thesis deadlines were looming. My friends were starting to go a bit crazy from the all-nighters devoted to the god of Thesis. I was clinging to sanity—very tenuously—with the help of a listserv.

The Black Men's Awareness Group on campus kept up an online site and e-mail chain where members circulated jokes and commentary on anything of interest. I'd been involved with the group ever since I'd volunteered to be an on-campus mentor to newly arrived black students my sophomore year. The listserv members were prolific and hysterically funny with their posts: mocking new Bush policy initiatives, teasing fellow listserv members about intramural basketball games gone terribly wrong, offering commentary on Kanye. I read avidly but contributed sparingly—until a new thread went up on the topic of illegal immigration. I clicked on the thread and began reading.

Two friends had summarized bills introduced in California and elsewhere to make undocumented immigrants eligible for in-state tuition rates at state colleges and universities. The posters supported the bills, and the first few comments in response to their posts were enthusiastically in favor. I'd been following the progress of the bills and believed strongly in them. After all, I'd been fortunate enough to land at Princeton, with its financial aid, but what would have happened if I'd ended up at a state university, having to pay out-of-state fees? Silently, I thanked my friends and the early commenters. But then I saw it: an anti-immigrant screed, the handiwork of one of my old freshman-year dorm mates. Here's the gist of it:

ILLEGAL immigrants getting these benefits? They're a drain on our country's resources. They're not citizens. My dad came to the United States from the Caribbean and became a citizen by following the rules. If they want to become citizens, they should follow the rules and wait their turn in line. As it is now, they're just free-riders. They take jobs. They send lots of money, TENS OF BILLIONS of dollars every year, back home in remittances. So they take jobs from hard-working Americans, they free-ride on benefits that good citizen Americans pay for with their taxes, AND they take all this money out of the US economy and send it back to their home countries. That doesn't anger anybody?

I didn't know what to do at first. I could just say nothing and wait for someone else to come in and hack his arguments to pieces. I could approach it just like I had the conversation with that girl at Forbes way back at the beginning of sophomore year: all dispassionate argument, no personal revelation. I could bang hard on how shortsighted it was of my old roommate to get suckered into this niggerizing discourse about undocumented immigrants. Good-for-nothing, lazy, take-shit-from-the-hard-working-American coloreds: How deaf are you if you can't hear the whispers of "Nigger nigger nigger!" in the background?

OR: I could reveal my own status and hitch that disclosure to other arguments I had at the ready: that many "illegals" actually do pay taxes; that they contribute a great deal to the U.S. economy; that there is no stupid fucking line to wait in unless you have the means and patience to put together an application for a U.S. visa in your home country—and even then you might not be approved; that if you came here legally and then fell out of status, it was hard as hell to dig yourself out of that hole. I knew that truth better than anyone.

I left my laptop and went on a walk. I thought about Juan Jo. Dude hadn't given two fucks about revealing his parents' status the year before. What did I stand to gain by continuing to keep my own status secret? Miriam had sent me the final draft of the *WSJ* article. It was scheduled to come out in less than two weeks' time. What was I scared of? I returned to my desk, revealed my status to the listserv, told everyone to keep an eye out for the *WSJ* profile, and sliced through my old roommate's arguments one by one. Twenty-five hundred words later, I had shared my essential truth.

The e-mail replies were fast and furious: my old roommate continuing to press his case, friends on the listserv writing to say they had my back. And then there was my boy C., who wanted to know just how and why the *Wall Street Journal,* of all publications, had become interested in my story. "Tell me more," he wrote. "Who is Dan-el Padilla Peralta? I'll keep it on the down low."

I laughed. Like my life would ever be on the down low anymore.

—— CHAPTER 15 ——

STEVE AND HIS OFFICE submitted my application for a retroactive change of status to the United States Citizenship and Immigration Services. Two weeks later, Miriam's profile came out in the April 15 Saturday issue of the *Journal*.

The night before, I'd gone into hiding to put the finishing touches on my classics thesis. From a room in a secluded corner of campus, I watched my in-box fill up. Princeton friends who'd graduated the year before and now worked in the financial sector wrote to ask why my face was on the cover of their mandatory daily reading. Derrick and my friends from Prep advising sent me love and tongue-in-cheek marriage proposals. My Collegiate classmates blew me up. But complete strangers—teenagers and adults and retirees—also wrote, wishing me good luck and thanking me for sharing. And students who shared my predicament wrote—high school students who'd only recently realized what it means to be out of status, and college students who, like me, were terrified of what awaited them after graduation. I lingered over their e-mails the longest.

After a few hours, I took a break from reading e-mails and editing my thesis to get lunch at Terrace. When I walked in, my friends came up to hug me. It was then that I noticed copies of the *Journal* scattered around. As we sat down to eat, my friends asked how it felt to be famous.

"It feels," I replied, "like I have a thesis due Monday."

WHEN I FINALLY submitted the edited and bound product, I celebrated by hosting daily Corona-drinking sessions in my room—I was firmly committed to keeping my senior-year spring as chill as possible. But soon media requests started coming in, and before long I was spending most of my free time on the phone answering questions from reporters.

Initially I tried to strike this pose of cerebral detachment: my story was not that special; I was one of many undocumented immigrants; immigration reform had to look beyond the achievements of specific individuals and take into consideration the suffering of an entire marginalized class. This public posture lasted until Steve got wind of some of my remarks and delivered me a short lecture over e-mail. Wasn't I speaking at cross-purposes? My whole application was effectively one sustained argument about how special I was. How could I say I wasn't?

I acknowledged the good sense of his advice and promised to change my ways. From that point on, I limited myself to the most anodyne remarks imaginable.

Miriam had been so confident my story would be a force for change, but in most of the follow-up coverage I was just the undocumented shelter kid who made it to the Ivies—*Ragged Dick* for the twenty-first century. On some days, the coverage grated on me. On most days, though, I had to face the truth of a different kind of inner emotional response: I *liked* being told I was a special Latino. I wasn't really all that removed from the seventeen-year-old who'd thrilled to Breimer's reference letter. After all, hadn't I fought for recognition my entire life? What was so wrong about the dream of fame finally coming true?

ABOUT A WEEK after the article's publication, the dean of the senior class asked me to drop by his office. Paranoia set in: clearly I had incorrectly footnoted a paper or inadvertently quoted an author without using quotation marks or been seized by some other ruinous spirit of academic carelessness. On my way to Dean Williams's office, I prepared myself for a stern talk—or worse. But when I arrived at his door, he was all smiles. We greeted each other and chatted for a bit about my thesis work. Then:

"Confidential news. No telling anyone until it's official."

"Yes, Dean Williams."

"You are going to be nominated as the salutatorian, to deliver the Latin speech at commencement. The nomination is subject to final approval by the faculty at the upcoming faculty meeting. But we don't expect any issues there. So congratulations!"

"What?"

Dean Williams laughed at my shock.

I was vaguely familiar with the history of the Latin Salutatory: ever since Princeton's original incarnation as the College of New Jersey, one of the graduating seniors had delivered the Salutatory every year. Holy shit: I was now about to become a part of that history?

I walked out of the dean's office beaming. For just the briefest moment, the intellectual weaponry trained on my self-conceit was muzzled. I was such a special Latino. I was the *platano*-eating all-star. I was the most ballinest player.

I called Mom, who screamed when I told her the news.

Then I returned to arguing with myself.

"STAY POSITIVE," Steve exhorted me. But within a few weeks of submitting the application, he and I were beginning to hear from well-placed supporters and contacts that the immigration service might decline to rule on my application, for fear of establishing a precedent. No change of status would come to fruition. The anxiety returned with a vengeance. All this work, all that publicity, for nothing! Now I was screwed.

We debated what to do. I consulted with the ad hoc team of supporters that had been advising me for the past few months. Would another round of publicity tip the scales in my favor? I agreed to do a few more interviews. To no avail: Steve and I soon learned from a senior official that although the service found my case "compelling" and desired to make me "whole," this desire fell well short of granting me a change of status.

I tried my hardest to shove this news into the most remote corner of my mind by concentrating on the short term: applying for a grant from the classics department that would allow me to stay on campus for the summer to refine my thesis for academic publication; drafting my Salutatory address; eating copious quantities of ice cream; and enjoying the perks of celebrity, such as the cards I kept getting from people who'd read the *Journal* article and wanted to send along checks or twenty-dollar bills. Most of the larger incoming donations were routed to a special fund for my legal bills, set up by one of the Sachs advisers—but I saved just enough of the twenty-dollar contributions to upgrade from a beat-up CD player to my very first iPod, purchased at the New York City Apple Store.

———

ONE NIGHT, Amanda knocked on my room door and quietly took a seat on my couch. "Hey," she asked after a few moments of silence, "so are you sure marriage won't work? I'd . . . I'd do it. I'd do anything to help you."

I noticed her lower lip was trembling.

"You know," I said, desperately trying to keep my voice as unemotional as possible, "it means so much to me that you'd be willing to do that. But I just couldn't live with myself if it went down that way. I can't have you making that kind of sacrifice for me."

I offered her a Corona from the six-pack in my mini-fridge and changed the topic. We were going to be normal seniors up to normal senior-year stuff, my *papeles* nonsense be damned.

BEFORE I EVEN HAD time to take a breath, I was face-to-face with Princeton's three-day graduation marathon. Early the first morning, I picked up Mom and Yando at the train station. Yando, now sixteen and sporting facial hair on his cheeks, had mastered the art of dressing preppy *comme il faut* and blended almost instantly into the campus landscapes of seersucker and cable-knit sweaters.

At Senior Prom that night, Yando got his dance on with my friend Christine's younger sister, to everyone's amusement. But when I started dancing, a curious expression came over his face. I thought he might be getting tired, so we took a break. On the dance floor sidelines, Yando asked me if he could meet the valedictorian, C.D., who happened to be a Terrace friend. "No doubt," I replied, and walked him over to the table where C.D. and his family were sitting. I introduced them to each other and expected them to hit it off talking about music—I'd told Yando that C.D. was a superbly accomplished musician.

Instead, Yando shook C.D.'s hand and, looking straight at me, said to him:

"You're the only person who's ever beaten my brother at anything."

C.D. deflected the compliment and turned the conversation to music. I pretended not to have heard him. I mean, the kid was tripping. Didn't he wipe the floor with me whenever we played ball? What was he talking about?

When Mom motioned to us and said she was tired of the *bulla,* we left the prom and set off for the house of the professor who'd offered to put them up. A few minutes into our walk, the expression I'd first noticed on the dance floor crept over Yando's face again. Mom asked him what was wrong. He began to yell.

"I don't want to be here! Everyone talks about Dan-el, about how cool he is or how smart he is and how I should be like him! Everyone keeps asking me if I'm applying to Princeton! I don't care about him and I don't care about Princeton and I don't want to be here!"

Mom tried to hold his hand and reason with him. She was not successful.

"*You* compare me to him! You've always compared me to him! Remember the time I was eight and I asked you for something, and you said to me, 'Why aren't you more like Dan-el?'"

Mom insisted she'd never said anything like that.

"You *did* say that! I remember it!"

"But please, *mi'jo*"—tears were falling from her eyes—"why are you so upset? Did I or Dan-el do something to upset you? Please, Yando, don't be like this. Please don't be angry; we've come through so much as a family. Please."

I stayed resolutely silent. Mom asked us to hug each other. By this point we were standing in front of our host professor's house. I stiff-armed the hug, wished them both good night, and went on a long, meandering walk back to my room.

I was furious. I knew it was selfish of me not to care about his pain, but I was in no mood to be understanding. All the shit going down in my life, and now I had to deal with the trials and tribulations of the aggrieved younger brother? He couldn't be happy for me the week of my graduation? He had the *luxury* of worrying about living up to my example—it's not like he had to worry about not having *papeles,* or about having to face a ten-year ban he couldn't do shit about.

Dan-el and President Bill Clinton,
Princeton Class Day, spring 2006

———

THE NEXT MORNING, I picked up Mom and Yando and brought them to the auditorium where the Phi Beta Kappa induction ceremony was being held. On the walk to the induction, Yando and I said not a word about what had happened the night before.

I dropped them off at their seats and went to take my seat onstage with C.D. Just as we were sitting down, one of the deans approached us and asked if we wanted to meet that afternoon's Class Day speaker. Our families would have to stay behind at the induction, but we'd be taken to where the speaker was prepping.

The dean's question was rhetorical. *Of course* we wanted to meet the speaker—who was Bill Clinton.

And so, halfway through the PBK induction, C.D. and I were spirited off to the Chancellor Green rotunda in East Pyne, which was now being patrolled by tall, extremely fit-looking men with earpieces. There, shaking hands and taking photos, was the former president. We got in line for a photo op. Five minutes later I was introduced to him.

"So great to meet you, Dan-el," he drawled, in that inimitably light southern accent. We shook hands. My first thought was that his hands were unbelievably soft. My second thought was that this whole scene was too crazy to actually be taking place and that I would not be able to contain my exhilaration when I saw Mom and Yando. *I met Bill,* I'd say, *and his hands were the texture of down!*

I have no idea what we talked about as the cameras snapped our photo.

C.D. and I were sent to take our seats for the Class Day ceremony, held outdoors behind Nassau Hall. Our classmates were filing into their seats when the president and his entourage crossed over from East Pyne to a makeshift podium erected on the lip of Cannon Green.

He saw me standing a short distance from the podium, came up to me, shook my hand again, and whispered:

"I've heard about you from my wife. We're going to do everything in our power to help you with your problem. Don't even worry about it." And off he went in a flash of cameras to take his seat for the ceremony.

I nearly swooned. I was *the* special Latino! No ten-year ban for me!

The next morning, I was still giddy when I woke up late and rushed to Nassau Hall with my graduation gown half on. Once there, I joined the line forming for the academic procession and practiced my Salutatory address. From a distance I could make out Yando and Mom guiding our graduation guests from the train station to their seats. I saw Yando break out in an enormous smile when Jeff, back stateside that week, finally arrived.

Soon the music began playing. Seniors swarmed to their seats. The academic procession exited Nassau Hall, looped around the massed crowds, and marched to the wooden platform. C.D. and I took our positions. My stomach tightened in anticipation. Finally, President Shirley Tilghman said:

"The Latin salutatorian, Dan-el Padilla Peralta."

I rose from my seat and began the slow walk to the speaker's rostrum. Taking in for the very first time the rippling sea of seniors and their families stretching from Nassau Hall to the FitzRandolph Gates, I was momentarily gripped with fear. But then I saw Carlos, Mom, Yando, Father Michael, and Jeff all smiling at me. Dad hadn't been able to make it, but everyone else who loved me was there. My friends and family were waving and cheering. Marveling at the good fortune that had brought me to them, and them to me, I cleared my throat and began declaiming:

"*O sodales mei hominesque Princetonienses . . .*"

The rest of graduation was a sweaty haze. An hour and a half later,

Family and family friends (and a Princeton Public Safety escort)
at the Terrace Club, Princeton commencement, spring 2006

C.D. and I were leading our class through the FitzRandolph Gates, mortarboards streaming through the air.

THE NEXT DAY was senior move-out. Since I'd received some funding to stick around and work on revising my thesis, I didn't have to worry about moving out; instead I helped my friends pack their suitcases, load boxes into their parents' cars, and throw out dorm-room detritus. We tried to keep ourselves upbeat with jokes and stories and vows to travel to see each other. It wouldn't be too bad, after all: we were all bound for grad school or law school; the world was small; and anytime we ached for the old camaraderie, a train or plane could work its magic. And if I happened to get stuck in England . . .

"We'll fly to see you! We promise!"

Amanda had accepted a place in a master's program at King's College London, so I'd be seeing her for sure. We were heading to England together.

After the other homegirls took off with their families, I helped Amanda with her bags to the Dinky station, where she was taking New Jersey Transit back to her parents' place in New York City. We traded idle talk until the Dinky pulled up. I put her luggage on the train. The doors began to close. And then, right as the train wheels creaked, she dropped the L-word and began to cry. I said it back. We waved at each other. The train pulled out.

I walked back to my room feeling very confused. I wasn't sure I'd meant it. I wasn't sure she'd meant it. And I had so many unanswered questions still playing games with my mind. If she really did feel that way, why were we not dating? Something didn't feel right.

FOR MUCH OF THE SUMMER, I shuttled back and forth between Princeton and New York. The first week of August, Nick and I caught up over some beers at an Upper West Side bar. He was a newly minted Yale alum with no job, no real idea of what his next step in life should be, and plenty of time to kill once he and his serious college girlfriend decided to take a "break."

"Well," I joked with him, "at least you made a relationship work for a while. I can't say I ever had that."

"Eh. What's going on with you and Amanda?"

"Mad awkwardness."

Amanda and I had started seeing each other, but she still seemed a little hesitant, and I was, too. I sensed she had other dudes on her mind—Salim, maybe, or one of the guys she'd crushed on near the end of our time at Princeton. And I was still thinking about a friend of hers I'd gotten involved with the last few weeks before graduation. Our relationship prospects didn't look terribly bright.

"Don't be such a pessimist. It'll be fine. What's new with immigration?"

"Everything and nothing, true Borges style."

The original change-of-status application had become moot the moment I graduated from Princeton and was no longer enrolled as a full-time student. I'd received a handwritten note from President Clinton informing me that he'd reached out to President Bush on my behalf; I'd been informed that the details of my case had even been brought up by Karl Rove at a private White House briefing. Very boss developments—and I wasn't afraid to humblebrag in front of Nick. But all this work hadn't translated to anything: no move to regularize my status seemed likely anytime soon. There were some whispers that nothing would happen *because* my situation was so "compelling"—that magic word again. So I'd made a final decision: I'd take the Sachs, leave the United States, and reapply for admission from abroad.

I wasn't beefing too hard. It could always be worse: at least I wasn't in deportation proceedings. I would be leaving the States "of my own free will," whatever the hell that meant. People were telling me it was so brave of me to take that risk. But I didn't see what was so brave about pursuing the only real option I had.

"What happened to the DREAM Act?"

Here I did have beef. I'd joined a lobbying group of undocumented students led by Josh Bernstein, of the National Immigration Law Center, on a trip to D.C. in late July. I hadn't allowed myself to hope for much, but I kept telling myself that the way to engineer real change was through advocacy, and Josh had been super-nice to me in encouraging me to get involved. The trip had been a whirlwind. We'd attended the Illinois constituents' coffee hour in the Hart Senate Building and met with Senators Dick Durbin and Barack Obama.

Durbin had spoken passionately about the importance and fairness of DREAM. We'd done a press conference at the offices of the National Council of La Raza. We'd done a briefing for Senate staffers in the Dirksen Building. We'd taken photos with Senator Ted Kennedy, another staunch supporter of DREAM. We'd met with the head counsel to Senator Hagel. We'd met with Congressman Lincoln Díaz-Balart. But the entire time, I'd grown more and more pessimistic about anything substantive actually popping off.

True, everyone had been unfailingly gracious. Everyone—especially Senators Durbin and Kennedy—had exuded passion for DREAM and concern for us. Everyone had praised our determination in the face of adversity. But whenever the question of a timetable for DREAM had been raised, the response had always been the same: there are these other legislative priorities, you see, and then there are all these members of Congress who want to pursue alternative forms of immigration reform. The final, definitive answer? There was no definitive answer. DREAM might happen this year—or it might not. Comprehensive immigration reform might happen—or it might not.

"Let's be real," I vented to Nick. "The undocumented are easy as fuck to forget. We can't vote, and we can't even come out in large numbers to agitate in public—cats are scared, because who wants to get deported? Still no light at the end of the tunnel."

"So there's no chance legislation gets passed?"

"Nah, kid. Another year will go by and DREAM will be swept under the rug. I'm not trying to wait while this shit plays itself out. I need to get out. Maybe I reapply for admission from abroad and don't get in. Maybe the immigration gods smile on me and everything works out. But I can't pause my life while Congress beats around the bush and does jack shit."

"You know," Nick said, trying to stay upbeat, "I'm coming to visit you over there once I get my job situation straightened out."

"You better, fam. And let me not even front like it's the worst possible outcome to go into 'exile' at Oxford. I'll have peoples on the other side. Not just Amanda, but my dude Derrick—he's gonna be doing a master's at LSE."

"Yeah?"

"So it's gonna be fine."

"We'll talk on the phone, Skype, whatever we need to do."

We finished our beers and dapped.

I saw him a few more times that summer. I found out one of our Collegiate classmates was also Oxford-bound and made plans to see him on the other side. I packed up my Princeton dorm room. I ate *mangú*. I worried about girls. I obtained a new Dominican passport from the Dominican Consulate General in New York. I applied for and secured a visa to study in the UK. To no one's surprise, DREAM stalled.

On September 15, 2006, Mom, Carlos, and Yando took me to JFK in a cab. I boarded a Virgin Atlantic red-eye flight and took off for Heathrow.

— CHAPTER 16 —

I DISCOVERED WITHIN a few days of my arrival in England that Oxford's constant rain and cloud cover would pose major problems for this sunlight-obsessed Dominican. But I had absolutely no complaints about Worcester College. The grounds were breathtaking: walls that dated to the English Civil War; a main quad of immaculately kept grass that flanked a row of thirteenth-century cottages; and a beautiful library whose three-century-old spiral-staircase entrance had recently been renovated through a gift from Rupert Murdoch—a proud Worcester man, or so I was told. There was even a charmingly duck-frequented lake. On its banks, my new Oxford friends and I would soon whittle away many afternoons feeding baguette pieces to swarms of large mutant carp.

At the lake's northern end, an all-purpose sports field—rugby pitch in fall, cricket field in spring, "football" field year-round—gave Worcester the distinction of being one of the few Oxford colleges to have its athletic facilities on-site. I lived about a hundred yards or so from that sports field, in a newly erected housing unit for Worcester graduate students standing directly across the street from the Middle

Common Room—the bar-cum-lounge around which graduate student life revolved.

When not in the MCR watching bad TV and sipping a beer, I was walking around the lake or reading on the sports field or exploring the town. In the weeks before the beginning of Michaelmas—Oxbridge jargon for fall term; winter term was Hilary, and spring term Trinity—I sauntered up into Jericho and stood outside the offices of the Oxford University Press; explored Port Meadow and retraced Lewis Carroll's walks; paced up and down the galleries of the Ashmolean Museum, two blocks from Worcester's gates; and ventured into town to gaze at and roam around the other colleges, with their grand names and distinguished histories: St. John's, Trinity, Balliol, Exeter, Lincoln, Jesus, Merton, Christ Church. It was a blissful time in the sandstone paradise.

I MADE WEEKLY TRIPS into London. On the very first, I met up with Amanda at her new digs. At the Gloucester Green bus station, in Oxford, I bought a twenty-quid return fare to London. An hour and a half later, I got off at Marble Arch in Hyde Park and took the tube up to Camden Town. Walking out of the station, I saw, in quick succession, a Foot Locker, a stretch of street peddlers, a dealer standing on a corner, and a dude hawking CDs of "conscious" rap.

So this, I thought, was what HarlemWorld in London looked like.

Past the tube station, a few fast-food joints, and a massive Sainsbury's stood the entrance to Amanda's apartment complex. She was waiting for me at the gate.

I hugged her and went in for a kiss. She turned aside and asked me how my bus ride had been. We made small talk on the way to her building. I tried to hold her hand; she gently pushed mine away, with no explanation. The small talk continued as she toured me around her floor and building. Then she asked me if I wanted to go on a twenty-minute stroll to the London Zoo. I said yes. We took off, chatting about God-knows-what while I waited for her to say what I sensed she had to say.

It finally came out as we walked along Regent's Canal, which stank to high heaven. The gist: in the craziness of senior year, she'd felt like she had romantic feelings for me. After thinking it over during the summer, she'd finally realized that she just cared for me as a friend. She didn't want to be in a relationship. She simply wasn't attracted to me that way. Besides, she wasn't at the stage where she could be in a serious relationship with anyone, really. She was so sorry.

I smarted at her admission that she wasn't attracted to me. *Physically* attracted, because that's what I was sure she meant. And in my head I railed at her for stringing me along until we'd gotten to England. See, she had family on this rain-battered, cloudy-as-fuck island—but whom did I have? Derrick wasn't arriving for another few weeks, and anyway I wasn't about to cry on my dude's shoulder.

I kept the hurt bottled up and remained on my most proper newly-dumped-boyfriend behavior the rest of our walk to the zoo and after.

TWO WEEKS OF exploring Oxford and London swiftly gave way to afternoons of study at the Sackler Library, lectures at the Examination Schools, and tutorials at St. John's College and the Oriental Institute. My supervisor, a tutorial fellow at St. John's, was fearsomely learned, so much so that I worried he'd wave me away once he realized how much of a dullard I was. Every tutorial, I felt like I was being flayed alive, and so after every tutorial I consoled myself with a trip to a pub.

Outside of tutorial, I made new friends. The crew consisted mainly of American expats. We had plenty of free time to spare: most of us were in multiyear programs that built up to a written thesis, but no real work was expected from us quite yet. So we met up several times a week to bemoan the policy failings of the Bush administration; play beer pong; and emulate—and, whenever possible, surpass—the achievements of our British peers, who somehow managed to remain functional students even after getting themselves shit-faced by 10:30 P.M. on weeknights and gorging themselves on extravagant, stomach-bursting amounts of kebab.

In moments of solitude, I still ached for Mom, Yando, Carlos, the sprawl and chaos of New York. And *mangú*. You couldn't get *platanos* in Oxford. The local Sainsbury's? Tesco's? Please. But then I'd chastise myself for obsessing over what I didn't have. And Mom kept sending me letters and cards reminding me to *focus on the present;*

Dan-el on the steps of the Clarendon Building just before matriculation in the Sheldonian Theatre, Oxford, fall 2006

seize this blessing; you're not missing anything in New York. But whenever I looked at her cards, dutifully pinned up on a corkboard above my desk, all I could think of was home.

MOM WOULD RING once a week. We'd talk about *O'ford* and my new surroundings, but she'd also want to know what was developing on the immigration front. At first, there wasn't much to report. Steve and I had been e-mailing from the moment I touched down in the UK. He was cautiously optimistic about the prospects of my obtaining a waiver from the ten-year ban. When I told him I wanted to apply for a tourist visa to return stateside for the holidays, Steve helped me put together the application. I submitted the application and scheduled a visa interview at the U.S. embassy in London for the first Friday in November.

"Mom, what's new at home?"

"Nothing, *mi'jo;* church and work. But please talk to your brother. You know, applying to colleges has him *tan nervioso*—it's hard to calm him down."

I thought about Yando all the time. One of the very first items I'd unpacked and put up on the wall of my room was a card Yando had sent me back in February of sophomore year. It was so unmistakably, idiosyncratically *him.*

> Well, as I reflect upon the many nuances of brotherhood,
> I come across a very important idea, the crux of the word,
> brother. It's simply amazing, though, how the second part of
> the word, hood, comes into play. It is, I guess, the hood that
> really unites people together, and it shows to me the real
> meaning of the word brother. Well, as I go off to school, and

Yando visits, spring 2007

you in college, just know that I'll always be here, humming the tune of "Different Strokes." Yeah.

Signedly,
Yando

The note never failed to make me laugh. I'd forgiven and mostly forgotten the graduation incident: maybe he was too self-involved to celebrate my moment, but it was mad self-involved of me to blow off his frustration the way I had, plus we'd gone through way too much together for me to hold that shit against him. I just missed him. And I missed our basketball games. I told him that when I came back stateside I would whoop his ass.

At first, Yando and I were instant-messaging and e-mailing and occasionally calling on a not serious tip—like whether Cam'ron's new single was even worth listening to. But soon every conversation we had became about Yando's fear of not being admitted to a top-flight school. Mom was right: my dude was worried sick.

"It's just that," he kept saying, "I don't have straight A's, and I don't have great SATs, and I don't have all the extracurriculars my classmates do."

"But you do have plenty of high grades. Your SAT I and SAT II scores are strong. You've been singing for ages. And your Riverdale teachers rave about you."

"You don't understand, though. I'm not you. What happens when I fail and don't get in anywhere?"

To this, I'd either reply with a hard edge—"Stop with this comparing-yourself-to-me nonsense"—or with gentler exhortation: "You are you, and you need to focus on yourself and your strengths."

Nothing I said reassured him. Kid was the ill pessimist. To put him in a better mood, we began to plan his trip out to see me—the Sachs stipend was so generous that I'd set some money aside to purchase a round-trip ticket for him. I promised I'd try to find a basketball court for us to play on when he flew over.

BUT MY VERY first transatlantic visitor was Nick. On a typically foggy morning, I picked him up bright and early at Heathrow. We talked the entire bus ride to Oxford. He'd landed a position in Yale's development office and wasn't feeling the grown-adult job life. Didn't think the job was quite right for him, but it was a job. And the lady life was set: my man was back with his serious girl-friend, but they argued all the time over seemingly inconsequential shit—arguments that quickly spiraled out of control into genuine unpleasantness.

My lady life?

"Very boring, dude. Just gaming the cuties of the MCR. And besides, none of these girls is trying to deal with my crazy."

"Stop it, kid. If you focused on one girl instead of spreading yourself so thin, maybe you'd improve your odds."

My man wasn't alone in saying that. Derrick, the sage of LSE and now himself wifed up (with an Indian hair model, no less), had been on the same tip, telling me over and over again whenever I chilled with him in London that my new strategy of spreading the love wasn't going to yield me a quality girl. I dismissed him and Nick with a wave of the hand. He and Nick were fortunate, and I envied them: their shorties were all about them. I wanted that—but then I didn't, because I really enjoyed being single, and was any chick really prepared to handle my flaming combination of academic obsessiveness and constant immigration-related anxiety? Truly a jump-off combination, let me tell you.

"There ain't no chick for me, kid, not right now."

Nick wasn't persuaded.

"Bullshit. You just need to stop being so hard on yourself."

"Me? Hard on myself? Never."

"That's what it's all about. You criticize yourself too much; then you talk to all these random girls you keep meeting here, or the ones you're still in touch with from the States; and when none of them falls head over heels for you, you're like, 'Oh, they can't deal with my shit.'"

"Nope. None of this is true."

I laughed and promptly changed the topic. Fuck my deficiencies; did Nick really know how much balling we were about to get up to in Oxford and London? No? Then gird your loins, child.

———

My next trip into London was for the visa appointment. On the morning of the fated day, I arrived at the embassy offices—a drab compound in Grosvenor Square patrolled by heavily armed American soldiers—was cleared by security, and took a seat in the waiting area for applicants. I sat for an hour, until my name was called and my paperwork was requested at a numbered window. A cursory exchange, then another four and a half hours while my paperwork was processed. Finally, my application number was called again. This time I was ushered to a window not in the main waiting room but at the end of a long hallway. There I was greeted by a young-looking and extremely dour-faced embassy employee. Once I'd pressed my thumb on the window's biometric scanner to confirm my identity, she addressed me in an emotionless monotone.

"We have reviewed your application for a B-1 visa. We understand that you overstayed an earlier visa and resided illegally in the United States. We also understand that you have family currently residing in the United States. You do not meet the nonimmigrant-intent standard of the B-1, and we will not be recommending you to the Department of Homeland Security for a waiver of the ten-year ban on admission."

She returned my paperwork to me.

"Have a wonderful day!"

I walked out of the embassy in a daze.

It was only when I boarded the Oxford Espress bus for the return trip to Oxford that the full significance of the consular officer's words hit me: the ten-year ban was really going to be enforced. Was it that surprising? Well, in a corner of my heart, I'd still believed that I was special. That somehow, some way, the embassy would send me off with visa and waiver. Now I was just one of the millions knocking on the door of America and being denied admission.

I fought my emotions the entire bus ride back to Oxford, kept telling myself that I'd find a way back to the States. But when I returned to my studio apartment, I gave in: I punched the wall, my desk, the bathroom door, until my hands were raw. Then I picked up my desk chair, threw it across the room, and cried.

I DIDN'T TELL anyone about my crying jag—stoic front till I die, for serious—but one of the first people I did tell about the B-1 experience was Dad.

We'd been slowly reconnecting. All throughout college, he'd tried to stay in touch with me by calling me at least once or twice a month. I wasn't the greatest on the phone, and sometimes I'd let his calls go to voice mail. After commencement, though, he'd called to ask for my e-mail address, and within a few weeks we were writing to each other regularly. Short little silly witticisms at first, followed by lengthier and more serious reflections. He had some life lessons to impart.

The first few weeks after my move to Oxford, we'd traded some messages about his youth. Way before Mom had come into the picture, he'd served a stint in the army; studied law in college; traveled to the States to take a course on credits and payments; traveled to Argentina to study advanced accounting. Slowly I learned that the man I knew as Dad—the man whose physical departure from my life I'd spent so much time trying to understand as a child and whose flaws as a father I'd been so quick to seize on as a teenager—had lived this extraordinarily rich and cosmopolitan life. He'd cast himself over and over again into the great unknowns of travel abroad and reemerged to tell the story. Shit, I'd had the Internet to prepare myself for

England. What had he had when he left Santo Domingo, first for the United States and then for Argentina?

The e-mailing helped me get over the undercover beef I had with him for having left me when I was small. Face-to-face with the full panorama of his life, I understood that decision for what it truly was: he'd been far removed from the boundless vitality of his youth when he tried to take on the final great unknown of raising a family in a country not his own. Maybe that unknown had defeated him; but he'd at least been willing to venture into it.

The night of the B-1 fail, I wrote to him. He replied the next morning with a two-sentence e-mail:

> *Tú eres un Triunfador. Eres dueño del mundo y USA es sólo un pedacito.*

> You are a winner. You are master of the world, and the USA is only a little slice.

I left that e-mail open on my laptop for weeks. It was the truth I had to convince myself of. The United States had been home—but the world was my home now. I had to embrace that. I had to be more of a *triunfador*.

I FINALLY CALMED DOWN when I remembered that I still had one thing going for me.

Before I'd come over to Oxford, my Princeton thesis supervisor and I had talked about the possibility of my doing some work for her as a research assistant. From her recently deceased dissertation adviser at Penn she'd inherited boxes of notes and files on the neighborhoods of republican and imperial Rome. The materials were arranged in binders, each containing passages he'd copied out from the ancient authors and inscriptions he'd studied, pages of his own (usually hand-written) commentary on various aspects of Roman urban life, and lists and diagrams.

Would I be interested, Harriet had asked me one day, in sorting through the material and turning it into some kind of searchable database? She was hoping to use the database to write a book on neighborhood culture and religious life in late republican Rome.

We'd met over lunch at Princeton about a month or so before I left for England to discuss what the arrangement would entail. I'd have to teach myself how to work with Adobe FileMaker, but that wouldn't be terribly hard. I'd benefit from the opportunity to im-merse myself more deeply in the study of ancient Rome, and she'd benefit from having a database of materials at her disposal. I could do most of the work for the project at Oxford—she'd xerox and post me copies of each binder's materials—but I'd have to return stateside from time to time, preferably during my Oxford vacations, to consult the binders.

Harriet spoke with the department, and the department with the university. Within two months Princeton had offered me a position as a research assistant on a casual hourly wage. But to return stateside to work on the project, I still needed a temporary work visa. I con-sulted with Steve and scheduled a second appointment with the U.S. embassy in London. Once again, the main hurdle would be the ten-year ban.

At the end of November, I returned to Grosvenor Square and was summoned to a window at the end of the first-floor embassy hallway. There, a consular officer interrogated me carefully and rigorously about the nature of the project and my participation in it. Then he informed me that the embassy would conduct an investigation before deciding whether to recommend a waiver. The investigation and (if approved) the processing of the waiver would take several months. The embassy would be in touch if and when the waiver had been approved.

I wrote to Harriet and Steve with the update and prepared for a long wait.

IN THE MEANTIME, I tried to be more of a *triunfador*. The Sachs had left me with plenty of money for jaunts across Europe, and Ryanair and easyJet made travel to the Continent very affordable, so I began planning a trip to France and Italy for the first week of December. I'd see Jeff in Paris, then hop over to Rome and live my dream of walking around the Roman Forum.

The first Saturday of December, I took the bus from Oxford to Luton Airport, boarded an easyJet flight, and touched down at Charles de Gaulle. From there I trained to Gare du Nord, switched to the Paris Métro, and got off at Montmartre, where I was spending the night at a hostel before meeting up with Jeff in the morning. I stepped out of the Métro station at Abbesses to a view of Paris at night, full moon casting its glow over Sacré-Coeur, Saint-Pierre de Montmartre, the Moulin Rouge. For a few moments I lost myself in silent contemplation, standing still in wonderment at the sights. The blustery wind finally sent me down the street and around a corner to my hostel.

Early the next morning, I took the Métro to the Thirteenth Arrondissement and met Jeff at his apartment on Rue de Tolbiac. He buzzed me into his building, wrapped his arms around me, and launched into a million questions. How was I doing? How was Oxford? How was my French? How long was I planning to spend in Paris? He had all these places he wanted to take me to.

First we went to the Louvre. After an indulgent meander through the antiquities collection, we headed to Café Marly—around the corner from the courtyard pyramid—for lunch. At the front desk, the maître d' asked us whether we had a reservation. When we replied that we didn't, he immediately excused himself, entered the café, spoke in very hushed tones with two of his colleagues, and returned five minutes later with a pained expression on his face. Two menus in hand and still looking terribly inconvenienced, he waved us into the main room of the café.

Which was completely empty. Jeff and I burst into laughter.

We glanced at our menus. A *garçon* came by to take our orders. Everything down to the smallest bowl of soup was exorbitantly over-priced, but Jeff insisted on paying and encouraged me to buy what-ever I wanted. While we waited for the food, Jeff and I reminisced about the past: our first encounter at Bushwick, his trips to Bradhurst, the afternoons of roller skating. In the stroll down memory lane, Jeff turned serious:

"You know, my family life became really complicated after I graduated college. My parents wanted me to pursue a lucrative career, but I loved photography. I loved travel. We fought so much over that. I wanted to become an artist, at all costs. And I wanted to teach kids about art, especially kids like you.

"Teaching art was amazing. You know, I stuck with it even after I got mugged at gunpoint walking from the Bushwick shelter to the Chauncey Street subway station. And I'll never forget stepping on empty crack vials every time I made that walk! But it was worth it. You and your brother were worth it. Just being around you was a source of healing for me as I went through my struggles with family and figured out what the next steps in my life would be.

"I left the States to start a new life in France because everything was getting too crazy for me, between family and relationships. I wanted a fresh start. My big regret is having been out of touch for as long as I was. I hope you and Yando didn't take that personally. I thought about both of you every single day."

It was the longest I'd ever heard him talk about himself.

I fumbled through an awkward response: how moved I was that he'd taken me into his confidence and shared with me what he had, how I'd wondered for ages what he'd gained from putting me on the path to Collegiate, how I was so happy he'd found some measure of happiness in helping my family.

"No more talking about me," he said. "What's up with immigration?"

I updated him on the ongoing waiting game with the embassy.

"For my country, *your* country, to put you through this—just ridiculous."

He resolved to keep my spirits up. The remaining four days of my trip flew by in adventures, sightseeing, and a visit to Café de Flore, on Boulevard Saint-Germain, to order an overpriced *jambon* San Daniele and commune with the spirits of Sartre and Beauvoir. My last evening, Jeff and I went out to an apartment party in the Eleventh hosted by one of his friends. The wine flowed copiously. I slept the sleep of an adopted Parisian that night—and missed my flight to Rome the next morning. Jeff had me get on the phone with Ryanair to see if I had any cheap rebooking options.

"Non, non," replied the customer service rep, *"on ne peut pas"*—unless I was willing to pay 250 euros for a flight leaving later that day.

"But I thought this was a discount airline!"

I pleaded, I raged—no luck. Instead of rebooking, I simply purchased a same-day Eurostar ticket back to the UK. Once my anger at Ryanair died down, Jeff and I grabbed a quick breakfast around the corner from his apartment building, then walked together to the Tolbiac Métro. We hugged. I made him promise to come see me at

Oxford. From the Métro I made my way to Gare du Nord and took the midday Eurostar back to London.

As my train rumbled beneath the Channel, I realized I wasn't too cut up about missing my flight to Rome. I could always plan a trip there later. What mattered was that I'd had an amazing time with Jeff. For years I'd known how fortunate I'd been to have had him as a father figure. But my feeling of good fortune was now leavened with pride: that, for all those years, he'd looked upon me as a brother.

FOR THE CHRISTMAS HOLIDAYS, I chilled at Oxford with my American expat friend Dave. We passed the time watching British

Dan-el at the Arch of Septimius Severus,
Rome, spring 2007

cable TV and drinking unmixed Pimm's straight from the bottle. The entire time, I didn't hear a peep from the U.S. embassy. After the New Year, Steve wrote to let me know he'd been busy rounding up support letters from some of the same politicians who'd put their names behind my original change-of-status application. But that was about it for updates. When the new term began, I put my head down and tried to impress my Oxford supervisor. Spring drew nearer; still no word from the embassy.

At the end of Hilary term, I enlisted Dave as a travel buddy for my long-awaited trek to Rome. One March morning, Dave and I touched down in Ciampino Airport and scored seats on a shuttle bus to Termini rail station. Standing just around the corner from the station entrance was my first glimpse of the classical past I'd studied: a stretch of the Servian Wall, Rome's primary republican-era fortification. The nerd in me danced.

Maps in hand, Dave and I found our way to the hostel we'd booked on Via Principe Amedeo, checked in, and headed right back out. A few blocks away at the church of Santa Maria Maggiore, we savored our first taste of Rome's monumental architectural splendor. From there we walked the length of Via Cavour, which sloped gently downward toward the ancient heart of Rome as it wound past low-rise apartment buildings and stores whose seedy aspect evoked the atmosphere of the Subura, imperial Rome's sleaziest neighborhood— part of which now lay buried beneath it. In twenty or so minutes we reached the Via dei Fori Imperiali. On our left, in the distance, was the Colosseum; immediately ahead, the Forum. We crossed the street, narrowly avoiding a collision with a city center metro bus.

At the railing that separated the street from the excavated Forum, we stopped and stared for a few minutes in awestruck silence, face-to-face for the first time with the heart of republican and imperial Rome.

Dave at the Trevi Fountain, spring 2007

"Shit," I finally exclaimed. "To think that my broke ghetto ass would finally make it here."

I laughed. Dave laughed, too. I sensed I'd found a kindred spirit in him—he'd confided in me back during our holiday Pimm's binges that he'd grown up broke in Florida—so I wasn't too embarrassed at disclosing my feeling that this was all just so . . . incredible. *Mirabile visu* for real. For so long, Rome had existed solely in my imagination; now I was able to wander and breathe it for the very first time.

The Rome of the Trevi Fountain and the Spanish Steps and Trastevere and the Vatican Museums lulled me into an exquisite delirium, a trance I couldn't and didn't want to shake. Sauntering later that morning through the Farnese Gardens on the Palatine, city unfolding before us as the cloud cover lifted, I began to nurse the dream that Rome, not Oxford or London, might one day become my second New York. Not shabby for a formerly undocumented *platano* eater.

—— CHAPTER 17 ——

WHEN DAVE AND I touched back down in the land of perpetual cloud cover, we headed to an airport computer cluster to while away the hours until our Oxford bus arrived. I checked my e-mail, began the task of identifying which messages were urgent and which weren't—and froze upon reading the sender and subject line of an e-mail sent on my second day in Rome:

From: Visa Coordination Unit
Subject: US Visa Application
Visa Coordination Unit
Embassy of the United States of America
24 Grosvenor Square
London, W1A 1AE

With the compliments of the American Embassy

Dear MR. PADILLA PERALTA Date: 19 March 2007

Please submit your passport. You have three months from the date indicated above in which to resubmit your passport.

I read and reread, took a break, and then reread again. The embassy was requesting my passport for visa processing—which had to mean that my visa application had been approved, and my request for a waiver of inadmissibility granted!

At first I kept the news to myself. I didn't want to get my hopes up too high, and I needed confirmation from Steve that the e-mail meant what I thought it meant. But a few days later, Steve wrote to inform me that my visa waiver had in fact been approved.

In the weeks that followed, I submitted my passport to the U.S. embassy after a short trip to Greece, the U.S. embassy processed and stamped it with a new H-1B visa, Harriet and I began working on a schedule for the creation and maintenance of the research database, and I bought a round-trip ticket to New York. In the dark about all of these developments? Mom. I was big into surprises.

Around 5:00 A.M. BST on April 22, I called her while I waited at the Gloucester Green Oxford bus station for the airporter to Heathrow. She picked up, her voice clogged with grogginess.

"*Haalooo . . .*"

"*Bendición,* Mamá. I hope I didn't wake you up."

"No, no, it's fine, *mi'jo.* Is everything okay?"

"I'm calling to let you know that I'm going to see you in a few hours."

"*¿Quéeee? ¿Cómo?*"

"Mamá, they approved the visa. I'm getting on a 9:00 A.M. flight out of London. It gets into JFK at 11:20 A.M. I'm going to see you!"

"Thanks be to God! He has been so good to us! I get to cook for you, *mi'jo*! Would you like some *mangú* for breakfast?"

"Yes, Mom."

"How long will you be back in New York? And when did you find out about the visa?"—and what must have been four more questions all flew out at me at once as the Heathrow airporter pulled in and travelers began crawling toward its doors.

"I'll tell you everything when we see each other in a few hours. Mom, the bus is here, but I'll call you once my flight lands in New York, okay? I can't wait to see you. *Bendición.*"

"*Te quiero, mi'jo.* May God and Saint Michael protect you on your flight."

A seven-hour flight and a forty-five-minute cab ride later, I was back in Spanish Harlem, stuffing my face with *mangú*. While Mom called her sisters to share the news of my return, I told stories of England to Carlos and Yando.

Later that day, I headed out on a long walk to slake my thirst for the neighborhood and the city. Seven months wasn't a long time: the streets of the hood hadn't changed much at all. I was the one who'd changed. I enjoyed no right to return to the places where I'd grown up except through the embassy's dispensation. I was and yet wasn't

Dan-el at the Parthenon, spring 2007

American: I was back home on a visa that marked me as the recipient of the U.S. embassy's beneficence.

But I'd achieved my *nostos*. And, in the inaugural Padilla Peralta tournament of 2007, I shook off the rust and slayed—*slayed*—Yando in a game of 21.

BEFORE LONG, I was back at Oxford for Trinity term and more tutorial papers. But I carried good news with me across the pond: Yando had gotten into college. The self-professed ill pessimist had three admission letters—from Duke, Amherst, and Bowdoin. He'd told me practically nothing when I got home; I'd had to pry the information from Mom. But when I asked Yando how he was feeling about the admits, he responded good-humoredly for what felt like the first time in ages:

"I'm leaving the hood, *nukka!*"

The week after my visit home, he took off on pre-frosh trips. After his final visit, he told me over the phone that he'd made up his mind.

"It's hard to explain, I guess, but I just felt so *right* at Bowdoin. Like the other students were my kind of people. And I think this whole go-to-the-best-school-you-get-into stuff isn't really me. I just wanna go to where I feel most comfortable, you know?"

He mailed in his intent-to-matriculate form a few days later.

About a week after, Mom called to check in on me while I furiously rewrote papers for my supervisor. She started telling me that Yando had shown her some Bowdoin materials and that she was so excited to move him in and visit him, even though she couldn't pronounce or spell his college's name to save her life (*Bodén? Baudín? Boudín?*). Then:

"*Mi'jo,* I told him this, but I want to tell you now, that I feel so blessed, because all of my dreams for you two have come true. Every day I think of you both and all you've done and overcome, and I can't tell you how proud I am."

"Thank you, Mom."

I didn't want to get too emotional over the phone—front so hard—so I changed the subject.

SUMMER CAME, and with it more travel. All of my friends bounced to the United States except for Derrick, who—swearing mighty oaths that he would never fall hard for a girl again, after getting played by his Indian hair model—was sticking around London to complete his LSE coursework before beginning a full-time job at Deloitte. He was missing out, I kept telling him. The newly returned expats were about to take over the East Coast with a summer of raging unlike any other.

But before the raging, there were some old friends I wanted to get back in touch with. First I spent an afternoon with Father Michael, now in his sixth year as pastor of Sacred Heart in the Bronx. Then I called the Resurrection boys and made plans to meet up at McDonald's with the ones still in the city. Over Big Macs they let me know what was good. I was the one out of the loop; they were still tight with each other.

I learned that they'd all joined the armed forces right after high school or a little while after. Not because they were passionate about the war in Iraq or the global war on terror or service to country in some romanticized sense. "I just did it for a job"—that's what they said. Besides, they had baby mommas and kids to take care of, and college right out of high school hadn't been an option. They'd served, done at least one tour abroad, been discharged, returned to civilian life.

A few weeks later, Pablo rounded up everyone he could, crammed us into his car, and burned down I-95 to Virginia Beach to visit Lawrence, one of the two old Resurrection cats still in the service. We got into Virginia Beach at around four in the morning and went straight to the beach. We skinny-dipped. We chugged energy drinks. We consumed mounds of pancakes at Denny's. We day-drank with wanton abandon. Finally, when night came, we hit the Virginia Beach club scene. As we got ready to head out, one of the boys pulled a massive stack of condoms out of his bag. I laughed.

"How many chicks are you gonna bone tonight, fam?"

"Can't have no little niggas running around down here," he said, smiling.

Late that night, Pablo dropped me off at the Virginia Beach bus station. I was taking an early Greyhound back to New York to finish some research for the Princeton project.

"Love you, kid," he said as we dapped. "Don't ghost."

On the bus ride up, my thoughts kept returning to the guys, who'd welcomed me back into the mix just like no time had passed and nothing had happened. I couldn't make myself pretend that everything about that was totally gravy. Yeah, I wasn't about to fault them or lord it over them because of where their lives were taking them. More now than ever, I believed with every ounce of my being that structures, contexts, and luck reigned supreme. I wasn't some Horatio Alger–regurgitating dummy, on some simplistic jump-off about the self-made man picking himself up by the bootstraps all the way to the Ivies. And I was proud of them for the choices they'd made: they'd served their country; they were trying to be fathers to their kids; they were working jobs; they were trying to expand their view of the world. I just didn't see how it would be easy for them to connect with the life I lived now, and I didn't have an easy time connecting to theirs. We could ball and drink and talk girls, basics. And then? I didn't have baby mommas to bitch about. I wasn't banging at clubs on the regular.

Somehow, though, we were still fam, now and forever.

AT THE END of the summer, I left the East Coast and reported back to Oxford for year two. Michaelmas was busy with research and graduate-school applications. By mid-December I'd applied to five stateside Ph.D. programs in classics. To celebrate the submission of my applications, I went on a trip to the French Alps. At the very top of Superdévoluy, I gazed at the snowcaps of the Hautes-Alpes and for the most ephemeral moment felt as old as Europe. From Superdévoluy I jumped across the pond to Spanish Harlem for New Year's, then flew back to England in time for Hilary term. *Très* boss, this intercontinental lifestyle.

I was at the Sackler Library typing up a thesis chapter when Mom called me one afternoon.

"How's *mi'jo* doing?"

"I'm good, Mom. Everything okay over there?"

"I found out something today and thought you should know."

"What's wrong?"

"Father Michael has cancer. It's advanced."

"What?"

"I found out from one of his parishioners and then confirmed it with his parish secretary. He just started chemo. You should call him. When is your next trip to New York?"

I'D BEEN PLANNING a second short trip stateside at the end of January to meet with Harriet and pick up a new batch of materials for the research project. I moved the trip up by a few days. On my second day back in the tristate area, I took the subway up to Father Michael's parish and rang the rectory bell. His secretary showed me to Father's rooms on the second floor.

"Dan-el," he said, rising to his feet and steadying himself on a cane as I walked into his living room. "What a pleasant surprise to see you."

He'd aged, like, ten years since I'd last seen him.

"Pops." I hugged him. "How are you feeling?"

"I'm fine, you know. The leg hurts, but I'm feeling much better, and the cane helps. I'm staying very positive. With God's help, I'm going to beat this. Sit down, tell me how you're doing. How's Oxford? What's your thesis about?"

I tried breaking it down. He was still so mentally alert that for a moment I could pretend he was the same lanky six-foot-six priest brimming with energy I'd met in the Resurrection rectory long ago. But when he got up again, this time to get himself some water, I saw that he couldn't really move his leg without wincing in pain. I went to fetch the water for him. He drank, then fell silent. I wanted to ask him about the cancer but was too afraid of what he'd tell me.

Finally he cleared his throat.

"I began to feel it when I was celebrating Mass, the pain in my leg. I ignored it for the longest time. Then the pain got worse. I prayed on it and went to the doctors. They did tests. When the results came back, I put my trust in the Lord. The chemo leaves me feeling exhausted sometimes, but I've handed over my suffering to him. On the hard days, I feel myself, my faith, growing richer. The Lord's will be done. He has been so good to me. The love I feel coming from him, from the parishioners, from you."

I sat there trying to contain my tears. I didn't know how to say what I really wanted to say: that he was Pops, that I loved him, that I was terrified by the thought of his mortality. And I worried I'd disappoint him if I opened the door to the other thoughts crossing my mind: that his suffering was one more reason for me not to believe, that there was no sense and no justice in the existence of a God willing to take away a caring, selfless man in the prime of his life from the people who loved him. I knew he'd smile and simply say, *God's ways are not our ways, Dan-el. You should know that.*

"If he wills it, I will beat this. My disease is in his hands. And don't you worry about me."

I tried forcing a smile.

"But tell me more about yourself. What are you working on besides the thesis? Your mom told me some months ago that you were starting to work on a book. How's it going?"

I'd started mulling over the idea of a book about my life a few months after the *Wall Street Journal* profile. I'd drafted a short piece about my immigration experience for the *Princeton Alumni Weekly* and then convinced myself—after some nudging—that I could write about my life for more than a few pages at a time. When I told Mom about the possibility of a book, she'd gotten very excited and mentioned it to all of her friends, and to Pops as well, apparently. I'd been excited, too, at first. But once the initial excitement faded—

"I drafted some material and showed it around. I got all kinds of feedback, most of it confusing. Some people say focus on immigration, others on growing up in Harlem, others on Collegiate and Princeton. Some people say write the story one way, others another way."

"What do *you* want to write?"

A few answers began tumbling out of me: I wasn't even sure if I wanted to write about myself; I wanted to write about the people who'd changed my life ("Like you, Pops"), I wanted to write about the hood, I wanted to write about private school and Princeton, but without any of that look-at-him-he-made-it! glossiness. And I kept thinking back to this splendid line of Proust's I'd recently come across in a lecture: "The beautiful things we shall write if we have talent . . ." The *if* was crucial. There was so much I wanted to write about, but I just wasn't sure I had the ability to pull it off, you know?

"Oh, stop it," he said, laughing. "You most certainly have that ability. Just remember, this is *your* book, *your* life."

"I'll try to remember that, Father."

"And then?" Pops had an intent look on his face now. "What do you want to write next? I know you're not stopping at one book."

I hadn't given that possibility much thought.

"Something on Roman history? And probably not for popular consumption."

He had more questions. Was I following the presidential primaries? What did I think of this Obama guy? I was a question-answering machine that afternoon.

I FLEW BACK to England for the last few months of the master's program. My expat contingent and I partied very hard and vowed to stay in touch once we all flocked back stateside. I accepted an admission offer from Stanford and grew excited at the prospect of interdisciplinary doctoral studies in California weather. But soon this excitement hit up against a ceiling.

I talked first with Steve, then with Stanford, and learned to my enormous chagrin that in order to enroll in the Ph.D. program I'd have to change my visa status from H-1B to F-1, since I couldn't be a grad student on a work-only visa. I also learned that there was no easy or speedy way of doing this. I could travel to the Dominican Republic to submit an F-1 application and reapply for the waiver of the ten-year ban at the U.S. embassy in Santo Domingo. Unfortunately, I would then have to contend with the nonimmigrant-intent standard used to adjudicate F-1 applications. No way my application would meet that standard to a consular officer's satisfaction, not with my immigration history and with Mom and Yando currently living in the States. The other option was to return stateside, continue working for the Princeton research project, and submit a change-of-status application to the immigration service while residing in the States. My odds of being adjusted to F-1 were marginally better this way, but Steve was quite clear: it would take time, and there were no guarantees.

In July, I returned to the United States to continue working on the Princeton project. While Steve's office put together my change-of-status application, I spoke with Stanford about deferring. Since the standard wait time for processing the change-of-status application was three months, the earliest I'd be ready to enroll would be January of the coming year. Stanford signed off; the change-of-status application was submitted at the beginning of September; the wait was on.

At first I didn't stress that much. The Princeton project kept me intellectually stimulated and gave some structure to my days. In my spare time, I went up to Columbia to hang out with Nick, now in law school; took up some tutoring; and began to take some real steps in my writing.

It was only when fall gave way to winter that the lack of a response from the service to my change-of-status application began to nibble at my peace of mind. The silence was too reminiscent of senior spring, plus this time I didn't have a real fallback plan. When the holidays passed with no word from immigration, I began to panic. Silently, though: I didn't want the tears to come streaming out if I opened up to anyone about how anxious the wait was making me.

———————

ON A LATE-WINTER AFTERNOON, I called Pops on my way to chill with Nick at Columbia. As always, he was ready with questions. What was new on the immigration front? When was I heading to Stanford? How was the research project? How was the writing? Did I have a girlfriend? Would I ever entertain a priestly vocation?

Steve and I had finally heard from the service about my change-of-status application, in the form of a note asking for evidence of my employment at Princeton. We'd sent off pay stubs and crossed our fingers. In the meantime, I was sitting in on two graduate seminars at Princeton to keep myself focused. The research project was coming along well. The writing, not so well. Girlfriend: none at the moment. And I knew myself well enough to doubt that a calling to the priest-hood was in the cards.

He chuckled, then coughed and said:

"It is so good to hear your voice. Will you come by?"

I promised him I would. I asked him how he felt.

"Some days, better than others. For a while I could celebrate Mass without feeling dizzy. The doctors said after the first few rounds of chemo that the cancer looked to be in remission. But then it came back—your mom must have told you. Our Lord has his reasons. I know he is taking care of me."

When news of the remission had first reached me, I'd been so happy that everything else had momentarily faded into insignificance. The immigration *mierda,* the personal-life stuff, the academic-ambitions stuff—all that seemed so trivial when put next to Pops's breakthrough. But then Mom had dropped the hammer about the cancer's return. And now, every day she reminded me that I had to call Pops, had to go see him. Every day, I kept finding reasons not to:

I'm going to be out of town. I'll do it tomorrow. He must be so tired after the latest round of chemo. I don't want to impose . . .

I knew they were excuses. I knew I didn't want to talk to him or see him because I was afraid of how I'd react when I saw him. I knew I would cry.

I was on the phone now because I was tired of feeling like a coward. But as I listened to his weakened voice, the tears began streaming down my face. I had to get off the phone. I didn't want him to hear me sobbing.

"Stop by and say hi whenever you like. We'll talk about politics. This Obama guy. You'll let me know what you're working on. God bless you, my son."

"Yes, Father. We'll see each other soon."

EARLY THE SECOND WEEK of March, Mom ordered me to call Father and plan a visit to Sacred Heart. I rang and left him a message. I don't remember what I said. I'd learn sometime later that by the time I finally called, he was already in the ICU. When I returned home from a trip to Princeton on March 13, the look on Mom's face as I walked in told me everything I needed to know.

I kept it together when she told me, and I kept it together for the rest of the day. I kept it together when Mom, Yando, and I took a cab to Sacred Heart two days later for his wake. But when we got to the front of the viewing line and I saw Pops's body, I turned away, walked to a corner of the church, and cried until my eyes were dry. Mom approached and put her hand on my shoulder.

"He's with our Lord and the Virgin Mary now."

I looked in the direction of the open casket and began crying again. That bloated, embalmed face wasn't him. I would never see him smile again while he listened to my chatter about the classes I was taking or the books I was reading or the books I hoped one day to write. Regret tormented me. Christ, how I'd wanted to tell him that even though I'd turned out to be the worst Catholic ever—with my agnosticism and my lusts and my very potty mouth—I loved him for having been my Pops. I hadn't even had the chance to thank him one final time for paying that Tower Records bill, or to apologize for not having paid him back. And now I'd never have the chance. Because I'd been too scared to spend more time with him.

By the end of the wake I thought I had myself under control. Then Pablo called. When I took the call and he said, "Pops loved us, bro," I burst into tears all over again. I knew he could hear me crying, but I didn't care.

I WAS IN a miserable mood for much of the next month, even after word finally came down from the immigration service at the beginning of April that my application had been approved and I'd be able to begin my doctoral studies at Stanford. "Congratulations!" Steve wrote. "The immigration (and classical) gods continue to look favorably upon you!"

The night I learned of the service's decision, I went out for a drink and tried to jump-start myself out of my chronic bad mood. Maybe the best remedy was to begin planning for my new life at Stanford. The next morning, I fired off e-mails to my new director of graduate studies. Now that I was on an F-1, I had to enroll as a full-time student as soon as possible. Stanford's spring quarter was already under way, but perhaps I could enroll at the start of the summer? In a matter of days, everything was settled: I'd be moving out to the West Coast to begin my doctoral program the last week of June.

Under my new status, I could no longer continue as a research assistant at Princeton, which meant I had much more free time to kill. I figured I'd eat up the idle days with reading, watching and rewatching my favorite seasons of *The Wire,* going to Yankees games. But Nick was trying to get me to go on dates.

"You seeing anyone these days?" he'd ask whenever I met up with him.

"Eh," was my usual reply.

I'd been on some dates back in the fall and early winter. The ladies I'd been hollering at mostly seemed interested in having me open up to them the great mysteries of life at an Ivy or life at Oxford. Maybe it was my conversational maladroitness, maybe it was theirs, but I'd grown tired of feeling like the object of assorted status fetishes. I just wanted something *normal.* I wasn't clear on what that meant, but if pressed, I might have said something like: I want to be more in a woman's eyes than just your typical high achiever bearing the very comforting stamp of top-flight institutional approval.

Nick was relentless in trying to hook it up.

"I can introduce you to some law school friends of mine."

Law school had been good to him. After breaking up with his girlfriend from college, he'd started dating one of his classmates. She was cool, her friends were chill, and generally Columbia Law's ladies seemed on point. But even after I met some of them, I didn't really feel like hollering. Where would I even start? With some stupid-ass date at a nice restaurant? I didn't want to be serious about anything.

I was doing absolutely nothing in my parents' apartment one afternoon when my college friend Mariaelena messaged me. Her high school friend Missy had an extra ticket to that night's Yankees-Athletics game and couldn't find anyone to go with her. Was I interested?

I'd met Missy the summer before at a Stadium bleacher outing organized by Mariaelena and sat next to her as the Yankees eked out a narrow win. She was a Jersey native and a graduate student in social work at Fordham. She had been so funny about how hot it had been that day—by the seventh-inning stretch we had all turned into desiccated shells of our former selves. After the game, I'd told Mariaelena that her friend was cool. A few days later, Missy and I had added each other on Facebook. Of course, I didn't holla—because who lays mack on Facebook? Not me. I was better than that. But now I was telling Mariaelena that I was down to go to the game with her friend.

That night, Missy and I met up at the Stadium and cracked jokes for three hours. I liked her sense of humor, and she seemed to like mine. In the background, the Yankees scratched out another close win. Before the last out, I proposed a second get-together the following week at Citi Field, the Mets' new stadium. She smiled and said yes.

So Missy and I went to another baseball game.

And another.

And another.

For one game, we rode the Yankee Clipper ferry that took off from Weehawken, New Jersey, and made stops in Midtown and lower Manhattan before steaming up the East River to Yankee Stadium. At one point during the ride, I remember saying, apropos of nothing in particular:

"I don't really open up to people. Not easily."

To which she replied:

"Yeah, me neither."

Self-protective lies. See, somehow we still fell into this long conversation about ourselves, our families, and our desires for the future. She told me about her father's fight with heart disease. I listened carefully and told her about Dad, Jeff, Carlos, Pops. She listened awesomely. And in the focus and warmth of her gaze, I felt so wonderfully at ease.

In the days and weeks that followed, we traded silly texts. But we'd also talk about the hopes and dreams that animated her. For her social-work internship, she met with truant schoolchildren rounded up by the police in my Spanish Harlem hood. Some kids struck that hard thuggish pose, others adopted this perpetually sullen mask—and they were all fronting. So many of them didn't have anyone to talk to about how poor they were, how unappreciated or disrespected they felt at their massive herding-pen public schools, how mistreated or abused they were at home.

She was there for the black and Latino kids. I admired that.

We started seeing each other several times a week. But before I knew it, it was early June and my departure date for the West Coast was imminent. We didn't talk much about it, mainly because I didn't really know what to say. The week of the ferry ride, I'd been planning flights and sorting out housing arrangements. All along, I'd been thinking that the best plan was to fly out late the second week of June and give myself a week to acclimate to my new Stanford surroundings before the summer quarter began. But this plan lost its appeal when I discovered that the day I'd originally earmarked for travel was two days before Missy's birthday. I couldn't spend just a few more days in the city hanging out with her? Maybe she'd like to see CC Sabathia pitching against the Nationals.

I rebooked my flight, told her I'd be around for her birthday, and offered to take her out on a birthday adventure. I didn't admit I'd changed my plans for her; I spun some yarn about unanticipated developments with Stanford housing, because I didn't want her to think I was a rushing-into-seriousness loser.

She saw through my front. Lucky me: I wasn't convincing enough.

Also not convinced: Mom, who, when I mentioned Missy and my change of plans, took a good, hard look at me before getting a tease in:

"¡Mi'jo 'ta enamorado!"

She was right.

I LEFT FOR California but came right back a month later to spend a weekend with Missy. A month later, she flew out to spend a few days with me. Thus began our transcontinental romance. My first year of doctoral coursework, I flew east to see her once a month, twice if I'd managed to economize enough on food purchases—very easy to do (grad student pro tip) if you eat only pasta and gobble up all the free snacks at department talks.

The entire time, on the phone and on instant messenger, Derrick—still working in London but now entertaining thoughts of returning stateside for law school—ragged on me: "Dude, you are sprung on a white chick."

"No denying: yes, yes I am."

"But a social worker—good call. Makes sense: chick needs a social-work degree to deal with your crazy ass."

Missy and Dan-el in Napa, California, summer 2009

I laughed. He spoke it how it was. I mean, I was even allowing myself to cry in front of her! She was having me open up about my feelings! No more stoic faces for this *platano* eater, at least not in front of her.

WHEN MISSY COMPLETED her social-work degree at Fordham, she decided to move out to the wild, wild West to join me. She drove three thousand miles in three days, her Mazda Protegé sinking under the weight of the life she'd packed to share with me. The moment she pulled into the parking lot of Hoskins Court, Stanford, and stepped out of her car, face flushed with exhaustion but still glowing with the most perfect smile, I was the happiest I'd ever been. I've been a happy alien every day of our lives together since.

EPILOGUE

EVERY DAY, I feel grateful to this country for the education it has given and continues to give me and my brother; for the teachers, mentors, homeboys, and homegirls it has provided me; but most of all for the life companion whose love and support push me to be the very best person I can be.

I'll never stop boasting, in the manner of Tennyson's Ulysses, that "I am a part of all that I have met." But it took me so long to learn how to live that line properly. The experience of coming out as undocumented during my senior year of college set me on the path to developing a more versatile and richly textured idea of myself—in large part by forcing me to confront the stories that could and would be told about me if I did not take charge of their telling. At the same time, the experience humbled me, by making me realize just how profoundly lucky I was to benefit from the public and private support of so many communities. But it was only as I digested the experience by trying to write about it that a third dimension of my experience presented itself: how much it would mean to me if the person I eventually fell in love with understood me fully as the product of those communities. I had and have no intention of ever being only a

Dominican, or a minority, or an undocumented immigrant, or a Spanish Harlem resident; or a Collegiate man, a Princeton man, an Oxford man.

Missy has pushed me to make sense of my involvement in those communities, the relationships that tie them together, the growth that I've experienced in each. To write something like this book ultimately requires a great deal of love, not just self-love of the most vainglorious kind—though I imagine that has left its mark on these pages—but love that empowers you to bring to life the connections among the friends and institutions you care about in the most dynamic and passionate way you can.

She also keeps reminding me to stop fronting, to be more honest about my feelings. Because old habits die hard, and my sentimental education is far from complete.

ODI ET AMO. As much as I love America, I'm angry with it, too, because my struggle to legalize follows directly from our country's ongoing failure to implement a practical and just immigration policy.

The fate of millions of undocumented immigrants remains in the hands of an improperly conceived, poorly structured, and misincentivized system. And don't even get me started about the escalation in deportations over the past five years—undertaken at the initiative and with the support of a Democratic White House whose advocacy for the suffering and downtrodden has not, to date, extended to the families broken or the lives mangled by deportations. The 2012 memorandum implementing Deferred Action for Childhood Arrivals (DACA) was a small step forward; it should not distract us from the evils wrought by these deportations and from the ongoing failure of both parties to enact comprehensive immigration reform.

The Greek historian Thucydides tells us that the Athenian statesman Pericles, in a speech delivered not long after the beginning of the Peloponnesian War, bragged that *his* city did not deport foreigners (a snide allusion to Athens's nemesis, Sparta). Twenty-four hundred years later, however, a zealous *factio* of anti-immigrant agitators and their administration enablers seems more determined than ever to brag about deportation figures. Like tearing families apart is something to be proud of.

Now, I have only partial control over how my life story will be interpreted, but I want to be very explicit in what follows on the lessons that can and cannot be taken from my experiences.

First: I was the beneficiary of overgenerous servings of good luck. This has made it tricky for me to advise the students who've come to me for guidance over the past few years. I wouldn't advise them to leave the United States to regularize status. But it makes equally little sense for me to tell them, "Go to a private school in New York, then an Ivy League university, then Oxford, and maybe by then you'll have amassed the contacts and friends you'll need to make your status problem more manageable." At first glance, then, it might seem that my life story has very little relevance either for those people demanding rigid adherence to the "law" or for those youngsters who matter to me most: the students trying to find a way around the current system and its debilitating constraints.

But, although my specific immigration experience is not a primer for how to obtain legal status, it does affirm the potential power of the undocumented-immigrant contribution to American society. E-mails and phone conversations and meetings with so many undocumented students over the past few years have reinforced my conviction that our community of DREAMers is uniquely talented, gifted, bursting with desire and ambition. How hungry we all are to learn and to achieve! How eager we are to contribute to American society: to lend our hands and our feet to its economy, our minds to its intellectual production; to expand its horizons of inclusivity and diversity; to enrich its democratic discourse. Yet every single day, the ambitions and aptitudes of the undocumented millions are trivialized and marginalized by an immigration policy lacking in rationality or justice. Lives are forced into a waiting pattern of alienation and anxiety as the undocumented among us wait for news of comprehensive immigration reform—their talents and abilities suspended between the poles of constantly deferred hope on one end and ever-present fear on the other.

My hope for this book is that it will communicate a sense of the power of their potential contribution. Along the path I took, many more are coming, not just to be migrant laborers or housecleaners or cabdrivers but to be students, academics, writers, artists, politicians. Our lives are a living testament to the exceptional potency of the American Dream that inspired our parents to surmount every obstacle in their quest to raise us here.

NOT LONG AGO, Missy and I were walking around the Upper West Side, holding hands as a sprinkling of winter flurries came down. A poem came to mind that morning, Whitman's "Mannahatta"—an old favorite from Collegiate, where I'd first read it in a one-day seminar on New York poems taught by Dr. Russell (who else?). I'm fondest of these lines:

> The down-town streets, the jobbers' houses of business—the houses of
>   business of the ship-merchants, and money-brokers—the river-streets;
> Immigrants arriving, fifteen or twenty thousand in a week . . .
> The beautiful city, the city of hurried and sparkling waters! the city of spires
>   and masts!
> The city nested in bays! my city!

Over the years I've marveled at how delicately Whitman's verses balance the prideful claim to the city—my city!—with the images, bodies, faces of those newly arrived, future contenders for the ownership of the city.

This balance is lost on those who are opposed to immigration in general and to undocumented immigrants in particular, most of whom tend to view immigrants as easily detachable from the authentic American experience. In their account, America is separate and separable from the immigrant invaders who swarm into America to milk social services, drop anchor babies right and left, and deprive hard-earning Americans of opportunities to work; these illegals are bodies to be rounded up, detained, and deported by the full apparatus of the surveillance state.

Every time I walk around New York, I think of how it is mine not only because I was raised there but also because my traces are all over its landscape. Traces that, for the most part, I alone can see—but their being visible only to my eyes is no argument against their existence. On a street in Queens, I cut my foot as a seven-year-old and bled on the pavement while Mom bandaged me and a kindly middle-aged woman gave me water to keep me hydrated. On a street on the Upper West Side, my pranking eighth-grade classmates wrote my home phone number in hardening concrete. The streets, *my* streets: I've walked practically every street in Manhattan. I've eaten at almost every McDonald's. I fell in love somewhere between Yankee Stadium and Citi Field.

So I lay claim to New York City as my city because my life has been staged on it, because I am embedded in it, because it does not make sense to take my life out of it. And from New York, I expand to America and to the entire scope of my wanderings across it, from New York to Princeton and California, to make the same point: that I am embedded, productively, in an American web of relations;

that I call America mine because my life has been and is fully American.

Immigrant brothers and sisters: Of course, people will yell at you that America is not yours. That you have no stake in America, no place in America, no right to belong in America. You must not let them get off lightly with saying that. You must argue, remonstrate, shout back that your hands and feet and minds are as much a part of America as theirs are. Together we must fight to ensure that America remains not the dream of the chauvinistically minded few but the fulfillment of hopes for many. *We* are in the ascendant. America is ours, and we must not concede otherwise.

And to the haters, a final word: Demography is a bitch. Holla at me if you want me to break it down for you. You can find me chilling with the Muses, *studiis florentem ignobilis oti.*

ACKNOWLEDGMENTS

"His present skills tend to lag behind his more exacting ideas, and he tends to need prodding to go beyond his initial efforts" (Mr. Mitch Cramer, eighth-grade art).

Truer words about me have yet to be written. I owe a special and unrepayable debt to the many teachers and mentors who prodded me to push beyond my initial efforts. At the Centro Educativo Siglo XXI and at the Colegio Jardín de la Enseñanza (Santo Domingo), Ms. Báez, Lic. Rosa Ariza de Valera, Ms. Dulce Alida de León Jimenez, Ms. Rossina Sánchez, and Ms. Alvarado; at PS 226 (Bronx), Ms. Seda; at PS 143 (Queens), Ms. Anton; at PS 148 (Queens), Ms. Beaudet and Mrs. Spinelli; at PS 2 (Chinatown), Ms. McGill; at PS 200 (Harlem), Ms. Mackey and Ms. Torrence. At Collegiate: William Abernathy, Don Austin, Johanna Barmore, Roy Bergeson, Koshi Bharwani, Adam Bresnick, Sidney Child, Dan Chisholm, Mitch Cramer, Susan Fine, Jessica Flaxman, Bunny Genkins, Lynn Hansell, Matthew Horvat, Diane Hulse, David Jelinek, Martha Lew, Sara McCoy, Massimo Maglione, Scott Mattoon, Paul Ness, the late John Nobile, Laurie Rubel, Michael Rubin, Ronald Schwizer, Richard Shanley, Sherwyn Smith, Don Sorel, Lauren Sullivan, Phuc Tran.

Several Collegiate legends not only prodded me beyond my initial efforts but altered the course of my life. Joanne Heyman saw enough potential in me to extend an offer of admission. Germán Llarch and Angela Pimentel looked after me and made sure I behaved himself, and Kathleen Sullivan magically manipulated my Upper School schedule so that I could take as many classes as I wanted. Ryland Clarke and David Fisher taught me how to think like a historian. Michael Gately taught me how to debate. John Beall encouraged me to think of myself as a humanist. Decent-sounding sentences together. Bruce Breimer advocated for me. Stephanie Russell gave me the gift of languages and of her unwavering support. Kathy Young has been and will always be my second mom.

At Prep for Prep: Joe Ayala, Diahann Billings-Burford, Ed Boland, Peter and Katy Bordonaro, Frankie Cruz, Erin Duffy, Louise Frazier, Aileen Hefferren, Geoffrey Howarth, Charles Guerrero, the late John Lawrence, James Mercado, Dominic Michel, Akobe Sandy, Niki Smith, Silva Valcarcel. Then there is Gary Simons, who exhorted me and so many others to Be The Dream and who had faith in me long before I had faith in myself; thank you, Gary.

At Princeton: Mark Buchan, Jeff Dolven, Caryl Emerson, Denis Feeney, Andrew Feldherr, Patricia Fernandez-Kelly, Michael Flower, Andrew Ford, John Gager, Constanze Güthenke, Bob Hollander, Bob Kaster, Joshua Katz, Anne Caswell Klein, Catherine Millett, Paul Muldoon, Michael Nettles, Elaine Pagels, Nathan Scovronick, Anne-Marie Slaughter, Marta Tienda, Froma Zeitlin. Nancy Weiss Malkiel's concern for me and hard work on my behalf made all the difference as I confronted the challenges of my junior and senior years. Harriet Flower has been the most selfless and supportive intellectual and professional mentor one could hope for, and it is a pleasure to record my gratitude to her here.

The Sachs community welcomed me with open arms, and it is

with particular delight that I embarrass its members with effusions of gratitude. Thanks to Joel Barrera, David Loevner, Harry Lord, Justin Pope, Bill Sachs, Paula-Rose Stark, and Michele Woods for making my interview with them one of the most intellectually stimulating and transformative moments of my time at Princeton. In the years since the interview, David and Cathy Loevner and Bill and Iliana Sachs have been unstinting in their generosity, good advice, and kindness; Joel Barrera has been a cheerleader and role model; and Charles Gillispie has dispensed wisdom that I hope to engrave on tablets of bronze one day. My thanks to the larger community of Sachs Scholars for inspiration and intellectual companionship, and to Harry Lord and the Class of 1960 for their continued support of the Sachs.

At Oxford: Cath Fraser, Josephine Quinn, Scott Scullion, and the porters of Worcester made me feel at home; Alan Bowman and Nicholas Purcell welcomed me into the circle of Roman historians and initiated me into (some of) the mysteries of the profession; Katherine Clarke (and Scipio!) guided me on my thesis ventures; Martin Goodman challenged me time and time again in tutorials; Sir Fergus Millar generously made time to take me out to coffee when I arrived; Jasper and Miriam Griffin welcomed me into their home for afternoon tea and Christmas dinner.

Finally, at Stanford: Alessandro Barchiesi, Giovanna Ceserani, Marsh McCall, Richard Martin, Joy Maxmin, Ian Morris, Andrea Nightingale, Josiah Ober, Grant Parker, Walter Scheidel (*Doktorvater* extraordinaire), Susan Stephens, and Jen Trimble. Ian, perhaps you'll be disappointed at my failure to include any Kenneth Dover–like vignettes. Giovanna, thank you for your words of wisdom when I had grown frustrated with the direction the memoir was taking.

From conception to execution to publication—a nine-year process!—this memoir relied on the vision and determination of a special few. Miriam Jordan's sensitive and thoughtful profile in the *Wall Street Journal* drew attention to my story, and it was in talking with her not long after the profile came out that the notion of an autobiography first took form. David Loevner introduced me to Nancy Karetsky, who demystified the world of rights and contracts and set me up with the folks at Janklow and Nesbit. Mort Janklow has been and continues to be a tireless champion for this book. Priscilla Gilman, who took me under her wing when I first signed on with J & N and represented me for many years, offered timely and invaluable feedback on every scrap of writing I sent her way (I calculate that she has read approximately 300,000 words from my pen, most of them utter dross). At Penguin Press, where Ann Godoff saw the promise of this project and gave it her full support, I have had the good fortune of not one, not two, but three editors: Vanessa Mobley acquired the book, poured herself into helping me formulate a robust idea of what the memoir should be, and shepherded it to the halfway mark; Eamon Dolan applied his laserlike scrutiny to the chaotic draft manuscripts that I sent his way; and Ginny Smith Younce guided me to the finish line with patience and rigor. I take this opportunity to thank Will Carnes and Sofia Groopman for their assistance as I crawled to the finish line, and the production and publicity teams at Penguin for their work in readying for publication the book you hold in your hands.

The ups and downs of my immigration saga involved numerous behind-the-scene movers and shakers, some of whom would rather not have their names in print. Of those who can be named, I thank from the bottom of my heart Stephen Yale-Loehr, for many years of legal guidance and advocacy; his former assistant Lindsay Schoonmaker, a model of organization efficiency when things reached a fever pitch; Josh Bernstein, for introducing me to DREAM Act advocacy and to the greater community of DREAMers; and the many supporters from Resurrection, Collegiate, Prep, and Princeton for writing to members of Congress and lobbying the immigration service on my behalf.

Maximas gratias vobis ago, stalwart friends: Christian Estrella, Jorge Pérez, and all my KRL for life; Bali Kumar, Akim St. Omer, and all the Prep advising heads; Zaak Beekman, Ted Clement, Nick Moscow, Steve Myers, and the great Dutchman class of 2002; Krista Brune, Terrace F. Club, Omet Ewoterai, Marya and Clark Fisher, Daniella Gitlin, Liz Hanft, Mariaelena Morales, Christine O'Neill and Matt Musa, Judnefera Rasayon, Kelly Sanabria, Rachel Zuraw and Matt Solomon; David Bagby, Tom Kelly, Will and Matt Motley; Federica Carugati, Matthew Loar, Carolyn MacDonald, Mark Pyzyk and Hans Wietzke. A special shout-out to Dave for agreeing in a pinch to serve as my book-contract-signing witness, and to Will, Ted, Nick, and Matthew McCann for providing invaluable criticism on early full drafts of the manuscript.

Last but most assuredly not least, my family. To my father, in DR but always an email away: thanks for expecting and demanding the very best from me. To my *abuelas,* Ciriaca Peralta and the late Lucia Rodriguez: thank you for modeling for me what tenacity means. Jeff: thank you for being there when my family had no one to turn to. Father Michael: if words can reach you, thank you for the example of your integrity. Carlos: thank you for showering Mom, Yando, and me with your singular combination of humor and strength. Yando: I am fortunate to have you as my brother and best friend.

Missy: I couldn't have completed this without you (and Señor Boots); thank you for making me realize that there is so much more to life than what I originally dreamt of in my philosophy. And finally, Mom, for your love invincible in battle: your dreams for Yando and me knew no limits, and you taught us never to back down in the face of adversity. It is an honor to dedicate this book to you.

Dan-el Padilla Peralta
on the third day before the Nones of March, 2015
Weehawken/Union City, New Jersey

GLOSSARY

NOTE: All are Spanish terms unless otherwise indicated.

Amor de Rey   "Love of the King" (slogan of the Latin Kings)

Angel de mi Guarda   "Guardian Angel," a traditional bedtime prayer, the opening four lines of which go:

> Angel de mi guarda *(O guardian angel)*
> Dulce compañía *(Sweet companion)*
> No me desampares *(Don't abandon me)*
> Ni de noche ni de día *(Neither by night nor by day)*

antes de   before

apagones   blackouts

Aquí están   Here they are

arroz   rice

arroz con habichuelas   rice and beans

asunto   issue

bacalao salted and fried cod

bachata, merengue two genres of music popular in (and some would say indigenous to) DR

basta enough

beca scholarship

Bendición See *'Ción* below

besando la mano "kissing the hand," metaphor for soliciting a blessing

blanquito, blanquita white boy, white girl (diminutives)

bochinche gossip

bulla noise

cabezas duras blockheads

calefacción heating

campo rural village

caprichoso picky, whimsical

chelito little bit of change

chin-chin itsy-bitsy bit

chismorreando gossiping

chula hottie

cibaeña bien educada a well-educated Dominican girl

Cicerón en latín, Platón en griego Cicero in Latin, Plato in Greek

'Ción (bendición) Bless me (as question and response; when a younger person says *"'Ción,"* he/she is *asking* for the blessing, which the older person then gives)

ciudadanos citizens

Claro que sí But of course

como un hombre like a man

como un tíguere like a hoodrat

compromisos commitments

concón the rice at the very bottom or sides of the rice pot, usually left to clump together and harden for a bit after cooking *cualquieras* "anybodies" (fem.) but with derogatory meaning of "loose women"

Cuidado Be careful

dando carpeta causing mayhem

Desde que Brutus mató a César, ¡los brutos viven sin cesar! From the moment Brutus killed Caesar, brutes have lived without ceasing. (The punch line hinges on the homophones *César* [Caesar] and *cesar* [to cease].)

diligencia errand

Dios mío My God

Dios te bendiga God bless you

dique (dizque) "apparently"; in DR slang, often the equivalent of interjectional "like"

endemoniado devil-possessed person

Ese niño va ser un genio That kid's gonna be a smarty-pants

¿Eso te interesa? Does that interest you?

factio (Latin) party

fieras animals, beasts

gangas gangs

hombre man

hombre de trabajo workingman, blue-collar man

hombrecito little man

Hören Sie gut zu (German) Pay attention closely (the audio-recording mainstay of any German student's existence)

indios Indians

la sala living room

licenciado college-educated

liderazgo leadership

madrina/padrino godmother/godfather (as referred to by a child; *comadre/compadre* is the term used by an adult to refer to the godmother/godfather of one's child)

malentendido   misunderstanding

mangú   a dish consisting of mashed plantains, hard-boiled eggs, and
   onions (with cheese and/or salami sometimes thrown in)

Materiam superabat opus (Latin)   The work surpassed the material
   (used to make it) [Ovid, *Metamorphoses* 2.5]

mentula (Latin)   dick

mesero   waiter

mi amor   my love

mi'jo (mi hijo)   my son

¡Mi'jo 'ta enamorado!   My son's in love!

mierda   shit

mira loco   look, crazy!

mirabile visu (Latin)   a marvel to behold

mojiganga   (what a) farce

moreno   dark-skinned

moro (short for *moros y cristianos*)   rice-and-bean dish very popular in
   the Caribbean

muchacha/o   girl/boy

mueble   couch

mujeriego   womanizer

música de tígueres   hoodrat music

necio   pig-headed/stubborn

negros   blacks

no más   no more

no sabe a na'   it doesn't taste like anything

no tan refina'o   not that refined

nostos (Greek)   homecoming

noticiero   news show

novias   girlfriends

O sodales mei hominesque Princetonienses (Latin)   O my companions,
   Princetonians

Odi et amo (Latin)   I hate and I love (opening three words of a
   famous Catullus epigram [*Carmina* 85])

¿Oh sí?   Oh yeah?

papeles   identification papers, legal documentation

pastelitos   empanadas

patria   fatherland

pela   spanking

pernil   roast pork

Pórtense bien   Behave yourselves

¡Qué desperdicio!   What a waste!

¿Queda muy lejos, no?   It's very far, right?

Quisqueya   Indigenous name for Hispaniola, adopted as nickname
   for DR

santos   saints

Si Dios lo quiere   If God wills it

sinvergüenza   shameless

sordomudo   deaf-mute

studiis florentem ignobilis oti (Latin)   thriving in the pursuits of
   inglorious leisure (a phrase from Virgil [*Georgics* 4.564]).

supplosio pedis (Latin)   the "stomp of the foot" whose correct use was
   upheld by Cicero, among others, as the mark of effective oratory

taller   shop

tan nervioso   so nervous

Te digo a tí   I'll tell *you*

Te dije   I told you

Te quiero   I love you

tía, tío   aunt, uncle

tíguere   macho

tígueres   macho boys, hoodrats

tostones   flattened fried (green) plantains

Tres Reyes Magos   Three Kings

trigueño   mixed-race

triunfador   winner

unos granitos de arroz   a few little grains of rice

¿Y cómo se aplica? ¿Dan becas?   How does one apply? Do they give
  scholarships?

yola   raft